PIZZA
BOMBER

PIZZA BOMBER

JERRY CLARK AND
ED PALATTELLA

PIZZA BOMBER

THE UNTOLD STORY
OF AMERICA'S
MOST SHOCKING
BANK ROBBERY

JERRY CLARK AND
ED PALATTELLA

BERKLEY BOOKS, NEW YORK

THE BERKLEY PUBLISHING GROUP
Published by the Penguin Group
Penguin Group (USA) Inc.
375 Hudson Street, New York, New York 10014, USA

Penguin Group (Canada), 90 Eglinton Avenue East, Suite 700, Toronto, Ontario M4P 2Y3, Canada
(a division of Pearson Penguin Canada Inc.) • Penguin Books Ltd., 80 Strand, London WC2R 0RL,
England • Penguin Group Ireland, 25 St. Stephen's Green, Dublin 2, Ireland (a division of Penguin
Books Ltd.) • Penguin Group (Australia), 250 Camberwell Road, Camberwell, Victoria 3124, Australia
(a division of Pearson Australia Group Pty. Ltd.) • Penguin Books India Pvt. Ltd., 11 Community
Centre, Panchsheel Park, New Delhi—110 017, India • Penguin Group (NZ), 67 Apollo Drive,
Rosedale, Auckland 0632, New Zealand (a division of Pearson New Zealand Ltd.) • Penguin Books
(South Africa) (Pty.) Ltd., 24 Sturdee Avenue, Rosebank, Johannesburg 2196, South Africa

Penguin Books Ltd., Registered Offices: 80 Strand, London WC2R 0RL, England

The publisher does not have any control over and does not assume any
responsibility for authors or third-party websites or their content.

PIZZA BOMBER

A Berkley Book / published by arrangement with the authors

PUBLISHING HISTORY
Berkley premium edition / November 2012

ISBN: 978-0-425-25055-6

BERKLEY®
Berkley Books are published by The Berkley Publishing Group,
a division of Penguin Group (USA) Inc.,
375 Hudson Street, New York, New York 10014.
BERKLEY® is a registered trademark of Penguin Group (USA) Inc.
The "B" design is a trademark of Penguin Group (USA) Inc.

PRINTED IN THE UNITED STATES OF AMERICA

10   9

ALWAYS LEARNING   PEARSON

For Danielle, Michael and Isabelle

For Chris, Henry and Nina

AUTHORS' NOTE

This account is drawn from personal observations, contemporaneous notes, interviews, court documents, transcripts and other official records, as well as news media reports, particularly those in the *Erie Times-News*. The opinions expressed in this book are the authors' alone and not those of the Federal Bureau of Investigation. In selected instances, we have chosen to identify individuals by initials. These include individuals who were informants or persons of interest but who were not charged nor shown to have credible or relevant information about the events chronicled here.

J.C.
E.P.
Erie, Pennsylvania
December 2011

It is easier to commit murder
than to justify it.

—Papinian, Roman jurist

There is nothing more deceptive
than an obvious fact.

—Sir Arthur Conan Doyle,
The Adventures of Sherlock Holmes

Introduction

Since the founding of the Federal Bureau of Investigation, in 1908, its agents have infiltrated the Mob, probed corruption and pursued terrorists. But fewer than three hundred of the FBI's investigations have earned Major Case status, which refers to the bureau's most complex and serious probes.

The first Major Case was the investigation of the Lindbergh kidnapping, on March 1, 1932. Six decades later, the FBI opened a string of some of its most famous Major Cases in recent times. OKBOMB, Major Case 117, covered the investigation of Timothy McVeigh's bombing of the Alfred P. Murrah Building, in Oklahoma City, on April 15, 1995. CENTBOM, Major Case 130, referred to the investigation of Eric Rudolph for bombings that included the blast at Centennial Olympic Park, in Atlanta, during the Summer Olympics, on July 27, 1996. The FBI gave the name PENTTBOMB to Major Case 182, which covered the investigations of the attacks on the Pentagon and World Trade Center, on September 11, 2001.

On August 28, 2003, what would become FBI Major Case 203 originated on the outskirts of Erie, Pennsylvania, a medium-sized industrial city on Lake Erie that usually makes the national news only because of its record snowfall. A pizza deliveryman by the name of Brian Wells robbed a bank wearing a time bomb locked around his neck. He was carrying notes that told him where to find clues to disable the bomb, but the plan went unfinished. As police questioned Wells and a television camera rolled, the homemade contraption exploded and tore a fatal wound into his chest.

COLLARBOMB is what the FBI called Major Case 203. The public came to know it as the pizza bomber case. Its investigation and prosecution would take more than seven years.

PART I

EXPLOSION

1

Final Delivery

Tony Ditomo heard a rush of wind on the other end of the line. He had picked up the phone to take an order at Mama Mia's Pizza-Ria, just south of Erie, Pennsylvania. Ditomo, the store's owner, could barely make out this customer's words: the deep male voice drifted in and out. It was 1:30 P.M. on Thursday, August 28, 2003.

"Do you deliver to upper Peach?" the caller asked.

Mama Mia's is squeezed in a strip mall at 5154 Peach Street, one of the busiest roads in Erie, a city of 102,000 that anchors Pennsylvania's northwestern corner, on Lake Erie. Fast-food restaurants, gas stations, car lots, banks, shoe stores, a hospital: they all line Peach Street. It gets more congested to the south, as it stretches away from Erie and into Millcreek Township, where Mama Mia's is located. Interstates 79 and 90 feed the traffic on the southern section, which includes the Millcreek Mall. That section is known as upper Peach.

Upper Peach soon would be busy for the Labor Day weekend. The tourists would arrive from Pittsburgh to the south, Buffalo to the east and Cleveland to the west; Erie is about two hours from each. The visitors would spend the day on the lake and at its beaches and drive Peach Street for dinner and shopping.

Mama Mia's delivered to upper Peach, to a point.

"It depends where on upper Peach," Ditomo told the caller.

"Across from New Motors," the voice said.

The spot is in Summit Township, a small, rural suburb south of Millcreek. The caller wanted the pizzas delivered to the site of the TV transmission tower for WSEE-TV, the local CBS affiliate. The caller said he and some guys were working at the tower site, across the street from the car dealership.

Ditomo thought the caller might be on the tower, he was having such a hard time hearing him. Ditomo kept hearing what sounded like the wind, but the wind was not blowing hard on this day.

Whoosh.

Whoosh.

Whoosh.

Ditomo said Mama Mia's would deliver to the tower site. The caller ordered two small pizzas with pepperoni and sausage. The caller started to give directions. Ditomo couldn't hear anything. He told the caller to talk to his delivery driver.

Ditomo handed the phone to Brian Wells.

———

Wells was forty-six years old, ten months younger than the forty-seven-year-old Ditomo. Wells had driven for Mama Mia's for about nine years. He got the job through the husband of his landlady, who owned a five-room cottage where Wells lived with his three cats. Wells took a break from Mama Mia's two years earlier, when he spent several months at his brother's place in sun-drenched Arizona to work in a tool-and-die shop. It closed, and Wells returned to Erie and its long and snowy winters. He resumed delivering pizzas.

Wells was never married and had no children. The delivery work let him keep his independence. He was distraught a year earlier, when he wrecked his car and temporarily lost his delivery job; he told his landlady he'd rather be homeless than move in with his mother. The landlady and her husband loaned him the money to buy a $1,800 1996 greenish-blue standard-shift Chevy Geo Metro. On August 28, 2003, Wells had paid back the loan about a week earlier. The Geo was about as small as a car could be for someone Wells' size: five feet nine inches tall and 175 pounds.

Wells, a recovering alcoholic, enjoyed Mama Mia's slow pace. One of his coworkers opened her own pizza shop some years earlier, and she asked Wells if he would like to deliver for her. Wells declined. The new shop was too chaotic, Wells said; if he worked there, he'd be driven to drink.

Acquaintances described Brian Wells as childlike. He wore oversize eyeglasses that drew comparisons to Elton John's. He had a large, oval-shaped head and was balding, with closely cropped gray hair. He liked the lottery, crossword puzzles, the TV show *Survivor* and the musical *Jesus Christ Superstar.* He played guitar. He didn't own a computer. He looked forward to an annual contest in the *Erie Times-News,* the local newspaper. Readers deciphered printed clues to find a key that unlocked a box full of cash. The contest was called the Great Key Hunt.

Wells had a GED. He got it after he dropped out of Erie's East High School at age sixteen in September 1973, as a sophomore. For his final grades the year before, he got two Fs, three Ds, two Cs, two Bs and an A, in swimming. He left school to work. Mechanics interested Wells. As an adult, he collected parts to build a car; he once stored two car doors inside the cottage.

Despite his simple manner, Wells was of normal intelligence, and in some areas he tested much better than his peers. His overall IQ when he was sixteen years old was 109, slightly above the average of 100, according to an Erie School District psychological study. In the same IQ test, Wells recorded a verbal IQ of 100 and a performance IQ, which measures nonverbal tasks, of a 120, higher than 91 percent of the population.

Wells got straight As until he entered junior high

school, according to the study, which a school psychologist performed because of Wells' poor grades. Wells' father suffered from multiple sclerosis; the study surmised his father's "physical incapacity" disconcerted Wells and contributed to his academic decline.

The study found Wells suffered from nascent psychological problems. "The . . . record appears to indicate psychopathic tendencies along with paranoid flavor," it said.

The school psychologist gauged Wells' "self-projection" by having him draw a person. Wells drew "a male figure that appears to be physically strong and dominant," according to the study. "This large figure appears to indicate slight manic and grandiose signs in this adolescent. It appears to be related somewhat to studies of aggressive psychopaths."

The study portrayed Wells as an intelligent but troubled and defiant loner with no need for authority. "He claims that he will not please others," the study said, "and he presently sees adults as being too demanding and that he will lead his own life in his own time."

———

Wells' only criminal case came in 1992. The Erie police charged him with threatening to shoot a magistrate over a dispute with Wells' neighbors. Wells had complained to the mayor, saying that "it would be cheaper to use $1 bullets" to fix the mess than sue his neighbors before the magistrate. Wells pleaded guilty to harassment as a summary, the most minor of offenses.

———

Wells kept a routine. He got up around 7:15 A.M., bought a copy of the *Erie Times-News*, ate breakfast at a McDonald's and drove to Mama Mia's. Wells worked from 11:00 A.M. to 2:00 P.M. On August 28, 2003, he told Tony Ditomo he wanted to leave by 2:00 P.M. or earlier. He said he and his sister that evening planned to eat pizza and watch videos with their widowed seventy-five-year-old mother at her apartment. His father, Harold C. Wells, a utility worker, died at age sixty in 1990.

Wells had few close friends. One woman he knew, Angie, who had a black boyfriend, visited him frequently at Mama Mia's. She always wanted money from him. Wells told Ditomo about another woman, Jessie. Wells said a black guy would drop her off near Wells' cottage, and she would walk there to see him.

———

Ditomo, who had owned Mama Mia's for seventeen years, liked Wells. He was reliable, unlike another of Ditomo's drivers, Robert Pinetti, who was forty-three years old. He was friends with Wells, and a recovering alcoholic, too. Ditomo never smelled alcohol on his breath, but Pinetti could be strange, Ditomo would later tell the FBI. Pinetti's eyes were glassy. He walked away in the middle of conversations. He liked gambling. He missed work for minor car problems and other small things.

———

Wells was Mama Mia's only driver the afternoon of August 28, 2003. Ditomo gave him the phone to get directions for the delivery to the TV tower. Wells jotted down the address, 8631 Peach Street, and the directions: "New Motors. Radio towers. 1st left." The delivery would be Wells' sixth and last of the day. Ditomo wrote up the bill—$6.99 for each pizza—but did not take down the caller's telephone number. His shop had caller ID.

Each of the pizzas took about five minutes and thirty seconds to bake. Wells stuffed the warm pizza boxes into his insulated bag and walked to his car. He wore white low-cut sneakers made by Franklin, clean blue jeans and a gray T-shirt embroidered with three small American flags below the word *AMERICA* written in white block letters. Wells turned his Geo Metro right onto Peach Street and headed south, toward upper Peach and the tower site. It was 1:47 P.M.

───────

A small white sign with blue numerals is stuck low to the ground where a dirt road bisects Peach Street. The sign, for 8631 Peach Street, displays the address for the TV tower, situated at the end of the dirt road in a weedy clearing surrounded by trees. A subdivision rises in the distance.

On August 28, 2003, a white house with an attached garage was located at 8645 Peach Street, next to the start of the dirt road. A For Sale sign was stuck in the front yard. Wells was familiar with the house, owned by an eccentric handyman by the name of Bill Rothstein. Wells had been with Rothstein at the TV tower site the day before.

Wells hadn't told his boss about that.

2

"I Don't Have a Lot of Time"

Like many suburbs, Millcreek and Summit townships, south of Erie, became the desired destination for retailers. The first stores spread over what was once farmland. Soon one retailer piled atop the other: Kmart and Walmart and Target and Lowe's and Best Buy. In Summit Township, the sprawl's epicenter was Summit Towne Centre, which opened in 1991.

Summit Towne Centre looks like any number of other commercial developments in the United States. Summit Township is just as nondescript. The city of Erie, the fourth-largest city in Pennsylvania, was founded along a natural harbor called Presque Isle Bay. The city has its rust-belt reputation, but it also has its downtown and its waterfront and the bay and the lake. Summit Township and Summit Towne Centre appear, from the view of a car window, anonymous and anodyne.

Brian Wells drove south on Peach Street, past the Millcreek Mall and into Summit Township. He traveled through a series of stoplights; the traffic moved swiftly on this sunny, warm and clear day. About halfway to Wells' destination, the Geo passed the Summit Towne Centre on the right. An Eyeglass World store, at 7630 Peach Street, sat about twenty feet from the road. Behind it was a McDonald's. Tucked behind the McDonald's was the Summit Towne Centre branch of PNC Bank, at 7200 Peach Street.

The Geo approached one of the most-traveled intersections in Erie County, of which Erie is the county seat: the interchange between the north-south Peach Street and the east-west I-90. The ramps leading on and off the highway often back up. Wells drove the Geo through the interchange, up a hill on Peach Street and through another intersection, this one with Robison Road. A Shell gas station occupies the intersection's southwestern corner. Its address is 8228 Peach Street.

Wells was getting closer. The Geo neared New Motors. Wells could see Bill Rothstein's house and then the small sign for 8631 Peach Street, the TV tower site. He turned left onto the dirt road. He had traveled three and one-half miles in about ten minutes.

Wells drove 1,225 feet down the dirt road. Crunching gravel broke the silence. He could see the red TV tower and the clearing, which included a vehicle turnaround. A chain-link fence surrounded the tower's base. Inside the fence was a cluster of shedlike buildings, a propane tank and satellite dishes.

The Geo stopped near the tower. Wells got out with the pizzas. It was 2:00 P.M.

A gun went off in the clearing.

———

The small bowl of Dum Dums lollipops sat on the long front counter of the PNC Bank at 7200 Peach Street. The tellers put out the lollipops; they were for anyone, but mainly children.

On August 28, 2003, at 2:27 P.M., a man wearing what looked to be a neck brace walked into the bank and strolled past the basket of lollipops. He didn't wait in line. He went up to the chief teller, who was busy working the counter and drive-through window. The man scratched the back of his neck. He was of medium height and stocky, with a smattering of short gray hair on either side of his balding head. He had on blue jeans with dirt ground into the knees. He wore two T-shirts: the one underneath was gray; the one on top was baggy and white, with *GUESS Jeans* written across the front in large dark letters.

A closer look at the white T-shirt showed the man was wearing not a neck brace, but a metal collar that encircled his neck. A box bulged under the white T-shirt. The man walked without a limp, but he carried a funky blackish-brown cane. The handle was curved, like the handle of a gun.

The chief teller, Barbara Lipinski, thought this impatient customer was wearing a body cast. She held a canister from the drive-through window. She told him she was working that window at the moment.

"You have to get in line and wait your turn," Lipinski said.

The man handed Lipinski a white envelope striped with blue from a highlighting marker. Lipinski, a veteran teller, knew what this was: a demand note.

Inside the envelope were four pages of 8 ½-by-11-inch paper. A blue stripe was highlighted at the bottom of each page. Hand-printed words the size of typewriter type covered the sheets of paper.

=RECEPTIONIST=

Do not cause panic or many people will be killed Sounding any alarm will interrupt this action and guarantee injuries and death. Involving authorities at this point will get this hostage and other people killed.

Immediately without causing alarm, you must contact the Bank Manager in private. The Bomb-hostage must accompany you.

Bomb is expertly booby-trapped and cannot be disarmed in time unless keys are found by following instructions immediately. Bomb-Hostage needs less than 20 minutes in the bank and 30 minutes to deliver. No money—no keys. If any one of us is stopped or apprehended we will detonate bomb or its timer will run out. We will retaliate if interrupted.

=BANK MANAGER=

No alarm, panic or Police! Close doors.

The note stated the man wanted $250,000, an unreasonably large sum for a bank to have on hand. The note stated sentries were watching to make sure he got the cash. The note explained how, after he left the bank, the man could find directions to deactivate the bomb. The note had so many instructions spread over all four pages.

Act Now, Think Later or You Will Die.

After receiving the money, we will provide Bomb-Hostage with the location of the final key and combination to disarm and remove bomb. Wait 1 hour after Bomb-Hostage returns to contact police or we will 1)-BOMB or 2)-RETALIATE.

If any of you fuck up this robbery, it will be our life's mission to fuck up your lives! We have followed your customers and employees home. We know where your families live!

That part of the note was signed: =The Troubleshooters=
The fourth page of the note was directed to the police. It warned them "stand down" and let the heist proceed.

You can only protect the Bomb-Hostage and everyone else by staying clear! Our team is in radio contact. If any of us is stopped or apprehended the bomb will

**detonate. If Bomb Hostage is delayed for more than
10 minutes he will not have enough time to continue.
Our team has spent combined 7 ½ years in prison
perfecting this plan. Do not think you can outsmart us
in less than an hour.**

Lipinski skimmed the pages. She looked at the man.

"I want to speak to the manager," he said.

Lipinski left the counter. When she returned, the man
was sucking a Dum Dums lollipop, which he had taken
from the basket. Lipinski told him the manager was at
lunch and would be back in about a half an hour, or
around 3:00 P.M.

"I don't have until 3:00," the man said. "I don't have
that kind of time. I need $250,000."

He lifted his baggy white T-shirt. A gray-colored device hung from his neck and rested on his chest. It looked
like a bomb.

Lipinski looked at the man. He still wanted $250,000.

Lipinski said she didn't have that kind of money; she
couldn't get into the vault. That is why the man's note
was also directed to a manager: that would be the person
with access to the vault. With the manager out, the vault
was off-limits. Lipinski would have to give him the money
from the cash drawers.

"Give me what you have," the man said.

Lipinski took money from her cash drawer. Another
teller bent down behind the counter and mouthed "911"
to a customer who had walked in to cash some checks.
Lipinski got more cash from other teller stations. She put

the money in a white canvas bank bag and gave it to the robber: $8,702.

"It's not enough," he said.

"What do you want me to do?" Lipinski said.

She told him that was all the money she had.

The robber turned and started to walk out of the bank. Eleven minutes had gone by since he arrived. It was 2:38 P.M. He did not run. He sucked the lollipop. He carried his cane in his right hand. In his left hand, he twirled the bag of cash. When he swung the bag like that, he looked like Charlie Chaplin.

———

The robber got into a bluish-green Geo Metro parked in front of the bank. Three 911 calls immediately went out to report the robbery. One caller was the customer who had been in the bank, to whom the teller had mouthed for help; at this moment he was in his car, watching the Geo Metro.

"I'm calling about that bank robbery at PNC Bank Summit Towne plaza," he said.

"What happened?" the operator said.

"The guy just walked out with I don't know how much cash in a bag. He had a bomb or something wrapped around his neck. He's sitting in the parking lot of McDonald's on upper Peach by Summit Towne plaza. I'm watching him in out my rear view mirror right now."

"You saw him with the bomb or whatever it was?" the operator said.

"Yes. He's got it strapped around his neck."

"Tell the state police," the operator said. "I'm ringing them."

At 2:40 P.M., a dispatcher sent the Pennsylvania State Police to the scene.

———

The robber did not drive out the main road of Summit Towne Centre and exit onto upper Peach Street. He tried to drive his Geo Metro through the drive-through lane at the bank. He could not, so he drove on to the main road for the Summit Towne Centre and pulled into the parking lot of the McDonald's. The robber got out. He walked to the McDonald's drive-through sign, which was posted in a flower bed. He got down, lifted up a rock that was embedded in the landscaping and grabbed a piece of paper stuck to the bottom of the rock. The robber stood, read the note and lifted his eyes. He looked toward an Eat'n Park restaurant on the other side of Peach Street.

The robber returned to the Geo. He drove a backstreet near the McDonald's and pulled into the parking lot of Eyeglass World. A state police cruiser with flashing lights stopped the Geo. Eleven minutes had passed since the robber had left the bank. It was 2:49 P.M.

A state trooper, Victoria Weibel, called to the robber over her cruiser's public-address system.

"Driver, turn off the vehicle!"

"With your left hand, reach out and drop the keys out the window!"

"Place both hands outside the vehicle!"

"Do not move!"

Weibel and another trooper, Chris Stafford, moved toward the robber. They drew their guns. Weibel saw the robber had something around his neck and protruding from under his baggy white T-shirt. The device reminded Weibel of a halo, worn by a victim of a broken neck. The robber, under orders from Stafford, got out of his car and onto his knees; Stafford handcuffed the robber's hands behind his back. The robber kneeled outside the Geo and near a police cruiser. Other troopers arrived.

The robber told Stafford he was wearing a ticking time bomb.

Stafford shouted a warning. The troopers fell back. Weibel called the Erie police, the only local department with a bomb squad. The call reached the Erie police station, six miles north of the Summit Towne Centre, at 3:04 P.M.

Two other troopers, James Szymanski and Terrance Dawdy, arrived. They had driven more than 100 mph on I-90 to get to the parking lot of Eyeglass World. They approached the robber.

"He's got a bomb," another trooper said.

The troopers walked on. Dawdy was skeptical. The state police got bomb calls all the time. They never turned out to be true.

Szymanski and Dawdy asked the robber what was going on.

He said he had a bomb on his chest. He spoke to the troopers in a voice that suggested his regular tone was of a high pitch; it was a bit higher now. He was nervous. He sounded exasperated.

"Can you lift it up and see how much time's left on it?" he said. "It must have the time on it. How much time is left?"

The troopers asked him what happened.

"He was black," the robber said.

He said a black man locked the bomb around his neck and ordered him to rob the bank.

Here we go, Dawdy thought. He had heard this story before.

"It sounded like he was just blaming it on a black guy," Dawdy would testify later.

The robber said three other black men, whom he did not identify, were to follow him to make sure he obeyed the instructions in the notes. They made him do it, the robber said. He asked the troopers to call his employer, Mama Mia's Pizza-Ria. He gave them the phone number.

The state police dispatched a cruiser to Mama Mia's.

The robber said he encountered the black guy while he made a pizza delivery to "the towers," across from New Motors. He said the black guy snuck up on him, and he tried to get away, but the black guy fired a gun. He wasn't hit, but fell to the ground, and the black guy locked the bomb to him. The black guy gave him written instructions, which were in the Geo. The black guy told him how and when he would rob the bank while wearing the bomb.

"What did he look like?" Dawdy said.

The robber did not respond.

"What was he wearing?"

No response.

"What was he driving?"

No response.

The troopers asked the robber if he had any mental problems.

No.

Was he seeing a psychiatrist?

No.

The robber said he didn't do anything wrong. They made me do it, he said.

"Let's go see if he's got a real bomb," Dawdy said.

Szymanski and Dawdy walked to him. Szymanski felt the white T-shirt, the one with *GUESS Jeans* on it. He used a knife to cut it from the hem to a few inches below the man's left armpit. Szymanski pulled the T-shirt away.

The box with the bomb was grayish blue and hung from the metal collar. In the lower corner of the box, to the robber's right, was a white plastic digital clock mounted sideways. Steel mesh covered the box's opening; behind the mesh were wires of red, green and yellow.

The metal collar around the man's neck resembled an oversize handcuff. It had a complicated locking mechanism. A little metal box fastened to the collar contained a small, three-dial combination lock, in which the numbers rolled, like those locks found on suitcases, and four miniature keyhole locks, side by side. A green lever stuck out a side of the lock box. A warning was engraved on a metal panel:

DO NOT OPEN

=DO NOT REMOVE.

A sticker was on the box:

+RIVETED CONSTRUCTION PRODUCES DEADLY SHRAPNELL [*sic*]+

+KILL ZONE = 100 YARDS, HIDDEN AND EXPOSED +

+BOOBY TRAPS+

Szymanski and Dawdy walked back to the cruiser.

"Was it real?" Dawdy said.

"It had a device with a clock on it," Szymanski said. "It looked real. It could be a bomb."

They fell back. Szymanski parked a cruiser in front of the robber and stood behind the open doors. Dawdy stood at the rear of the cruiser. They asked the robber how long he had to rob the bank before the bomb went off.

"Twenty minutes for me to get the money. And then I had like another fifty minutes."

The robber said he was to use the fifty minutes to follow the instructions the black man had given him, the instructions on the notes in the Geo.

"They tell you where to get the keys," he said. "Then

you go to the next site in the car. Which one of you guys can go get the keys? Maybe if you get the keys, you could . . . I don't know if I have enough time."

"I'm not lying," the robber added.

Szymanski asked the robber why he didn't call the police.

At least three other people were watching him, the robber said. He said they were to make sure he followed the directions and robbed the bank.

"What's your name?" Szymanski said.

"Brian Wells."

Jerry Clark flicked on his unmarked car's lights and siren. In his eight years as a special agent for the Federal Bureau of Investigation, he rarely did that. Usually Clark could drive a reasonable speed and get through traffic without flashers or siren. This was different. He had to drive fast.

Clark had taken the call on his cell phone at lunch: a man wearing a bomb had robbed the PNC Bank in the Summit Towne Centre. Clark had planned on spending the day quietly, catching up on the mail before he took off the next day, a Friday, for the Labor Day weekend. Clark wasn't wearing his usual suit; he had come to work, at the FBI Resident Agency office in downtown Erie, in a polo shirt and slacks.

He had a busy weekend planned. Clark, forty-two years old, was to celebrate his twenty-five-year class reunion at

Erie's Cathedral Preparatory School, from which he graduated in 1978. He was set to go to a Prep football game on Friday night and attend the reunion celebration with his wife on Saturday night. Clark would see lots of his buddies at Friday's game. He hoped to catch up with some of them tonight, Thursday night, after they had arrived in town.

First, Clark had to deal with this strange bank-robbery call. This was no "note-job" case, where a desperate guy strolls into a bank, gives the clerk a demand note and leaves with some $50 bills in a bag. Clark had seen plenty of those. He had investigated bank robberies where the suspects said they had bombs, but the devices turned out to be phony. One robber's "bomb" had been radio antennas sticking out of a lunch bag.

The FBI two years earlier assigned Clark to its Resident Agency office in Erie, his hometown. He worked the six previous years at the FBI Resident Agency office in Dayton, Ohio, part of the Cincinnati Division. It had been like the Wild West. In six years, Clark helped round up two thousand fugitives as part of a violent crime squad that focused on the Cincinnati region. Dayton, in one year, had seventy-eight bank robberies.

Before joining the FBI, Clark investigated large-scale drug trafficking as a special agent for the Drug Enforcement Administration, in Cleveland; before that, he had worked as a forensic therapist, a probation officer and a special agent with the Naval Criminal Investigative Service, the NCIS. Clark had more experience with bank robberies and other violent crimes than any of the six other FBI agents in Erie at the time; his whole FBI career he had been assigned to violent crimes—fugitives, kidnappings, bank robberies. He had a bachelor's degree in psychology and a master's degree in forensic psychology. He had wanted to be a psychological profiler, who used clues to develop the portrait of the criminal.

Clark speeded south on upper Peach Street. He pulled into the parking lot of Eyeglass World and saw the bank robber. Clark walked to his supervisor, Bob Rudge, the head of the FBI's Resident Agency office in Erie, a satellite of the FBI's Pittsburgh Division. What a waste of time this is, Clark and Rudge said. It has to be a hoax.

"Would this guy just fucking stand up and end this thing?" a trooper said.

Clark, six feet one inch tall and 200 pounds, pulled on a bulletproof vest. He was sweating. It was seventy-five degrees. Where was the bomb squad? Time was dragging. Everything seemed to have stopped; the police had closed upper Peach Street to traffic. The silence was eerie.

The man who had identified himself as Brian Wells talked to the troopers. Clark wanted to jump in. He specialized in interviewing techniques. He was sure he could use those skills and his psychological training to draw out the robber. But the troopers seemed to have built some kind of rapport with Wells; Clark didn't want to ruin that. He could talk to Wells later, once this was over. Clark watched.

Wells now sat cross-legged, with his left knee bent high

above his right. He told the troopers he wanted to stand. He said he was uncomfortable.

"Can you at least take these freaking handcuffs off? So I can hold this thing up? It's killing my neck," Wells said.

The troopers told him to stay seated.

Wells asked when the bomb squad would arrive.

In a while, the troopers said.

If this was bullshit, you'd better end it now, one of the troopers said.

"It's not bullshit," Wells said. "I didn't do anything."

"Do you think I could have a cigarette?" he said. He said it would probably be his last one.

The troopers said no.

Wells asked for a priest.

The troopers said no.

"Why isn't nobody trying to come get this thing off me?" Wells said. "I don't have a lot of time."

His voice rose. He talked about the notes in his Geo, about the black guy who jumped him.

"He pulled a key out and started a timer," Wells said. "I heard the thing ticking when he did it."

"It's gonna go off," Wells said. "I'm not lying."

Wells shook his head.

"Did you call my boss?" he said.

"Yeah," one of the troopers said, "we called him."

Wells said the bomb was beeping. He wanted it unlocked from his neck. He wanted the handcuffs off.

For ten seconds the timer droned: *Beep!*

Wells turned slightly.

Boom!

Orange flames flashed.

———

The blast blew Wells straight back.

Shrapnel flew over the head of Trooper Dawdy, twenty feet away from Wells; a piece of metal landed fifty feet behind Dawdy. The trooper shuttled backward on his buttocks. He felt like he was falling.

The boom sounded like an exploding M-80. A percussive wave flowed over the head of Jerry Clark, thirty feet away.

Wells' chest rose and fell. Then it stopped.

Clark realized this was no joke.

"Holy shit," he thought. "This man is dead."

It was 3:18 P.M.—ninety-one minutes after Wells left Mama Mia's, seventy-eight minutes after he left the TV tower site, fifty-one minutes after he walked into the bank, forty minutes after he left the bank, twenty-nine minutes after Trooper Weibel stopped him in the parking lot, fourteen minutes after Weibel called the bomb squad.

Clark and others rushed toward Wells. They thought he might be alive.

"Watch out for secondary!"

Someone had shouted to warn about the possibility of another bomb. Clark and the others backed off. Three minutes after the detonation, at 3:21 P.M., the bomb squad pulled up; they had driven as fast as they could through the traffic.

Bomb technicians in their protective suits examined the body. Wells wore no other explosives.

The blast had slammed the metal plate on the back of the bomb into Wells' torso. The plate ripped a butterfly-shaped divot the size of a paperback into his chest, cutting into his heart and killing him. The explosion fractured his ribs and shattered his left eardrum. It looked like someone had taken an ice cream scooper to the layers of flesh around Wells' broken sternum.

Clark walked to Rudge, his supervisor.

"I gotta have this one," Clark said. "You gotta give me this case."

"It's yours," Rudge said.

———

A state trooper entered Mama Mia's Pizza-Ria about twenty-five minutes after the explosion. A trooper had been there earlier, while Wells was in the Eyeglass World parking lot, to get the address of the final delivery.

The trooper in the store at this moment told Tony Ditomo a bomb blast had killed Brian Wells. The trooper examined the pizza parlor's caller ID box. He wrote down the information for that day's incoming calls, including the one Ditomo took from the deep-voiced man at 1:30 P.M.

Investigators soon determined that call had come from a pay phone.

3

Prelude to a Murder

On Erie's lower east side, on a spot near Presque Isle Bay, once rested what is known as the Erie Stone: the marker surveyors used as a starting point to lay out the wilderness town of Erie, named after a local Native American tribe, in September 1795. The surveyors placed the Erie Stone on the site of what had been Fort Presque Isle, which the French built to repel the British during the French and Indian War. The Native Americans destroyed Fort Presque Isle in 1763. Presque Isle Bay, which forms one of the most naturally protected harbors on the Great Lakes, went unsettled again for more than thirty years, until around the time the surveyors arrived.

The surveyors placed the Erie Stone in a potato patch next to the Presque Isle Hotel, the first American structure erected along Presque Isle Bay that was not a garrison. The hotel doubled as a homestead for settlers and as a tavern. The combination presaged what would become the character of Erie: a city with many taverns, a city whose largely blue-collar populace first relied on Presque Isle Bay and Lake Erie for its commerce.

During the 1920s, Erie was known as the freshwater-fishing capital of the world; as many as 120 commercial fishing boats jammed its docks to unload perch and the even more precious blue pike, which is extinct today. The commercial fishing waned later in the twentieth century, but Erie grew into an industrial powerhouse. It teemed with factories that churned out boilers and washing machines and castings and locomotives.

The locomotive plant remains to this day: GE Transportation, located in a small town just east of the city of Erie, where more than five thousand people work. So many other businesses have left the Erie area. The heavy-equipment company Bucyrus Erie departed long ago, and so did the boiler plant and a shingle factory and International Paper's Erie operations.

Erie, in the early years of the twenty-first century, had hanging over it an air of decline that threatened to smother hope. Erie reveled in the beauty of Presque Isle Bay and the tourism it attracted, but deep problems beset the city: its poverty, its collapsing manufacturing base, its residents' willingness, all too often, to dwell on how great things had been instead of pondering how great they could be. Erie, at its worst, desperately clutched to the remnants of its past.

At its best, the city mined its heritage to its benefit. Erie became famous in the War of 1812 as the port where Commodore Oliver Hazard Perry built the ships he used to defeat the British fleet near present-day Put-in-Bay, Ohio, in the Battle of Lake Erie, on September 10, 1813. "We have met the enemy and they are ours," Perry wrote in his victory letter to President James Madison. Landmarks throughout Erie—the main square, a street, a school—were named after the city's adopted hero. In the early 1990s, Erie got the state's help to build a full-scale replica of Perry's flagship, the U.S. *Brig Niagara*, as well as a bay-front museum. More waterfront construction, including a convention center and a Sheraton, was to come.

The development helped revitalize a section of Erie's bay front that had deteriorated decades earlier, as the fishing industry vanished. In the summer of 2003, one commercial charter boat operated out of the port of Erie. Fishing was still popular; not as a livelihood, but as a pastime.

A favorite spot for the recreational anglers is Erie's South Pier, not far from the *Brig Niagara* and the plot where the surveyors planted the Erie Stone. The South Pier forms half of the channel that connects Presque Isle Bay to the open waters of Lake Erie. Those who fish the South Pier enjoy views of the lake and the bay to the north and Erie's downtown to the south. The fishing is usually good. If not, the sailboats and yachts and private charter boats that pass through the channel make for a lively diversion. Everyone in Erie seems to know someone who fishes the South Pier.

———

If you fished the South Pier in the summer of 2003, before the bomb blast killed Brian Wells, you might have seen her: Marjorie Diehl-Armstrong, once one of the most infamous women in Erie County. She was a fixture at the South Pier, where she fished with her live-in boyfriend, Jim Roden, and their friend Ken Barnes. Diehl-Armstrong, known as Marge, was hard to miss. She was foulmouthed and talked incessantly and loudly, and, at five feet eight inches tall and 186 pounds, she was built like a fullback. She wore her dark black hair long, stringy and wild, like Medusa's.

Diehl-Armstrong was fifty-four years old in the summer of 2003. She lived on $580 a month in Social Security benefits. She had received them since January 1984, for a diagnosis of a bipolar disorder, or manic depression. She had no children and was estranged from her widowed father. He taught her how to fish when she was twelve years old and they were still close.

Diehl-Armstrong spent most of her time in 2003 with her fishing buddies, including Barnes, who regularly visited her at the small Cape Cod she owned on the city's east side. Another of Diehl-Armstrong's companions in the summer of 2003 was Bill Rothstein. She had known him for thirty years; they had been engaged once. As long as she had known him, Rothstein had lived at

8645 Peach Street in Summit Township, next to the dirt road.

On the day the bomb killed Wells, the dead body of Jim Roden, Diehl-Armstrong's boyfriend, was stuffed in a freezer inside Rothstein's garage. Diehl-Armstrong and Rothstein had hidden the corpse there three weeks earlier.

Some nights on the South Pier, Diehl-Armstrong would laugh with Barnes about another murder—how, twenty years earlier, she shot and killed another live-in boyfriend on July 30, 1984. She would chuckle at how she was acquitted in the case that established her notoriety.

"I shot the motherfucker six times," Diehl-Armstrong would say. "I got away with it."

"How'd you do that?" Barnes would say.

"I told them he was beating me up."

Years after Diehl-Armstrong killed that boyfriend in 1984, Erie residents would still debate whether she should have been convicted or acquitted. She had known the victim, Bob Thomas, for some time, but five months before she shot him, she had reconnected with him while waiting on line for free government-surplus cheese. Diehl-Armstrong, then Marjorie Diehl, never denied she killed Thomas, a U.S. Navy veteran of the Vietnam War diagnosed with post-traumatic stress disorder and schizophrenia. She never denied she was no more than five to seven feet away when she opened fire on him at 7:10 A.M. on July 30, 1984, as he rested on a couch in their rented house at 3917 Sunset Boulevard in Erie.

She blasted Thomas with a six-shot .38-caliber Smith & Wesson Model No. 10 short-barrel revolver. All six bullets ripped into him. They hit him once behind the left ear, once on the left wrist, once in the left arm, once in a shoulder blade and twice in the left shoulder, where one of the bullets cut downward and severed his aorta. Powder burns covered the front of Thomas' shirt.

Diehl was thirty-five years old, had a master's degree in education and worked sporadically as a teacher, social worker and secretary. She had purchased the revolver five days earlier at a sports store. She was on antidepressants at the time. The store clerk told police Diehl said she needed the revolver to protect herself from prowlers. The clerk said Diehl asked her if the gun would kill someone.

Diehl told the jury she bought the gun as a belated birthday present for the forty-three-year-old Thomas. She testified she walked into the living room in her silk nightgown and fired away. He regularly beat her and sexually abused her, she said. They argued the night before after watching *An Officer and a Gentleman*. Diehl said Thomas accused her of being attracted to Richard Gere, the movie's star, and that Thomas forced her to perform oral sex on him. Diehl said Thomas cut her arm with a cooking knife as they argued in the kitchen. She said she shot Thomas in self-defense, not in cold blood, before he could shoot her. She said he had reached for the Smith & Wesson.

"I was scared to death at that point," Diehl testified. "I had no other choice. It was him or it was me, and I couldn't think. I didn't have time to think and I just fired the gun."

The jury deliberated for eleven hours and acquitted Diehl of homicide and possessing an instrument of crime and convicted her of carrying a firearm without a license. Diehl wept as the judge read the verdict, on June 2, 1988. Her next step, she said, was "to talk to God."

———

A battered-woman defense, still something of a legal novelty in Erie County in the mid-1980s, made Marjorie Diehl's case a local cause célèbre. So did the testimony about her mental illness, and how the mania and depression from her bipolar disorder derailed a promising career in education and counseling.

Her father, Harold Diehl, one of nine children, sold aluminum awnings door-to-door. Her mother, Agnes Diehl, who had degrees from the University of Pittsburgh and Columbia University, taught in the Erie public schools for decades. Marjorie Eleanor Diehl, an only child like her mother, had an intense desire to make her mother proud. She also felt unwanted by her parents, or caught between them. "My mother loved me madly," she reflected later, "but my father was jealous of the love my mother had for me."

When Diehl graduated from Erie's Academy High School in 1967, she boasted straight As and, with a class rank of twelfth out of 413, spoke at commencement. She taught private classes in piano, organ and cello, and considered herself a musical prodigy. She excelled at Erie's Mercyhurst College, where she graduated in 1970, a year early, with bachelor's degrees in sociology and biology.

Diehl liked to remind people her family had been in Erie a long time, that her maternal grandfather had been a police sergeant and successful builder and that Erie's Diehl Elementary School was named after a cousin, John C. Diehl, a deceased Erie schools superintendent the newspaper called "the grand old man" of Erie education. In college, she styled her brunette hair in a bouffant hairdo. She prided herself on her straight and bright-white teeth. She wore fashionable clothes that accentuated her 120-pound figure. She considered herself the prettiest girl in town. She liked being smart.

"I was more of an egghead," she once said.

Diehl said her mental problems started when she was twelve, when she suffered from anorexia and weighed as little as eighty-five pounds. She stopped eating, she later recalled, because of pressure to be faultless and a fear of puberty and sexual attention from boys. She wanted to be thin and perfect for her mother. She felt trapped, she once said, like a bird in a gilded cage.

The trouble never left Diehl from this point, the point in her life when her mental illness took root. Her mental health worsened, even after she recovered from the anorexia. For the rest of her life, she would never escape what her many psychiatrists and psychologists would diagnose as a bipolar disorder marked by extreme narcissism—her grandiose belief that she was perfect and deserved perfection, that she was worthy of only the best.

Diehl's mental erosion accelerated into adulthood. She grew to fear commitment. She first received psychiatric treatment in 1972, when she was twenty-three years old. What had begun to surface, according to one evaluation, was "a deep-seated hatred of men and passive-aggressive personality traits."

"I told them I wanted to find the right marriage partner" is how Diehl explained why she first sought mental-health treatment. "I was having problems with relationships and I wanted to seek analysis, more or less voluntarily, to help me overcome any neurotic tendencies that might be hampering me finding the right marriage partner."

Diehl, unmarried, worked as a part-time high school history teacher before getting her master's degree in education from Erie's Gannon University in 1975, where she took courses toward a doctorate. Her master's degree emphasized guidance and counseling.

The first criminal case against Diehl resulted from her work for an abortion clinic. The Erie police charged her in a sting in April 1980. The police accused her of telling an undercover female Erie police officer that the officer was pregnant, based on the results of her urine sample. The police said Diehl recommended the officer pay at least $150 for an abortion at a clinic in Buffalo. The urine sample was that of a male police officer. The police charged Diehl with conspiracy and attempted theft by deception.

Without pleading guilty, Diehl entered a program for first-time, nonviolent offenders. She got two years of probation, which included sixty hours of community service.

She performed them at the Pennsylvania Soldiers' and Sailors' Home, in Erie.

"Marjorie was an excellent volunteer, helping out with office work, activities and field trips," the volunteer coordinator wrote Diehl's probation officer in September 1982. "They were very pleased with Marjorie and said she's the best volunteer they've had in some time."

Two years later, Diehl emptied the revolver into her boyfriend.

———

At 1:00 P.M. on July 30, 1984, Bob Thomas' dead body was slumped on Diehl's living room couch. Diehl carried a blue bank bag stuffed with $18,000 in cash and visited the home of a friend. Diehl had met the woman a week earlier while they waited on a line for free cheese and butter.

"Could you keep your mouth shut for a lot of money?" Diehl said.

Diehl pulled out the $18,000. She had cashed a Social Security check that morning; the rest of the money was from a payment she previously received from a car accident. Diehl offered the woman a total of $25,000 to get rid of Thomas' body. Diehl clutched her purse and two yellow plastic grocery bags. The bags were filled with tissues, the revolver she used to kill Thomas and a telephone. Diehl took the phone from her house. She didn't want Thomas to wake up and call the police.

Diehl met with the woman for hours. Diehl talked about how to dispose of Thomas' body: cut it up with a chain saw, bury it, dump it off a pier, burn it. The woman telephoned the woman's sister. Diehl offered the woman's sister money to make Thomas' body disappear.

The woman and her sister called their mother, who called the police. Officers entered Diehl's house and found Thomas dead on the couch. Diehl told the police what she had done.

———

Court-ordered evaluations of Diehl's mental condition prevented her from going to trial until four years after she killed Bob Thomas.* The defense said she was not insane, or incapable of differentiating right from wrong, but mentally incompetent to stand trial, or incapable of understanding the case against her and assisting in her defense. Her lawyers said her bipolar disorder was so acute she would remain incompetent unless medicated. The Erie County District Attorney's Office wanted her found fit for trial; prosecutors said she comprehended the legal system.

The defense seemed to have a great deal of evidence in its favor. Diehl had been under some form of psychiatric

———

*While Diehl was incarcerated and awaiting trial, another death occurred in the rented house on Sunset Boulevard where she had killed Thomas on July 30, 1984. On April 4, 1985, the owner of the house, E.C., a sixty-five-year-old man whom Diehl-Armstrong once dated, was found hanging from a nylon rope in the house's entranceway. The coroner ruled the death a suicide and reported that E.C. left two suicide notes and was suffering from throat cancer but was also distraught over Thomas having been killed inside the house. A friend of E.C. told the coroner that E.C. "had been extremely distressed since this murder," according to the coroner's report. "He has been the object of much harassment."

care for more than a decade and was first prescribed medication in 1976, as part of psychotherapy. She was on the antidepressant Tofranil when she killed Thomas. In addition, Diehl was a hoarder.

When detectives walked into her rented house at 3917 Sunset Boulevard, where she killed Thomas, the stench overwhelmed them. Diehl had packed the four-room bungalow with government-surplus food, and it was rotting. She had visited food pantries throughout the city to collect butter and cheese and other perishables, including thirty-seven dozen eggs. She jammed the food into her cupboards, her closets and her attic, where the temperature had reached ninety-five degrees.

One back bedroom had no furniture. A three-layered pile spread over the floor: clothing was on the top, and as many as six hundred wire hangers were in the middle; the base was composed of books, newspapers, magazines and garbage. Among the reading materials were what police described as "war magazines," such as *Soldier of Fortune*, as well as photocopies of more than ten scholarly articles on psychiatric disorders, with titles such as "Psychoses in Adult Mental Defectives, Manic Depressive Psychosis," "Medical and Social Needs of Patients in Hospitals for the Mentally Subnormal," "Mental Deficiency and Manic-Depressive Insanity" and "Schizophrenic and Paranoid Psychoses."

The "rats were having a heyday in the attic," one official said. The condition of the house stunned a detective. "It was dirty, it stunk, the kitchen counter was filthy," he said. "There were plates and food lying all over the place.

There were open pastries and pies. Green bread was stacked up in the refrigerator and freezer."

A county official, cataloging the fraud Diehl perpetuated on the public-assistance system, tallied her take. The list took up three legal-size pages. In addition to the eggs, the items Diehl had collected included 389 pounds of USDA butter, 727 pounds of cheese, 111 five-pound boxes of dry milk, 59 two-pound bags of rice, 33 five-pound bags of flour, 36 five-pound bags of cornmeal, 180 boxes of macaroni and cheese, 44 boxes of pancake mix, 15 ten-ounce packages of matzo balls, 93 three-pound jars of honey, 26 jars of spaghetti sauce, 18 pounds of pinto beans, 26 cans of beef stew, 9 pork chops, 2 bags of prunes, 50 boxes of corn flakes, 39 jars or tubs of peanut butter, 12 jars of jelly, 314 cans of soup, 6 bottles of syrup, 5 pieces of spoiled sausage, 58 bags of egg noodles, 111 cans of tuna, 20 boxes of stuffing mix, 13 cans of beef gravy, 4 boxes of Cap'n Crunch and 1 container of Tang. Crews carted away 4 tons of food. They threw it into a garbage truck.

———

Diehl hoarded money, too, like the $18,000 in cash she carried after she killed Thomas. Money had captivated her since she was eight years old, when her maternal grandparents kept a safe in their house. They would show Diehl the cash in the safe, all stacked up, and let her take some of it to the bank to deposit every Friday. "They would tell me how someday that was going to be my inheritance," she said.

The mental-health hearings delayed Diehl's trial in the Thomas case. So did allegations that, while out on bond in November 1984, she offered $5,000 to an escaped felon to kill two people. She disputed the claims and the felon's credibility, but an Erie County judge revoked the bond and sent Diehl back to the Erie County Prison. For more than three years she shuttled between the prison and Mayview State Hospital, a mental institution near Pittsburgh. Forensic psychiatrists told the judge seven straight times that her bipolar disorder made her mentally incompetent to stand trial. While she was at Mayview, awaiting trial, doctors from July 1985 to December 1987 prescribed Diehl lithium carbonate and other antipsychotic drugs, including Tegretol, an anticonvulsant used to treat manic depression.

In December 1987, Diehl complained of unbearable side effects and swore off all medication. Lithium carbonate brought on anaphylactic shock, and Tegretol gave her hives that resembled chicken pox. Her mania returned: an obsession with her personal appearance, nonstop talking, constant arguing. The prison psychiatrists changed their opinion of her competency on January 29, 1988, six weeks after she had discontinued medication. They said Diehl's manic depression had gone into remission. She was fit for trial, they said, with the caution that she was likely to regress under stress and would need medication in the future. An Erie County judge ruled her competent on February 17, 1988.

———

At trial, the Erie County District Attorney's Office argued Diehl planned to kill Bob Thomas and that she was guilty of first-degree murder. A conviction would have sent her to prison for the rest of her life. If the psychiatrists would have continued to find her incompetent, she could have been held in prison for years longer, possibly indefinitely. When the defense prevailed and won the acquittal on the murder count and the one weapons charge, on June 2, 1988, Diehl was free. Her conviction on the charge of carrying the revolver without a license got her fifteen months of probation.

The judge sentenced her on July 7, 1988. He said he was concerned Diehl might need more mental-health treatment. She cut him off.

"I do believe the only person who can control myself, is myself," she said. "I know when I need medication or need a psychiatrist. I'm not a dangerous person and I know myself. I am familiar with monitoring my own situation."

Diehl's lawyers were pleased with the sentence. Fifteen months of probation when she was charged with shooting an unarmed man six times at close range? Who wouldn't be satisfied with that? Marjorie Diehl wasn't. She complained the judge should have never revoked her bond and that she should have never spent time in prison.

"I should have been released on my own recognizance," Diehl told reporters outside the courtroom. "I've learned my lesson. I've done my time, and I'm not going to get into any more trouble."

Marjorie Diehl became Marjorie Diehl-Armstrong in 1991. Her first and only marriage ended in death. Her husband, Richard Armstrong, suffered from paranoid schizophrenia and had such a fear of germs and bacteria that he drank bleach with meals. Diehl accused him in April 1990 of threatening to kill her, mutilate her and burn down her house. He entered into a plea bargain and was sentenced to a month in prison in early January 1991. Richard Armstrong married Marjorie Diehl while he was on parole, on January 23, 1991.

Armstrong died twenty months later. Paramedics arrived at Diehl-Armstrong's new house, at 1867 East Seventh Street, in Erie, the afternoon of August 22, 1992, and found him sitting on the floor, having vomited, and resting against a couch, unable to walk. He said he had been suffering from headaches for two days, had become increasingly dizzy and fell that afternoon and struck his head on a table. He said, according to Diehl-Armstrong, that it felt as if something had busted in his head or a hammer had hit him. The damage left him with a brain hemorrhage. Armstrong fell into a coma at the hospital, was declared brain dead and died on August 24, 1992. He was forty-four years old.

Diehl-Armstrong blamed the hospital for her husband's death. She filed a wrongful-death suit in 1994. She got $175,000 in settlement four years later. She was known to keep some of the cash around her house.

———

Diehl-Armstrong's IQ of 118 gave her a higher score than 88.5 percent of the population. She looked down on those she considered beneath her, such as her psychiatrists. She fought with them when they wanted to prescribe her psychotropic drugs.

As part of her therapy following her acquittal in the Thomas case, Diehl was prescribed Prozac and the anti-anxiety medication Buspar. In 1999, a psychiatrist said she was displaying "schizoaffective disorder" and added Klonopin, used to treat panic attacks. In 2000, she was also prescribed Risperdal, used to treat schizophrenia, and Synthroid, to address hypothyroidism. While on all these medications, Diehl-Armstrong firmly believed, as she told the judge in the Bob Thomas case, that she alone knew how to best diagnose and treat her mental health, including what her psychiatrists called her intense and erratic "hypomanic" behavior. Her endless talking had a clinical term—"pressured speech."

"Hypomania can be a blessing," Diehl-Armstrong once said. "It is like a sixth sense: you can tell the games that are going on behind the games. Everybody is different. I am a unique person."

Hypomania, she said, didn't make her a psycho, like someone who jumps out a window because she thinks she can fly. Her hypomania kept her optimistic and gave her energy.

"It gives you resilience," she said.

———

Marjorie Diehl-Armstrong, who liked nothing more than to talk about herself, had a self-awareness that could be captivating. Many of the things she said made no sense in the context of her actions—for example, her insistence to her psychiatrists and lawyers that she was neither dangerous nor a hoarder. Even when she uttered rapid-fire remarks that seemed ridiculous to anyone but her, she did so in a striking manner—effortlessly mixing historical and literary references with astrological musings, pop-culture trivia and current events. She talked a lot, but often what she said was insightful, or even humorous, albeit in a grim fashion.

"I'd rather have a friend than an enemy," she once said. "I don't like enemies."

It was hard not to feel a little sorry for Diehl-Armstrong, though her obnoxious behavior made the sympathy difficult to sustain. Here was a woman who, during her childhood and into her twenties, displayed intellectual virtuosity akin to that of a wunderkind, only to have mental illness spur the decay of her personality into that of a highly gifted but self-centered and overbearing killer.

"If there was anything for a panacea for me, don't you think I would take it?" she said in one of her many reflections on her mental illness. "You have to remember, and I am not just bragging about it, but it has been linked to genius. Lincoln, Churchill, Teddy Roosevelt, Van Gogh,

Beethoven, Hemingway—some of the greatest artists and writers who ever lived were bipolar."

Diehl-Armstrong considered herself a part of this illustrious group—the rarified ensemble of the socially and artistically brilliant and praised—rather than a member of a certain class of murderers.

"I am not," she once said, "one of these people that goes around like Ted Bundy and does these horrible things."

———

Though she was unmarried or widowed for much of her life, Diehl-Armstrong was rarely alone. Despite killing a boyfriend, despite keeping a house filled with fouled food, despite having a mental illness whose primary symptom was hypomanic behavior, including her inability to stop talking, Diehl-Armstrong surrounded herself with other people, most of them men. "Sex has never been a worry to me," she once said.

Jim Roden, Diehl-Armstrong's boyfriend in the summer of 2003, the boyfriend whose body would end up frozen, had been with her sporadically for ten years. He was forty-five years old. Diehl-Armstrong and Roden met in a bar when she was on a blind date with someone else. After Richard Armstrong died, in 1992, she met with a psychic at Lily Dale, a spiritualist enclave in nearby Chautauqua County, New York. Diehl-Armstrong said she went to the psychic to connect with the spirit of her deceased husband, but the psychic predicted she would meet another man, who would become the love of her life.

Roden came along. Diehl-Armstrong said he matched the
psychic's description: a native of the Cleveland area with
thick red hair and a beard.

Roden, tall and skinny—six feet tall and 140 pounds,
with a waist size no bigger than twenty-seven inches—was
an alcoholic who, when he worked, laid carpet. After he
met Diehl-Armstrong at the bar, Roden called her repeatedly and showed up one day at her house at 1867 East
Seventh Street, the same house where Armstrong was
found dizzy and suffering from a head wound. Diehl-
Armstrong got upset and then calmed down. Roden was
like a dog that had followed her home. She said she was
fated to love him.

4

Body in a Freezer

Bill Rothstein, Diehl-Armstrong's erstwhile fiancé, disliked Jim Roden. The animosity intensified in mid-August 2003, three weeks before Brian Wells was killed.

Perhaps it was Roden's drawn-in, pointy face that so aggravated Rothstein. Perhaps it was Roden's long hair and scruffy beard and teeth so rotten Diehl-Armstrong paid to have them all pulled, though she never bought him the promised dentures. Rothstein had seen Diehl-Armstrong carry on with men before. Roden was different for Rothstein, who called him "a rat without a tail," playing off Roden's last name, which Rothstein said was missing a *t* on the end.

Roden stuck around. Diehl-Armstrong let him, despite Rothstein's contempt. Roden and Diehl-Armstrong started living together in 1993. Violence plagued their relationship for a decade. He cut her thigh by pushing her into a broken glass panel of a stove door in July 1994. He pleaded guilty to simple assault and got three months to a year in the county prison. He got another six months later in 1994 after police charged him with violating a restraining order Diehl-Armstrong had taken out against him. Roden threatened "to kill me" and also to burn down the house, Diehl-Armstrong wrote in the complaint. A year later, in July 1995, Roden got another six months in prison for violating another restraining order. Roden, Diehl-Armstrong said, "threatened to burn down the house with me in it."

The one constant through the turmoil was the fishing. Diehl-Armstrong took Roden to the South Pier to keep his mind off the alcohol; she didn't drink much herself. He often fished without her and with his friend Ken Barnes. One day in the mid-1990s, Roden introduced Diehl-Armstrong to Barnes, a former television repairman with a history of dealing drugs.

Barnes, like Roden, was good with his hands. In the spring and summer of 2003, in the months and weeks before Brian Wells was killed, Diehl-Armstrong put both men to work. She and Barnes were close enough friends by then that they called each other by their nicknames: Margie and Kenny. Barnes and Roden remodeled an attic room in the house she and Roden shared on East Seventh Street. The room was to be an apartment with its own kitchen and bathroom, so Diehl-Armstrong could tell the state that she and Roden were not a couple, but living apart in the same house. That way, Diehl-Armstrong and

Roden could both continue to get government subsidies for utilities and other expenses.

Roden and Barnes, then forty-nine years old, worked on the apartment. The conditions made getting around complicated. The four rooms in Diehl-Armstrong's Cape Cod on East Seventh Street were, like those in her bungalow on Sunset Boulevard, packed from floor to ceiling with all types of stuff: food, clothing, toys, furniture, trash, animal feces from her many dogs and cats, an artificial Christmas tree. Fleas and cockroaches had taken over the place. One room contained a large entertainment center overrun with stuffed animals as well as bags of garbage, broken furniture and a set of box springs. Bags of trash teetered on the kitchen counters and up against the stove; at the top of the heap, the wheel of an upside-down baby stroller nearly touched the ceiling. Diehl-Armstrong carved out narrow passageways in which to navigate through the filth. Bill Rothstein later told police she drove around on garbage night, pulled bags of trash from the curb and squeezed the rubbish into every inch of the 1,010-square-foot house. He said she was compensating for her parents not getting her enough toys when she was a child.

"I've dealt with a lot of things," a longtime Erie police officer later said of Diehl-Armstrong's East Seventh Street house. "I've dealt with corpses with the flesh falling off. This is worse."

———

Diehl-Armstrong's hiring of Ken Barnes to help remodel her house in 2003 was peculiar. She considered him a violent thief who victimized her. She and Roden accused Barnes of breaking into their house at 3:50 A.M. on May 30, 2003, the Friday of Memorial Day weekend. They said Barnes helped rob Diehl-Armstrong of thousands of dollars in cash in a zippered bank envelope she kept in a plastic grocery bag. She had been lying on top of the bag as she slept in her nightgown on a sofa bed in the first-floor living room, near the picture window. Diehl-Armstrong called the Erie police, reported $2,300 was missing and fingered Barnes. She called him a cocaine dealer and a pimp.

The Erie detective assigned the case, Sergeant Frank Kwitowski, filed no charges. Diehl-Armstrong, who said she was heavily medicated when she was robbed, changed details. She said $2,800 was stolen, not $2,300. Diehl-Armstrong and Roden went to a magistrate's office and filed a private criminal complaint for review by the district attorney's office. The complaint went on for twenty-five pages. She accused Barnes and a "crackhead" biker of hatching the plan, in which she alleged the biker held a knife over her heart and stole her bag of money while Barnes watched. She eventually put the amount of stolen cash at $133,000. She wrote that the biker told her "I'm going to kill you, bitch," three times.

> I didn't ask to be attacked, and it is not my fault. I don't have to beg at people's feet for justice. I am entitled to it and won't cease legally until I get it!
>
> I've lived here 16 years. It's a school zone with a good crime watch. There has never been any trouble.

Barnes said he had nothing to do with the robbery. He continued to work at Diehl-Armstrong's house, even as she and Roden investigated the case on their own and pleaded for someone to press charges. The district attorney's office opted not to pursue a case. The prosecutors made the decision after something else happened at Diehl-Armstrong's house that would require much more of their time.

———

By May 2003, Diehl-Armstrong was prescribed a cocktail of mood-stabilizing drugs. They included Buspar; Klonopin; Stelazine, used to treat schizophrenia; and Wellbutrin, an antidepressant. Her final treatment with a psychiatrist, outside of a prison setting, occurred on May 21, 2003. She struggled to focus her thoughts, and she "kept talking, not making any sense," according to the treatment notes. The psychiatrist advised Diehl-Armstrong to keep taking all her medications. She did not.

She stopped taking them nine days later, after her house was burglarized, on May 30. Diehl-Armstrong said the drugs made her sick and slowed her down so much that she couldn't react quickly enough to defend herself against the robbers.

"It would have killed a horse or a cow with all the shit I was on," she said.

———

Tom Rupczewski, an Erie resident, placed a classified advertisement that was published on page 5C of the *Erie Times-News* on Saturday, August 2, 2003.

SHOTGUNS Remington shotguns $235; 1887 hunt-
ing & trap, nice; $450 ea or offer.

Rupczewski got a lot of calls as soon as the ad appeared. Only one inquiry came from a woman. She drove
to Rupczewski's house in a red Jeep Cherokee about an
hour after she called. She wore canvas tennis shoes, a
loose-fitting top and shorts. She seemed tired and anxious
and smelled of cat urine. Rupczewski later identified the
woman to police as Marjorie Diehl-Armstrong.

Diehl-Armstrong knew her mental-health history, including her commitment to Mayview State Hospital, would
prevent her from buying a gun at a store. She decided to
buy a shotgun out of the newspaper, though she never told
Rupczewski of her past. He asked her why she wanted the
12-gauge shotgun. Home defense, she said; burglars struck
her house on May 30.

The shotgun was a semiautomatic Remington Model
11-87, twenty-six inches long. It could hold three
rounds—one in the chamber and two in the magazine.

"That's the one," Diehl-Armstrong said.

The shotgun was beautiful. Its stock was made of
American walnut that had been shined to a sheen. The
high-gloss blue metal glowed. Rupczewski asked Diehl-
Armstrong if this was the kind of gun she wanted for
home defense. This was a high-end gun. Other guns
might work better for home defense, he told her; gun
shops would carry those types of firearms.

"I have the money and I want this one," Diehl-
Armstrong said.

They talked about how the shotgun worked.

"If I was to shoot the gun, if I needed to use the gun in the house," she asked, "would it put a big hole in the wall?"

Rupczewski chuckled. The Remington had a full choke, which creates a tight pattern. The pellets would spread very little when the shells were blasted from this shotgun.

"Yeah, it's going to put a big hole in the wall if you miss whoever or whatever you're aiming at," Rupczewski said.

"I don't want to kill anybody," Diehl-Armstrong said. "I would just shoot them in the foot and scare them."

She babbled about taking out a restraining order against an old boyfriend. She was ready to go.

Rupczewski refused her requests to load the shotgun and sell her shells. She said she didn't want anyone to see the gun. She asked Rupczewski for a tarp or paper bags to wrap around it. He declined.

Diehl-Armstrong bought the gun for $450. She paid with cash, all crisp $20 bills, with one $10 bill. Rupczewski fingered the bills. They felt new. He asked her if the money was counterfeit.

"Are you a cop?" Diehl-Armstrong said.

She said her husband had died, and she got a settlement. This cash was good, she said.

Diehl-Armstrong went home with the shotgun.

———

A week later, on August 10, 2003, a clothed Jim Roden lay on the bed in his upstairs apartment at 1867 East Seventh Street about 2:00 A.M.

Rain hammered the roof. Thunder boomed in the distance.

Diehl-Armstrong walked up the fifteen stairs from the first floor. She inched along amid the junk. She walked into Roden's bedroom. She held the Remington shotgun with the nice stock made of American walnut. She stood five to seven feet behind the bed.

Roden was facedown, resting. He might have been asleep.

She fired twice.

The blasts hit Roden from behind, in the middle of the back, just below the right shoulder blade. The wounds were nearly side by side.

The tightly patterned shot spread through the rear of Roden's body to the front. It shredded his spine, neck and right lung.

Roden shrank into the fetal position. The seeping blood soaked his bed.

Roden's dead body stayed in the upstairs apartment at Diehl-Armstrong's for two days. The high temperature reached seventy-eight degrees.

During that time, Diehl-Armstrong called Bill Rothstein's house at 8645 Peach Street. After she shot Roden, she had taken to living in her Jeep, parked at the Walmart on upper Peach Street in Summit Township. She washed in the store's restroom.

Diehl-Armstrong finally reached Rothstein at his house and said Roden was dead and she needed his help. She pulled out $78,000 in cash and offered it to Rothstein to get rid of Roden's body. He accepted. They went to work.

Bill Rothstein was dressed for the job, though he always looked like he was dressed for a job. He was fifty-nine years old, six feet two inches tall, weighed 319 pounds and had feet so wide—size twelve EEE—he complained he could not find shoes that fit. Rothstein had a big gut and was built like he had swallowed a wooden barrel. He had a full beard, which was mostly gray; and as long as anyone could remember, Bill Rothstein, a certified electrician, jack-of-all-trades, amateur-radio enthusiast and substitute shop teacher at the local high schools, wore the same type of clothes, every day: thick-rimmed glasses, a work shirt, denim bib overalls, boots.

Rothstein and Diehl-Armstrong talked about the best way to dispose of Roden's body. Dismemberment would be efficient, Rothstein said. "It's best to chop it up into as many pieces and spread it around," he would later testify.

She wanted to cut up Roden's body. He insisted they do not. They decided to wrap up the body and stuff it into a freezer.

They drove to the East Seventh Street house and arrived at about 10:00 P.M. on August 12.* She grabbed a green plastic tarp from one room. Rothstein opened his brown 1988 Ford Econoline van and got a blue plastic

---

*Court records are uncertain as to when Rothstein visited the house and saw Roden's body; he told police it was between August 11 and August 13, but he could not be sure. Based on all the evidence in the Roden case, August 12 is the most plausible date.

tarp, and clear plastic tarp, items he had specifically brought over for this task. He and Diehl-Armstrong walked up to Roden's apartment. Flies buzzed everywhere, which was nothing new for Diehl-Armstrong's house. Rothstein pulled the bedcover onto the floor. Roden's body came with it. He and Diehl-Armstrong wrapped Roden's body, which was still clothed and in the fetal position, in the green tarp. They wrapped the tarp with clear plastic tape and yellow nylon rope. The blood smeared all over. At one end of the tarp, Roden's head stuck out.

Rothstein grabbed Roden's shoulders and lugged the body down the stairs. The wrapped body oozed blood as it hit the fifteen steps. Rothstein dragged the body into his van, and wrapped it in the clear plastic tarp. He drove to his house, at 8645 Peach Street, where he left Roden's body on the floor of the garage. He and Diehl-Armstrong needed to do something quickly. The garage was hot like a greenhouse.

———

The white chest freezer, a W. C. Wood Company model C25NAB, featured a lid that lifted open. It was the type of freezer you put in a garage or basement to store a side of beef. The freezer was six feet one inch long and two feet three inches wide. Its capacity was twenty-five cubic feet. The freezer cost $379.67. Rothstein paid cash for it on the afternoon of August 13, 2003. He bought the chest freezer at the Rex TV & Appliance store at 7200 Peach Street, in the Summit Towne Centre.

Rothstein pushed the freezer into his garage, where the corpse was on the floor. Rothstein could not lift Roden's body into the freezer. He threw a rope over the rafter beam above the freezer and attached a one-lever pulley to it. He hauled up Roden's six-foot frame and lowered it into the freezer. The body remained in the fetal position; Rothstein was able to fit it in completely. He shut the lid, pushed the freezer to the garage's back wall and threw a black plastic tarp over it. Since the time he had driven home from the appliance store, the job had taken him two hours.

Rothstein concentrated on the shotgun. He cut it into little pieces. It was like dismembering a body. He destroyed the gun in his kitchen and his breezeway with a reciprocating saw and an acetylene torch.

He drove around Erie County at 2:00 A.M. and tossed the melted pieces of the gun out the window. He also tossed out the remains of the twenty-two shotgun shells. He had cut up the shells, too.

Rothstein had experience disposing of a murder weapon. On February 2, 1977, a friend, Louis Allessie, told him he had just killed someone in Erie. Rothstein testified he unsuccessfully tried to burn the murder weapon, a .25-caliber pistol. He said he put it in a plastic bag and threw it in the trash.

Rothstein did not tell anyone about the pistol for two years. When he did, he testified for the prosecution in 1979. He helped convict Allessie of shooting the boyfriend of Allessie's former girlfriend in the head. Allessie got five to ten years in state prison.* Rothstein, then thirty-five years old, got nothing. In exchange for his testimony, he received immunity.

———

With the gun gone and Roden's body in the freezer, Diehl-Armstrong and Rothstein focused on Roden's apartment. Soon it was the cleanest room in Diehl-Armstrong's house. They scrubbed it of blood and cleaned the rest of her house: her dogs had left bloody paw prints everywhere. Rothstein used some of Diehl-Armstrong's $78,000 to buy Clorox, hydrogen peroxide and other chemicals from the Summit Township Walmart. He ripped up the bedroom's vinyl flooring and painted the walls and ceiling. He replaced the fifteen bloody steps. He took apart Roden's bed: the frame, rails, headboard and the mattress, which was splotched with blood. Rothstein wanted to cut up the mattress, but that would have been too tricky, trying to steer a saw through cotton batting and steel coils. Rothstein drove the mattress and box springs to his house and stuck them in his garage.

The new chest freezer, draped in black tarp, hummed on the back wall. By the time Brian Wells drove his Geo Metro down the dirt road and past Bill Rothstein's house on August 28, 2003, Jim Roden's body would be frozen solid.

———

*Allessie was paroled in 1982 and died at age forty-six in 1992.

5

Search Warrant

The police cruisers poured onto the dirt road. Troopers and FBI agents swarmed to the site of the TV tower. They did not see Bill Rothstein. They were not looking for him. They were looking for the immediate suspect, the black guy who Brian Wells told the troopers had ambushed him and strapped the bomb to his neck.

The investigators did not find a black man at the tower site on August 28, 2003. They found no pizza boxes, no guns, no shell casings. A state police helicopter circled overhead, taking aerial photographs. Evidence specialists crawled in the dirt and gravel. Led by State Police Corporal Richard Pottorf, whose exactness impressed Jerry Clark and his FBI colleagues, state police investigators lifted tire-track impressions and footprints.

The investigators pinpointed the pay phone from which

Wells' final order was placed. It was located outside the Shell station at 8228 Peach Street, at the corner of Robison Road. Agents snipped the handset from the kiosk. They hoped to lift fingerprints.

Jerry Clark stood in the parking lot of Eyeglass World. He struggled to figure out where to begin. He was the lead FBI agent on the case, the case agent, the one who had to find out if anyone put Brian Wells up to the heist, and why Wells wore the bomb. Clark was overwhelmed. In a typical bank-robbery investigation, he handled most everything. He interviewed the tellers, got a description of the robber, put the surveillance photo on the local news and in the paper and worked with the local police to reel in a suspect. In this case, in which the robber had been killed, a flood of troopers and FBI agents gathered the details. Clark didn't even get inside the bank.

Was this an organized bank robbery? Clark had investigated a crew that knocked off five banks in Dayton. The Wells case was an isolated event; no other local banks had been hit, but it had been a planned robbery. Had someone put the bomb on Wells? Was it a stranger? Someone Wells knew? Clark could not dismiss the possibility—he was not dismissing anything at this point—of a stranger accosting Wells, but Wells most likely knew the person who did this to him.

When he was in Dayton, Clark went out on calls with the local homicide cops, the guys on the force who were the real pros, and learned the complexities of determining who killed whom and why. He got on-the-scene tutorials on the angles bullets took as they careened through the human skeleton; on how the position of a collapsed body reveals clues about the fatal assault; on the amount of time needed for bodily gases to build up to the point they would send a corpse bobbing to the surface of Dayton's Great Miami River. Through all these grisly lessons, Clark traced a theme: the manner of death might vary, and the weapons might be different, but rare was the homicide in which the victim did not know the killer. The media trumpeted those kinds of cases—the case of a pretty young coed slain by the creepy stalker she had never met— but they were far from the norm. That was not the way it happened.

Clark tried to focus. Chaos was edging in. About thirty investigators roamed the area near Eyeglass World and Summit Towne Centre: FBI agents, state troopers, members of the Erie police's bomb squad. The FBI set up a command post in the parking lot of a Texas Roadhouse restaurant on Peach Street, across from Eyeglass World. A crew placed a large trailer, like one at a construction site, in the middle of Peach Street as the headquarters for evidence collection. Clark and other investigators gathered under its awning, to avoid baking in the heat.

The FBI and police evidence specialists divided the scene into four zones and started to pick up the remnants of the bomb blast. Investigators took photographs from an aerial platform on a fire truck. They cataloged 162 items, among them an EverActive AA battery, shards from two white Sunbeam kitchen timers, the remains of a black toy cell phone and a bone fragment from Wells' upper neck. Preliminary findings indicated the collar held two pipe bombs, filled with smokeless powder like the kind packed into shotgun shells, and that an electrical charge, probably from batteries, detonated the pipe bombs.

The deputy Erie County coroner examined Wells' dead body, with the collar attached to his neck. Agents with the Bureau of Alcohol, Tobacco, Firearms and Explosives x-rayed the collar to make sure it was not booby-trapped. The deputy coroner pulled a white sheet over the body and slid it into a body bag for transport to the county morgue, at the Erie County Courthouse, in downtown Erie.

The chief federal prosecutor in Erie, an assistant U.S. attorney by the name of Marshall Piccinini, drove up from downtown and met with Clark. Clark was baffled. This was so crazy, he said, that this bomb actually went off. What was almost as wacky was that Wells robbed a bank, hoping to get $250,000, a huge amount of cash, but died with the money he did get. Why would you hold up a bank knowing you were going to die? Was Wells a "bomb hostage," as the notes said, or a willing participant?

Clark could not get the image out of his mind: Brian Wells, cross-legged and shouting, getting blown backward in a ball of flame, his chest rising once and no more. Clark had just seen a man get blown up as he watched. "Oh my God," the investigators around him kept saying. "I can't believe it."

Clark had to get beyond that shock. The investigation would not be simple; wending his way through the bureaucracy would be a challenge in itself. The FBI took the lead because of the bank robbery. The state police had jurisdiction over the homicide. The use of a bomb brought in the ATF. Clark recalled an adage: "Big cases, big headaches. Little cases, little headaches. No cases, no headaches." This was a big case.

The cane that Wells carried in the bank was not a real cane. It was a homemade shotgun. The handle of the cane, which was shaped like an upside-down letter *J*, concealed a wooden trigger. The metal shaft of the cane was the barrel of a shotgun. A wooden box attached to the handle contained the chamber. Loaded inside was one Remington 12-gauge shotgun shell. Investigators found the cane gun on the front passenger seat of Wells' Geo Metro. It was unfired.

———

Whoever locked the bomb to Wells gave him the cane gun. That was the scenario outlined in a two-page note investigators found in the Metro. It was not a suicide note, as Clark thought might be the case. Wouldn't that have been ideal, to find a suicide note that answered all the questions and ended the case with one read? The two-page note looked like the four-page note Wells handed the chief teller in the bank. The same block lettering, as if someone had typed the letters and then traced them by hand; the same phrases; similar instructions. A blue stripe highlighted the bottom of the four pages of notes, but a yellow stripe marked the bottom of these two pages.

=Bomb Hostage=

You are to go to "PNC" bank at Summit Town [sic] Centre on Peach St. "Quietly" give the following demand notes to a receptionist or Bank Manager. Do not cause alarm. Get required money and deliver to a specified location by following notes that you will collect as you race against time. Each note leads to the next note and key until finished. You will collect several keys and a combination to remove bomb. After, police won't charge you because you where [sic] a hostage.

MOST IMPORTANT RULE! Do not radio, phone or contact anyone. Alerting authorities, your company or anyone else will bring your death. If we spot police vehicles or air craft [sic] you will be killed.

This powerful, booby-trapped bomb can be removed only by following our instructions. Using time attempting to escape it will fail and leave you short of time to follow instructions. DO NOT DELAY. You have less than 55 minutes until detonation. Spend no more than 20 minutes in bank. You will need 25 minutes travel time. You have a safety margin less than 10 min. Use all remaining time to retrieve and obey our instructions. You will gain additional time by finding the first of several keys. As you follow our instructions, you'll be given all keys and combinations after the money is received and safely counted. We will leave keys and combination as you progress.

If you delay, disobey or alert anyone you will die! It is your choice to live, or bring death. If you do not obey and leave bank without money YOU WILL DIE. So will others.

Stay calm and do as instructed to survive. We're following your moves in 3 cars to make sure you obey. 3 sentries are driving and looking out for authorities. We are scanning police radio frequencies and cell phone calls. If police or aircraft are involved, you will be destroyed. Alerting authorities or anyone else will prevent you from completing the mission.

Go to the bank and "quietly" enter with the weapon you were given *Give* the demands to the receptionist or manager. Avoid panicking the tellers or customers. Use the weapon if anyone does not cooperate or attempts to leave the bank. Weapon instructions are near the trigger

You must deliver the money alone. You must return all weapons/notes to us. Turn yourself into bank and police after we release you to safety.

"ACT NOW, THINK LATER OR YOU WILL DIE!"

The second page of the note was headed "Step #1: PROCEED NOW." It instructed Wells to get $250,000 from the bank, leave his driver's license at the bank and promise to return, and to exit the bank with the cash in a black garbage bag. "Cooperate quickly and you will survive," the note said. "There is only one way you can survive and that is to cooperate completely." A hand-drawn rendering of a McDonald's drive-through sign appeared on the note, as a visual aid. Near the bottom of the sign, looking like something out of *Peanuts*, was a drawing of a small rock. Above it, just to make certain of no confusion, read the word *ROCK*.

EXIT THE BANK WITH THE MONEY AND GO TO THE McDONALDS RESTURAUNT *[sic]*. GET OUT OF THE CAR AND GO TO THE SMALL SIGN READING— DRIVE THRU/OPEN 24 HR IN THE FLOWER BED BY THE SIGN THERE IS A ROCK WITH [A] NOTE TAPED TO THE BOTTOM. IT HAS YOUR NEXT INSTRUCTIONS.

The McDonald's note was in Wells' car. It had two pages; one included a reproduction of a professionally made map of upper Peach Street and southern Erie County. After he left the McDonald's, the note said, Wells was to drive to the Eyeglass World parking lot, remove a piece of orange tape stuck to the collar bomb "and tie it around the fire hydrant at Peach Street to signal that you have the money and left the bank." Wells never completed that instruction.

From the Eyeglass World parking lot, Wells was to turn right, drive to the interchange of Peach Street and I-90— where traffic usually backed up—get on I-90 headed west, drive two miles, get on I-79 headed north, drive two and one-quarter miles, and get off at Exit 180, for the Mill-creek Mall. When done, Wells would have nearly driven in a circle.

At the mall exit, Wells was to pull to the side of the exit ramp and stop at a sign that cautioned a traffic light was ahead. Wells was to walk into the woods just east of the sign and search for a container; the note included a drawing of the traffic-signal sign to show Wells where to look.

> **The container with the orange tape has your next instructions. Place all notes, containers and tapes in the money bag and proceed.**

The note repeatedly said the bomb was live, and it would go off unless Wells hurried and found the keys, which he could use to unlock it from his neck. The note instructed Wells to drive 60 mph "throughout coarse" and to "use only 2 or 3 minutes at each stop." If Wells dawdled on this scavenger hunt, he would die. If Wells called the police, he would die. If Wells tried to disarm the bomb without the keys, the note said, the trip wires would detonate, and he would die. Whoever locked the bomb to Wells had sent him on a race against death, a race very much stacked in favor of his demise.

———

The FBI agents and state troopers who marched into the woods at Exit 180 came out with a red-lidded plastic Folgers coffee canister. A piece of dark orange marking tape, like surveyors use, was tied to it. Inside the canister was a one-page note, written like the others, with the same map as the McDonald's note. This note directed Wells to drive up the ramp for I-79 Exit 180, take a left onto an overpass and turn left again to get back on I-79, this time headed south. Wells was to drive two miles and stop along the highway at a small sign marking the boundary for McKean Township, which borders Summit Township to the south. The location was just north of the interchange of I-79 and I-90. At the McKean Township sign, the note said, Wells was to "walk into the woods and follow orange tapes to the container with instructions inside."

Investigators found several pieces of orange marking tape at the spot near the McKean Township sign. The pieces were located between the berm and a wire deer fence in the woods to the west of the berm; a dirt road was on the other side of the fence, perpendicular to the highway. The longest piece of tape was about seventeen feet and stretched mostly straight, perpendicular to I-79. The end of the tape closest to the berm was tied to the neck of an empty and upright Red Dog beer bottle; it was weathered, with its label worn away, as if it had been roadside trash. The far end of the tape was tied to the branch of a pine tree that was six feet from the deer fence. A second, smaller piece of tape was tied to another branch of the pine tree. On that piece of tape was scribbled, in black marker, *VIETNAM*, in wavy capital letters, with a series of numbers written under the letters: "8438626." The numbers corresponded to the letters, following the pattern on a telephone keypad. Tied to another branch of the same pine tree was a third and smaller piece of marking tape. It had nothing written on it.

The way the pieces of tape were placed suggested someone had made a path. The path started with the beer bottle, nearest the berm, and the tape directed the visitor to walk west to the deer fence, where the path ended; a piece of marking tape was tied to a section of fence nearest the pine tree. In that same section, someone had woven weeds and tree branches through the wires of the fence. That section of fence looked like a curtain. The weeds and tree branches that made up the curtain were still green. They had not been woven into the fence for long.

The first trooper who arrived at the McKean Township sign spotted a white van on the dirt road on the other side of the deer fence. He radioed for cruisers to check on the van, but it drove away before the backup arrived. During their search amid the marking tape, the FBI and police found no coffee canisters or other containers along the makeshift path. Someone had gotten there first.*

———

Jerry Clark learned secondhand about what his fellow agents found along the highway. He had left upper Peach Street late in the afternoon of August 28 for the FBI office in downtown Erie. It was not where he wanted to be. He wanted to stay at the scene of Wells' death and then go on the scavenger hunt himself. He wanted to interview people; he wanted to talk to the other investigators.

———

*Investigators also found no containers, notes or other items at two other locations that were supposed to have been part of the scavenger hunt. The two locations were mentioned in the bomb-hostage note found in Wells' car. The note instructed Wells: "If you can't find all instructions = alt drop sequence. Use only in emergency = may be deadly." The note told Wells to stop, only if necessary, at a trailer park off I-90 and then walk to a nearby overpass on the highway to get further instructions.

Instead, he was stuck inside. He and Marshall Piccinini, the chief assistant U.S. attorney in Erie, were writing the search warrant for Wells' cottage, at 2421 Loveland Avenue, in Millcreek.

Piccinini, a thirty-eight-year-old former U.S. Army prosecutor, was known for his meticulousness. Every case, he liked to say, was a big case to him, whether the offense involved organized gangs trafficking in kilos of cocaine or the desecration of federal forestland by some nitwit camper. The significance of the Wells' case had become quickly apparent, adding to the import of the search warrant for Wells' cottage. No one wanted to see evidence suppressed because of a faulty search warrant and a Fourth Amendment violation.

Clark shared Piccinini's concerns. He liked Marshall, and he could talk frankly to him, though he thought him too cautious sometimes. The search warrant for Wells' place would be critical; the search of the cottage could end the investigation, depending on what the agents discovered. Bomb-making materials, a suicide note, maybe even another bomb—whatever agents pulled out of Wells' house was bound to help Clark answer his questions: Was Wells in or out? Was he an innocent victim in the bomb plot? Was he a willing participant? Or was he both?

With the lollipop in his mouth and his Chaplinesque saunter, Wells seemed nonchalant inside the bank, as if he had no worries about the bomb around his neck exploding. Wouldn't someone forced to wear a bomb have been more nervous, even frantic? And why hadn't Wells called the police? Had he been in on the plan, and was confident it would succeed? Had he been plucked at random and told the bomb was a ruse? Was he a dim-witted dupe? Was he a twisted and violent thief?

Clark and Piccinini drafted a nine-page search warrant. It was getting late. They needed special permission to execute the warrant after 10:00 P.M. Clark and Piccinini drove to the house of the federal magistrate judge in Erie, Susan Paradise Baxter. She was in her bathrobe when she sat down at her dining room table to review the warrant. Piccinini apologized for bothering her at such an hour. She signed and sealed the warrant at 10:20 P.M.

———

Millcreek Township police officers, using explosives of their own, blew open the front door of Wells' cottage at around 1:25 A.M. on August 29. The whole neighborhood lit up, like a fireworks display had gone off overhead. Wells' cottage was not rigged with other bombs; that possibility had led Clark to have the police explode the front door rather than break it down.

Shards of splintered wood littered the floor as Clark walked in. The welcome mat—WELCOME, in huge red letters, over large drawings of Sylvester and Tweety, of Looney Tunes fame—had come to rest in the front room. Except for the splinters and the dust from the explosion, Wells' place was spotless.

Wells' cats wandered about; their litter boxes were lined up, by the kitchen, not far from a broom and a dustpan. The kitchen counters were clean and uncluttered.

The kitchen sink and stovetop looked like they were scrubbed regularly.

The front room contained the most stuff: two desks with no chairs, a small chest of drawers, a sofa chair, a table, a TV set, a VCR, a stereo amplifier, a CD player, speakers, a pair of shoes stored in a cardboard box. A box of tools sat on the floor near a tangle of jumper cables.

Wells slept on a mattress on the floor. He had a room upstairs. The furniture included a large chest of drawers, a small bookshelf with no books and three mismatched tables. A single pair of blue jeans and a white towel hung in his closet.

One of Wells' brothers, in later administering Wells' estate, put the total value of Wells' stereo equipment and all his other belongings at $1,425, including the 1996 Geo Metro, whose worth the brother set at $850.

The austerity of the cottage deflated Clark. Where were the obvious clues?

———

Among the items the FBI took from the cottage were two spiral notebooks that had been on a desk. Handwritten names—mostly just first names—and corresponding telephone numbers filled a page in one of the notebooks. One woman was listed on the page as Angie. Another was listed as Jessica.

6
Another Death

J erry Clark never made his twenty-fifth high school class reunion that weekend. Clark instead directed a group of investigators that had grown to seventy-five people from different agencies: the FBI, ATF, state police, local police, the Erie County District Attorney's Office.

The FBI set up a command post at its downtown Erie office. On Friday morning, August 29, agents used software with the FBI's Rapid Start Information Control System to establish a toll-free hotline for tips from the public. The investigators broke into teams. Each got specific people to interview, including Wells' coworkers and the people named in his notebook.

Clark tried to monitor the activity as best he could. He was concerned that a significant tip would not get immediate attention because of the sheer volume of information agents had to evaluate. As soon as the FBI disseminated the number for the tip line, hundreds of calls streamed in from all over the country. Clark took one from a psychiatrist in San Diego, offering help. The FBI had to catalog and address every call, no matter how loony.

Clark was still spending most of his time inside, rather than out in the field. His main job was to keep the information flowing to FBI headquarters, in Washington, D.C. It was draining, sending what the FBI calls an "Urgent Report" to headquarters for review by FBI Director Robert Mueller. The reports updated the leads and summarized the daily briefings Clark held—one at 8:00 A.M. and the other at 4:00 P.M. Clark found the collection of the information painful. He was the case agent. When would he get a chance to sit down and analyze the criminal behavior in this case? When would he be able to finally conduct some interviews?

———

Clark would have liked to have interviewed Bill Rothstein. FBI agents stopped at his house on the afternoon of August 28, after Wells was killed, because the house was so close to the dirt road and the site of the TV tower. No one answered the door. Pieces of metal and auto parts and oil drums cluttered the backyard. The house was dark. So was the garage.

A man who identified himself as Bill Rothstein answered the door the next day, on August 29. The agents asked him whether he saw or heard anything unusual the day before. Nothing, he said. The agents asked him if he knew anything about the pizza deliveryman getting blown up. No, he said. The agents asked him what he knew about the TV tower.

"I never go down there," Rothstein said.

The agents never went inside Rothstein's house on August 29. They never walked into his garage. Some of the agents quickly came to believe that Rothstein had no part in what happened to Wells. They said it made no sense that Rothstein would be involved. The agents could not imagine someone living so close to the TV tower participating in a plot that had unfolded there.

"There was no way he would do it," one agent told Clark.

———

Federal agents arrived in waves. They came from Pittsburgh; Washington, D.C.; and elsewhere. Evidence specialists and bomb experts stopped at the spots along I-79. They flew bomb parts to the FBI lab in Quantico, Virginia. Agents studied the footage that the local ABC affiliate, WJET-TV, filmed of Wells' final moments, including the unaired section that contained the full explosion. Profilers with the FBI's Behavioral Analysis Unit (BAU), which specializes in urgent cases as an offshoot of the Behavioral Science Unit, reviewed the nine pages of handwritten notes.

Clark went home to his wife and two children for a short time on Saturday, August 30. He got some sleep—his first since Wells had been killed. On Sunday, August 31, Clark returned to the command post by 7:00 A.M. He wanted to get a handle on the day; Monday was Labor Day, but Clark had no intention of taking it off. He reviewed reports, held the morning briefing, met with his supervisor, Bob Rudge. The Erie County district attorney, Brad Foulk, had offered the assistance of his staff. Sometime after 9:00 A.M., with Foulk present, Rudge sought out Clark.

"We've got another body," Rudge said.

———

The man was clearly dead. His body, 187 ½ pounds and five feet seven inches tall, was lying on a twin bed in a bedroom in a one-story ranch house on Dobbins Road, in Lawrence Park, a small town just east of Erie known mainly as home to the GE locomotive plant. The man wore pajama bottoms with no shirt. The bedcovers were undisturbed.

The man's mother had found him on the bed at 9:00 that morning and called for an ambulance. The deputy Erie County coroner, Dennis Suscheck, got to the house at 9:45 A.M. He pronounced the man dead and spoke to the police officer on the scene. The dead man, Suscheck was told, was Robert Pinetti, who had worked with Brian Wells at Mama Mia's.

Suscheck called his supervisor. Soon the state police, FBI, ATF and Erie police pulled up to the house. The Erie police's bomb squad inspected the house and found no explosives.

———

Pinetti's mother told investigators her son suffered from alcoholism and depression; she said the death of Wells, his friend, had left him despondent. On Saturday, August 30, Pinetti got to Mama Mia's early; the shop needed him to cover what would have been Wells' shift. Pinetti delivered pizzas until midnight. "The decedent told his mother he went to his sister's house after work and consumed a quantity of beer," Suscheck wrote in his report. "The decedent arrived at his home that he shared with his parents at 02:30 hrs [A.M.] and, according to his mother, 'was asleep standing up.'"

His mother had called paramedics twice that morning—when she found her son dead at 9:00 A.M. and at 5:00 A.M., when she woke to find him unconscious in the bathroom, where he had vomited. Pinetti was snoring on the bathroom floor when paramedics arrived after 5:00 A.M. One grinded his knuckles into Pinetti's breastbone—a technique called a sternal rub—to rouse him. Pinetti sat on the living room sofa and told the paramedics he had drank a lot of beer that night. He said he did not want to go to the hospital. Pinetti signed a refusal form by barely marking his name on the piece of paper. The paramedics helped Pinetti to his bed and told him to sleep on his side, in case he vomited. The ambulance left without him. Four hours later, his mother found him dead.

Pinetti appeared to have died of a drug overdose. He had a drug problem; a local hospital had treated him for an overdose that spring. Investigators found no signs of trauma. They found no suicide note. The autopsy showed Pinetti's urine contained methadone and the ingredients found in the antianxiety drug Xanax, for which Pinetti had a prescription. No one knew where he got the methadone.

―――――

That Sunday morning, after Rudge spoke to him in the hallway, Clark had two death investigations to track—one on Wells and the other on Pinetti. The state police had jurisdiction over the Pinetti case. An unattended death wasn't a federal matter, but the FBI and ATF were still interested in Pinetti's relationship with Wells. The agents looked into the past of Pinetti. Before he worked at Mama Mia's, he got a real estate agent license and owned a pizza shop, Picasso's Pizza. He was unmarried, childless and, when he wasn't delivering pizzas, had spent much of his time caring for his elderly parents and his younger sister, all of whom had health problems.

Pinetti had few friends. He owned a $35,000 rental house in Erie but had few other assets; his next most valuable possession was a $1,500 1995 Nissan Altima. He had credit-card debts totaling $21,542. He owed his mother $17,725 for a loan. Pinetti's checking account had a balance of $63.49 when he died. His savings account totaled $27.67.

Wells' death concerned Pinetti. He told a relative the day after the bombing that Wells "wouldn't do anything like that." Pinetti told the relative he himself "was scared to deliver pizzas." Pinetti unsuccessfully tried to get a gun from his sister after he got off work at Mama Mia's around midnight on Saturday, August 30. He told her he was frightened.

————

The Erie County Coroner's Office ruled Pinetti died of an accidental overdose of Xanax and methadone. Pinetti would not have died had he swallowed only the liquid methadone or the Xanax. Taken together, in the amounts he ingested, the two drugs killed him.

The coroner's ruling left unanswered where Pinetti got the methadone, which is prescribed to heroin addicts. Pinetti was not addicted to heroin. The Erie police said drug dealers rarely traded in methadone on the city's streets. No methadone turned up at Pinetti's parents' house, "which probably suggests he may not have taken it at home," said the chief deputy coroner for Erie County, Korac Timon, who ruled on Pinetti's death. "We're not sure he even was aware of what methadone was."*

Pinetti's death perplexed the FBI. Was it related to the Wells' case? Were the two deaths coincidental?

"At this time, no connection has been made

————

*Timon wrote in the coroner's report: "Based on all of the findings, it is my opinion the decedent died as the result of Combined Drug Toxicity with a History of Alcohol Abuse as a contributory condition to which effect this office signed out a death certificate. In conclusion, due to the absence of evidence suggesting suicide, to include the levels of drugs detected in the victim's system, the manner was ruled Accidental."

linking Mr. Pinetti to the bank robbery that occurred on Thursday," a state police spokesman said at the time. "Investigators are, though, continuing to explore the link between the individuals."

———

The FBI had interviewed Pinetti on Saturday, August 30, two days after Wells was killed. Pinetti was at Mama Mia's. He was nervous and vague and kept saying he couldn't talk to the agents then because he had stuff to do. The agents said they would get back to him. After the agents left, Pinetti said he could not understand why the FBI wanted to talk to him. The agents never talked to Pinetti again.

It was another slip in the investigation. Jerry Clark was troubled. The Wells investigation was so sprawling, he had to fight to stay on top of it. How many more shortcomings would Clark have to untangle later? He already regretted he didn't interrupt the state troopers and talk to Wells. Now Pinetti was dead, with who knows what left unsaid. Clark believed Pinetti's death had something to do with Wells', but he was unsure how. Two drivers at a pizza shop dead within three days of each other? Maybe Pinetti knew what happened to Wells. Why didn't the agents press Pinetti on Saturday? If you are going to interview someone, interview him right then and there. Don't wait, especially in a case like this.

"We certainly would have liked to have talked to Pinetti in a little more detail," said Bob Rudge, Clark's supervisor.

7

Persons of Interest

eathbed confessions occupy a sacrosanct place in American jurisprudence. The Federal Rules of Evidence, like the rules of evidence for the state courts, prohibit most hearsay testimony, mainly because it is unreliable and prevents the defendant from exercising the Sixth Amendment right to confront witnesses. The law makes an exception for dying declarations. The prosecution can present such statements as evidence, even though the witness, being dead, cannot be cross-examined.

American law has recognized the exception since the nation's founding; a jury is allowed to hear, according to the Federal Rules of Evidence, "a statement made by a declarant while believing that the declarant's death was imminent, concerning the cause or circumstances of what the declarant believed to be impending death." A note to the Rules offers insight into why the law considers dying declarations inherently credible: "While the original religious justification for the exception may have lost its conviction for some persons over the years, it can scarcely be doubted that powerful psychological pressures are present."

Powerful psychological pressures were bearing down on Brian Wells when he spoke to the state troopers with a ticking time bomb locked to his neck. His deathbed confession was that a black man forced him to wear a bomb and that a group of three other black men was watching to ensure he abided by their plan. Why would Wells lie if he knew he was going to die? Why would anyone make a false deathbed confession?

The FBI took Wells at his dying word. The agents believed him when he brought up the black man and the group of black men. Clark counted himself among those investigators who could not dismiss the fact that Wells accused a group of black men of killing him. Clark remained annoyed at the investigatory gaffes, including the aborted interview of Pinetti, but in the early stages of the investigation, the scenario involving the black men still sounded as promising as any. No one—certainly not Rothstein or Pinetti—had provided information to disprove what Wells' had said about the black guys.

———

The results of the autopsy on Wells' body emphasized the ferocity of the bomb—the butterfly-shaped wound, 7.1 by 3.7 inches wide, torn into his chest by the bomb's metal backing plate; the lacerations to his heart, the bruises to his lungs; his broken ribs and sternum; his obliterated left eardrum. Erie County's forensic pathologist, Eric Vey, M.D., conducted the autopsy on Brian Douglas Wells the morning of Friday, August 29. Vey examined a cluster of reddish-orange bruises on Wells' right thigh that surrounded a gaping hole, 1.5 inches by 0.7 of an inch wide. "Explorative dissection is undertaken within this wound tract," Vey wrote in his thirty-page report, "revealing the presence of a single lead pellet consistent with a shotgun pellet. Also, a small shard of metal is recovered." The FBI took the pellet and the shard as evidence.

At first, the existence of the pellet appeared to support Wells' statement that a black man fired a gun at him; the weapon had to have been a shotgun, hence the pellet in Wells' thigh. However, the downward angle of the wound, as well as the evidence collected from the Eyeglass World parking lot and its environs, pointed to another possibility, one that the FBI eventually accepted as accurate.

The collar bomb had indeed featured two pipe bombs, side by side, arranged vertically inside the metal box that hung from the collar. One of the two pipe bombs blasted the pellet into Wells' thigh; the shard of metal was a piece of shrapnel. Evidence specialists recovered only twelve pieces of shot, including the embedded pellet.

Whoever made the device had packed the two pipe bombs with smokeless powder consistent with the powder inside the Remington 12-gauge shotgun shell loaded into the cane gun; Walmart exclusively sold the type of shell found in the gun. The black smokeless powder from the explosion sprinkled Wells' chest and arms. In emptying the shotgun shells, the bomb maker inadvertently included the twelve pellets in the explosive mixture. To sift out all the pellets would have been difficult. The FBI lab determined that the two pipe bombs contained enough smokeless powder to fill 273 shotgun shells, the equivalent of about nine boxes of shells, with a count of 30 per box. Cartons of pure smokeless powder are easily available for purchase; whoever made the bomb chose the more time-consuming option of emptying shotgun shell after shotgun shell, by hand.

Vey, the forensic pathologist, found no bruising on Wells' neck or other evidence, such as scratches, that indicated defensive wounds. Wells did not appear to have struggled when the bomb was locked to his neck. The lack of defensive wounds fit with what investigators immediately noticed: that the *GUESS* T-shirt, before Trooper Szymanski cut it away from Wells with a knife, fit neatly over the metal collar. Wells had to have cooperated as he or someone else pulled that T-shirt over his head to conceal the bomb. Had Wells put up a fight, the shirt would have been torn or stained with dirt or blood. The investigators also noticed the dirt stains on Wells' jeans. Maybe he had fallen. Maybe he had been pushed.

The autopsy revealed no drugs or alcohol in Wells' system. His body had no tattoos or other unusual markings, though his pubic hair had been previously shaved. The eight people who attended the autopsy studied the handcuff-like collar locked to Wells' neck. Like a small handcuff, this large handcuff was made up of two semicircular arms—one fixed and one hinged—that formed a circle when locked. The collar was spring-loaded; ratchet teeth tightened the two arms and prevented them from loosening. Thin tubing, filled with clear blue liquid, encircled the collar; the tubing was woven through the small holes in the interiors of the two semicircular arms. Three copper wires were twisted around the tubing.

Two ATF agents and two FBI agents—Clark was not among them—wanted to get the collar and the rest of the contraption out of the Erie County morgue as soon as they could and fly it to the FBI lab in Quantico, as intact as possible. The collar seemed to be the best piece of evidence; no one wanted to ruin it by cutting it from Wells' neck. The agents were not entirely certain the bomb was free of booby traps; they saw the liquid-filled tubing and the wires and worried that sawing through the metal collar would trigger an explosion. One agent told Vey there was a 99.9 percent chance the collar would not explode, but Vey wanted a 100 percent assurance. No one wanted to cut the bomb off Wells' neck. Vey, using a newly sharpened dissecting scalpel, cut off his head instead.*

———

The FBI's Behavioral Analysis Unit in Quantico analyzed the nine pages of notes. The profilers put the notes in the

---

*The FBI never determined the composition of the liquid in the tubing, though the liquid, the tubing and the wires around the tubing all turned out to be harmless. The FBI suspected the liquid was hydraulic fluid and that the tubing and wires were meant to confuse bomb technicians.

context of the bomb and the cane gun and the methodical manner in which someone had arranged for Wells to die. The profilers developed key personality traits of the person, or persons, behind the plot. They noticed the note Wells had in the car directed him to "Summit Town Centre"; the profilers theorized whoever wrote the note knew the plaza well enough to remember it was spelled "Centre" rather than "Center." The caller who phoned in the pizza order specified "upper Peach." Whoever wrote the notes and whoever made that call, the profilers and other FBI agents said, most likely lived in the area. The profilers theorized:

The offender likes power. He's obsessive. He manipulates people. But he's also patient.

This offender invested a great deal of thought and planning into this scheme, which could have evolved over a long period of time, even years. It's possible Wells knew the offender and misjudged the level of danger. It's also possible getting the bank's money was not the motivating factor.

Revenge is a theme repeated throughout the letters, along with certain dire consequence if instructions were not strictly followed.

For whomever locked the bomb around Brian Wells, the ordeal was about control and manipulation. It was "game-like" with rules and penalties. The reward was less specific. "Cooperate quickly and you will survive," the offender printed in a letter to Wells.

But the offender probably didn't expect Wells to survive and was most likely watching when the bomb blew up at 3:18 P.M. This offender needed to observe the events that day—in and around the bank—as Brian Wells walked inside, stood in line and then exited the bank. This offender was probably in or near the Summit Town [*sic*] Centre on Aug. 28 to observe what happened.

The profilers said a complex man or woman locked the bomb to Wells. The person was

Skillful at working with wood and metal, and would have possibly received vocational and technical training.

Known to friends as a handyman.

Fascinated with building or acquiring weapons or implements of war.

Fascinated with lethal products that could kill humans or animals. The behavior would have progressed over the years.

Secretive. The person would have worked on items such as the cane gun or collar bomb in areas unavailable to others.

Someone who would build things with inexpensive materials or would make things out of items on hand. That might reflect on the person's socioeconomic status.

Patient, with a lot of time on his or her hands.

Deceptive.*

---

*The FBI's Behavioral Analysis Unit alerted the agents in Erie to these characteristics early in the Wells investigation. The FBI released them to the public later, at a news conference on September 25, 2003.

The writer of the notes, said Bob Rudge, Clark's supervisor, "is a manipulator who manipulates the actions of others. He is like a puppeteer."

FBI agents interviewed the woman by the name of Angie, whose name and number were in Wells' notebook. Angie had left a message on Wells' answering machine before he died. Her comments to the agents intrigued Clark. The information she grudgingly provided strengthened his belief that, early in the case, he and the other investigators were pursuing a legitimate theory by tracing leads gleaned from Wells' last words about the black guy and group of black men. Angie was a twenty-five-year-old Erie resident, the same woman with the black boyfriend who used to visit Wells at Mama Mia's and bother him for money. Angie had worked as a prostitute.

Angie lied to the FBI. She said she did not know Wells, as if the agents would ignore that her name and number were in his notebook. She said Wells was her cousin. She acknowledged her record for prostitution but said Wells was not a client.

The FBI was unconvinced. Clark reminded himself of another adage: "In a homicide investigation, there are no such things as coincidences." Surely Angie's connection to Wells was not inadvertent. The agents questioned her boyfriend, J.J. His answers turned him into an investigative target.

J.J. was black. In addition, he possessed characteristics the profilers said applied to Wells' assailant: a deceptive person skilled with machines and familiar with weaponry. Even J.J. described himself as mechanical. He was a forty-six-year-old former U.S. Marine who, according to the FBI, handled munitions when he was in the military. He was unemployed but had last worked maintenance at an Erie plastics plant, where he handled complex engineering equipment. J.J. liked to return after hours, when he had free access to the plant's shop floor. He would use the equipment for his own projects.

J.J. had a criminal record for theft and possessing a crack pipe. J.J. said he never knew Wells, though he conceded that Angie left a message on Wells' answering machine right before he died; investigators found that message after Wells' death. J.J. said Angie wanted Wells to give her a ride. J.J. said he was waxing his car outside his apartment, on Erie's lower east side, when Wells was killed. J.J. babied that car, an older-model Lincoln Continental, candy-apple red with a white ragtop, whitewalls, spoked rims, curb feelers and a V-shaped antenna on the trunk roof. J.J. said the neighbors would back up his alibi.

On Friday, September 5, 2003, eight days after Wells was killed, the FBI searched J.J. and Angie's apartment. The agents took tools and J.J.'s laptop. They looked for firearms, explosives and ammunition, though none turned up.* The FBI considered this search pivotal; Clark got out

---

*The items the FBI agents were looking for were listed on a two-page warrant agents left with J.J. The affidavit of probable cause for the search warrant, which explains the reasons for the search of J.J.'s apartment, remains sealed.

of the office for it. As agents walked around upstairs, Clark sat with J.J. on the front porch. He tried to calm him. More than forty people crowded the street in front of J.J.'s apartment house, watching the FBI at work. J.J. fumed.

"This ain't Nazi Germany," he said. "And that's how I feel: like I am being persecuted. I fix and build things. But I have no knowledge of munitions. I've never been exposed to that stuff. I don't mess with guns."

The FBI said nothing to reporters about the search and whether J.J. was under suspicion in the Wells case. J.J. derided what he said was the FBI's classification for him: "a person of interest."

———

The FBI found the other woman whose name was in Wells' notebook—the woman named Jessica. She worked as a prostitute who frequented West Eighteenth and Cascade streets, in Erie's Little Italy, a neighborhood that once pulsed with working-class prosperity. Now it was where Jessica could solicit customers at all hours.

Jessica was the same woman as Jessie, of whom Wells spoke at Mama Mia's. She was the woman, Wells said, whose black boyfriend would drop her off at the corner and who would walk to Wells' cottage for visits. Her full name was Jessica Hoopsick. She was twenty-four years old. She had been turning tricks for years.

On July 22, 2003, about five weeks before Wells was killed, Erie police charged Hoopsick with loitering for the purpose of prostitution on West Eighteenth Street. She was addicted to crack. The arresting officer noted

Hoopsick's dimensions in the criminal complaint—five feet five inches tall and 200 pounds—and his report reflected her desperation. "This can't happen again," the arresting officer wrote Hoopsick told him. "I'll tell you anything you want to know." She pleaded guilty and agreed to receive counseling for drug use.

The agents in the Wells case found Hoopsick walking the streets in early September 2003. Like Angie, Hoopsick denied knowing Wells, though he had written her name and number in his notebook. Hoopsick did not cooperate in the early days of the Wells investigation, but she was someone the agents thought they might turn to later. Finding Hoopsick would be less of a problem, now that the agents knew where she worked. The challenge would be to catch her when she was not high.

The FBI's hotline brought in more calls than agents could handle quickly. Every tip, every potential lead, had to be cataloged and pursued.

One of the calls to the hotline came on September 5, from a sixty-four-year-old labor arbitrator and retired college professor with a good memory. The caller, Tom Sedwick, relayed what he saw on the afternoon of August 28. He said he made the observations on I-79, near the interchange of I-79 and I-90. That section of the highway includes the McKean Township sign, whose importance to the Wells case the FBI had yet to disclose to the public.

An FBI agent took notes of Sedwick's call. Sedwick

said he was driving south on I-79 when a car going the wrong way passed him.

> He observed a heavily tanned female driving a late 1970's GMC or Chevy Sedan, brown or bronze in color, traveling northbound in the southbound lanes on the burm *[sic]*. Sedwick stopped on I-79 momentarily, then past *[sic]* the woman who was traveling in the opposite direction.
>
> Sedwick further described this woman as in her 40's, with shoulder length dark hair.
>
> Sedwick could not provide any additional details as to the description of the woman or vehicle.

Another detail of what occurred that day came from Melissa Shearer, a twenty-nine-year-old stay-at-home mom who lived on Honeysuckle Drive in Summit Township, in the subdivision just north of the TV tower. The FBI canvassed Shearer's neighborhood on September 13, 2003. She told an agent that, at 1:30 P.M. on August 28, she put down her one-year-old son for a nap and looked out an open window at the sunny day. Between 1:30 P.M. and 2 P.M., Shearer said, she heard a loud boom emanate from the direction of the TV tower. She said the noise sounded like a single gunshot.

Shearer's statement led Clark to conclude Wells was fired upon in the clearing. Someone—maybe a black man—had shot at Wells, as he had insisted.

———

Two weeks after Wells' death, at about noon on Sunday, September 7, the Erie bomb squad suited up for another call. The squad's armored truck rumbled up to a bank at a corner of Twelfth and State streets, one of downtown Erie's busiest intersections. Police closed off the streets. The bomb technicians walked up to a wooden box resting against an outer wall of the bank. Reporters from the national media, still in town for the Wells case, watched. The techs blew up the box. Christmas ornaments and Christmas dolls flew about.

Around 12:30 A.M. that morning, a thirty-year-old Erie resident had removed the wooden box from his car's rear seat to make room for his friends; he had placed the box outside the bank, across the street from a bar. The man intended to retrieve the box later that morning, but he forgot. The box was filled with Christmas decorations he had received from his grandmother.

A bank employee spotted the box as he walked into the bank late Sunday morning. The employee was taking no chances, not with the case of the blown-up pizza deliveryman on everyone's mind. The bank employee called the police, who dispatched the bomb squad.

"With the recent event," the employee said, "I'm a little more cautious."

———

Any rookie detective knows the first days of an investigation are the most important for gathering evidence. The first days of the probe in the Wells case went by with no arrests and nothing that definitively pointed to a suspect. A potential lead sputtered on September 8. The FBI early in the day released composite sketches of two people who passersby said were acting strangely around upper Peach Street about the time Wells was killed. One sketch was of a skinny white man with stringy whitish-blond hair. He was seen carrying a cell phone and dodging traffic on a road outside the Millcreek Mall, not far from the exit where Wells was supposed to have picked up a note. The other sketch was of a muscular black man seen jumping a cement divider along upper Peach Street, near the mall.

The FBI stopped traffic near the mall and asked motorists if they were in the area on August 28; none of the motorists identified the white man in the sketch. By the end of the day on September 8, the agents found the black man. In person, he looked just like his sketch. The man saw the sketch on the local television news, recognized himself and contacted the FBI. Agents questioned the man for an hour and let him go. He was a New Jersey construction worker in Erie to build a store near the Millcreek Mall. When he jumped over the cement divider on August 28, the man was rushing to catch a bus.

8

A Design to Kill

FBI headquarters sent the word on September 9: the bureau had designated the Wells investigation Major Case 203, the highest status an investigation can get. The FBI agents in Erie debated what to pick as the name for Major Case 203. The public, having seen the footage of Wells on the network news, was already referring to it as the pizza bomber case. But labeling the investigation PIZZA BOMBER struck some in the FBI as too flippant, and possibly demeaning to pizza-delivery drivers. Clark and the other agents came up with something based on the signature element of the case—the bomb. It was wholly unique to crime in the United States, though it looked like something terrorists were known to use in South America. Major Case 203 henceforth was known, by the FBI, as COLLARBOMB.

Headquarters, which approved the name, treats a Major Case as priority. The cases get more agents, more funding, more equipment and more immediate access to the FBI's specialists. The FBI in Erie set aside a vacant floor in its downtown headquarters for the Wells investigation. Soon all the new equipment arrived: desks, fax machines, computers, cell phones. It was like Christmas. Another of Jerry Clark's jobs was to account for all of the new stuff, some of which the agents, though not usually him, were trying out on the street.

———

Brian Wells had been killed in a plan likely developed over months with the type of precision usually reserved for criminal masterminds on the order of the Unabomber. One look at photos of the collar bomb's remains, one look at photos of the injuries to Wells, reminded Clark and his fellow agents of the malicious nature of the plot and the collar bomb. It was like a demon had fashioned the device in a fury of malevolence.

"A lot of work went into this," said ATF Special Agent Jason Wick, who would become a key part of the investigation.

Wick, an ATF agent since 1989, had worked on the downing of United Airlines Flight 93 on September 11, 2001, and the 1993 bombing of the World Trade Center. Wick considered the collar bomb the most sophisticated improvised explosive device (IED) he had ever seen.

The device was a one-off. It was made by hand, by someone skilled enough to use machine tools to cut and assemble pieces of metal. The device had a rudimentary design, in terms of the bomb components. A metal box, made out of angle iron and sheet metal plates and with an open front, hung from the collar; its approximate dimensions were six and two-tenths by ten and one-half inches. Like with most IEDs, a pipe bomb—or, in this case, two pipe bombs, each five and one-half inches long and one inch in diameter—held the explosive materials. The pipes were arranged side by side vertically. Smokeless powder filled them. They were sealed on the ends with square metal plates connected to one another with threaded rods. Bolts held the plates to the rods, creating airtight containers that would blow under pressure.

Only one of the two pipe bombs—the one closest to the side of the metal box—detonated. When it blew, the force separated some of the metal on the second pipe bomb and made it inoperative. The one explosion was enough to kill Wells.

The pipe bombs in the collar bomb resembled a pipe bomb incorporated into what the FBI calls the Moody device—a boxlike mail bomb that a Georgia resident, Walter Leroy Moody Jr., was convicted of using to kill three people, including a U.S. Circuit Court judge, in 1989. By the time Wells was killed, a schematic of the Moody device had been floating around the Internet for years.

———

What made the collar bomb sophisticated, what made it a once-in-a-lifetime device, was the mechanism that triggered detonation. Evidence specialists recovered enough fragments of the collar bomb for the senior forensic examiner at the FBI's explosives laboratory in Quantico, chemist Kirk Yeager, PhD, to reconstruct it.

The device's fusing mechanism was composed of a series of switches that, when all of them were closed, completed an electrical circuit. Power from two AA batteries, placed in a RadioShack battery holder on the device, flowed through the closed circuit and supplied the charge to ignite the pipe bomb.

Whoever put the device on Wells first pushed a green plastic lever that snapped into place the two semicircular arms of the collar. To unlock the collar required the insertion of two keys into two of the four keyholes at the front of the collar—the keys Wells was to find on his scavenger hunt. Only two of the four locks functioned; the others, Yeager said, were meant to be decoys.

The activation of the bomb came after Wells had it locked to his neck. This is where the device's two particularly critical pieces—two Sunbeam kitchen timers, like those sold at Walmart—came into play. Only one timer had to be activated for the bomb to have worked, though both had been set by the time the bomb was locked to Wells. A metal bar was screwed into the face of each timer. Another screw was inserted into the twelve o'clock position of each timer. Copper wires attached the kitchen timers to the batteries. When the metal bar on a timer touched the screw, a switch closed.

Before Wells was sent off to rob the bank, the bomber—the person who activated the device—turned

the timers clockwise, so that as much as fifty-seven minutes had to elapse before each timer's metal plate touched
the screw; the insertion of the screws at the top of the
timers shaved off three minutes from each. As long as the
timer ran, that switch was open.

After the bomber turned the kitchen timers, that person stuck two cotter pins in holes in the device's front
panel. The cotter pins, attached to key rings, blocked the
timers' movements. Both timers were behind a metal
plate. The bomber activated the timers before he or she
installed the plate; the covering made the timers inacces-
sible to Wells or anyone else.

The bomber then pulled another cotter pin to arm the
collar bomb. The pulling of this pin released a spring-
loaded bolt in the device's interior; the bolt touched another metal plate that was wired to the collar bomb's
power source—two AA batteries. The spring-loaded bolt
was the device's arming switch; when the bolt contacted
the metal plate, another switch closed.

With the bomb armed, the bomber pulled out one of
the two remaining cotter pins and restarted the one
kitchen timer as Wells was sent on his journey. As Wells
told the state troopers: "He pulled a key out and started
a timer. I heard the thing ticking when he did it."

The bomb detonated when the kitchen timer reached
its end. The metal bar on the timer's face touched the
screw; that switch closed like the arming switch had
closed. The electrical circuit was complete. Investigators
never found the initiator, or fuse, that was powered by
the current and ignited the smokeless powder. Yeager said

it could have been a match, an exposed lightbulb filament or a thin piece of copper wire. He wrote in his report:

> The device functioned in the following fashion: the smokeless powder main charge was confined in two lengths of pipe. An improvised fuzing [sic] system consisting of a metal plate, spring-loaded bolt arming switch, two modified kitchen timer firing switches, two AA batteries, multiple lengths of wire, and an ignition source was connected to the pipe bomb main charge. The device was armed by releasing the spring-loaded bolt allowing it to make contact with the metal plate. Countdown was then started by activating one of the modified kitchen timers [by pulling the cotter pin]. When the timer reached the end of its countdown it closed a switch and allowed current to flow through the wiring connecting the power source to the ignition source. The ignition source created enough energy to ignite the smokeless powder.

Whoever made the bomb knew what he or she was doing. By requiring both the activation of the timer and the spring-loaded arming switch, the bomber guarded against an accidental explosion. "Bombers, if they're smart, have multiple switches to make sure that they don't get hurt when they're activating the device," Yeager would testify later. "So nothing could happen until this bolt was engaged."

Wells could have gained more time to keep the pipe bombs from exploding. Evidence specialists found one cotter pin still inserted in the metal panel. If Wells had pulled that pin, he would have released the second kitchen timer—which the bomber had activated—and opened another switch and gained fifty-seven more minutes. "This would have delayed the initiation of the device until the second timer reached the end of its countdown," Yeager wrote.

The full activation and release of both timers would have allowed Wells as much as one hundred and fourteen minutes to find the keys and unlock the collar. Wells never attempted to pull the third cotter pin, though it was inserted in the plate in front of him. He never told the state troopers about the pin. He almost certainly did not know about the importance of the second timer.

The device featured a way to deactivate the bomb altogether, though whether Wells knew of that option is uncertain. What Yeager described as a "kill arm" was located inside the metal box; the arm consisted of a long metal bar customized to block the movement of both kitchen timers. A miniature brass padlock controlled the kill arm. Opening the padlock with a key would have freed the kill arm, stopped the kitchen timers, opened a switch, and prevented ignition. A groove cut in the angle iron of the metal box allowed for access to the keyhole. The key for that lock, like the keys for the locks that would have opened the collar, were never found.

———

No fewer than eighteen warning labels covered the outside of the collar bomb. "LOCKS ARE BOOBY TRAPPED," read one. "BOOBY-TRAPS REDUNDANT SYSTEMS ACTIVATED UPON ARMING," read another. One message referred to the toy cell phone bracketed to the device. Another warned about "SEVERAL OTHER HIDDEN DANGERS." Someone had used red marker to inscribe an arrow on the front of the device to point to a hole for a screw.

Many of the supposed dangers, such as the liquid-filled tubing interwoven in the collar, turned out to be innocuous decoys that played no role in the functioning of the device. The black cell phone, powered by two AA batteries, one of which was of the EverActive brand, distributed by Walmart, was a toy; it "appeared to have been added to make the device appear more complex and thus slow bomb technicians attempting to render it safe," Yeager wrote. The LED timer on the front of the device was unmodified and not attached to the fusing system. The LED timer, powered by three AAA batteries, allowed the bomber to know how much time was left. The LED timer emitted the beep that preceded the explosion.

But the collar bomb was indeed booby-trapped: the whole thing was wired to go off if anyone tried to tamper with it. The device had parallel circuits. The kitchen timers governed the one circuit. The component that governed the other circuit was wire mesh, which was inside the metal box and in front of the pipe bombs and the timers. The mesh constituted what Yeager called the collar bomb's "anti-tamper switch." The mesh was wired to the battery pack. If the mesh came in contact with any part of the metal box, the connection would close another circuit, unleash the charge from the batteries and ignite the pipe bombs. "Thus," Yeager wrote, "any bomb tech who attempted to gain entry into the front opening of the device covered by the wire mesh could potentially set off the bomb if they made contact between the mesh and the box."

As he reviewed this finding, Jason Wick, the ATF agent, thought the late arrival of the Erie bomb squad had been a blessing. If the bomb techs had arrived before the bomb exploded, they might have moved the wire mesh to get to the guts of the collar bomb. Then not only Wells would have died.

The threat of death exuded from the entire collar bomb, from every component, whether the item was meant to be a red herring to confound rescuers or whether the item was designed to destroy. The backing plate of the collar bomb, the piece of metal that ripped into Wells' chest, had a nefarious purpose. The backing plate supported the pipe bombs, kitchen timers and the other elements of the device's innards. Lines had been scored into the backing plate. The scorings weakened the metal and guaranteed it would bend or shatter into shrapnel during an explosion. The scoring on the plate served the same purpose as the pineapple pattern on a World War II hand grenade—to send as much metal flying in as many directions as possible.

Once the pipe bomb ignited, Brian Wells had no chance.

———

Wells would have run out of time to disable the bomb, no matter how it ended up locked to his neck. Clark made that conclusion after he had agents drive Wells' would-be route on a Thursday (the same day Wells had died) at 1:30 P.M. Clark wanted to see how long the race against death would have taken.

When Wells walked into the PNC bank, he had "less than 55 minutes until detonation," according to the bomb-hostage note. Wells left the tower site seven minutes before he arrived at the bank. If the bomber had activated the kitchen timer at fifty-seven minutes, Wells would have had fifty minutes left, at the most, on that timer when he entered the bank.

Wells was in the bank for eleven minutes; once he left, he had an estimated thirty-nine minutes, and probably less, remaining on the one timer. He had a total of thirty-nine minutes to find and read the note under the rock at McDonald's, drive Peach Street and the interstates, stop to get the other notes, read them and carry out their orders.

The agents who drove the route determined Wells would have needed at least twenty minutes to drive from the bank to the two pickup points along I-79. The twenty minutes did not account for the amount of time Wells would have needed to get out of the Geo Metro at each spot, walk into the woods and retrieve and read the notes. The twenty minutes of driving time assumed the pickup spot near the McKean Township sign was the final location where Wells was to have found a note. That might not have been the case. The note that was left near the McKean Township sign, the note that no one found, could have directed Wells to drive somewhere else, thus taking up more time.

Based on the eleven minutes Wells was in the bank and the twenty minutes of estimated driving time, Wells would have had only nineteen minutes to execute the rest of the plan and ultimately unlock the collar.

"There's no way he could have done it," an agent who drove the route told Clark. "He's not going to make that route, even if everything is perfect."

Clark drove the route himself. He agreed: Wells would not have survived. In an ideal situation, Wells would have hit no red lights, found the notes easily and comprehended them quickly. No way, Clark thought as he sat in traffic at red lights along upper Peach Street. No way would Wells have had enough time to unlock the collar bomb. The only thing that could have saved him, Clark thought, was if someone was waiting for him at one of the pickup spots for the notes. That person could have pulled the third cotter pin, which would have restarted the second kitchen timer and given Wells fifty-seven more minutes. That person, perhaps the bomber, would have controlled whether Brian Wells lived or died.

———

Clark once again reviewed Wells' relaxed behavior in the bank. Clark once more listened to Wells' last words, his dying declarations.

Wells' story about the black guys had failed to yield solid leads; the investigation of J.J. had stalled. Clark determined Wells had lied about the black guy and the group of black men. Someone, in a show of criminal genius, had persuaded Wells to lie about the black men; the prevarication was meant to throw off the investigators and buy valuable time for the bomber and any confederates. Wells did not tell the state police what really happened to him. He decided to stick with a script. He blamed imaginary black guys.

Clark wondered whether Wells lied out of a desperate hope. The bomber threatened to detonate the device immediately if Wells deviated from the plan, according to the nine pages of notes. As he sat in the Eyeglass World parking lot, Wells must have thought he had two choices: break from the script and have the plotters kill him, as they said they would in the notes, or follow the script and keep alive the prospect, however slim, that the bomb was fake or could be disarmed in time. Wells chose to follow the script. He chose to parrot the story about the black men. It was a story, Clark believed, that the bomber told Wells to say—or else.

That is why Brian Wells lied in his deathbed confession: despite fate closing on him, he was still grasping at the chance he might not die.

9

"I Helped Her Do Some Stuff I Shouldn't Do"

Jim Roden's body could not stay in the freezer much longer. Sooner or later, someone, maybe Roden's family in Ohio, maybe a friend, would report him missing. The trail inevitably would send police to Marjorie Diehl-Armstrong's house, and probably Bill Rothstein's, and to that freezer under the black tarp in his garage. Rothstein and Diehl-Armstrong had to make Roden's body vanish.

They had done a good job of erasing much of the evidence of his murder. They had scrubbed and refurbished Roden's apartment and moved his mattress and box springs to Rothstein's garage. Rothstein dumped most everything else from the apartment: vinyl flooring; the bed's headboard and footboard, rails and frame; other bloody objects. He deposited the stuff at Lake View

Landfill, owned by Waste Management, on Robison Road in Summit Township, a five-minute drive from Rothstein's house. Rothstein's garbage became indistinguishable from the rest of the mountain of trash. Investigators were never able to find any of it.

Rothstein visited the landfill as many as seven times after he hauled Roden's body out of Diehl-Armstrong's house. His first stop was hours after he handled the body; he dumped his pair of Carhartt overalls and boots, all soaked in blood. His last trip to the dump was his biggest. On the late morning of September 13, 2003, Rothstein unloaded 1,040 pounds of debris, none of which, he would tell investigators later, was from Diehl-Armstrong's house. The stuff in the final load, he said, was from a self-storage unit he had rented at Summit Storage Center, at 8971 Peach Street, just south of his house. He cleaned out the storage unit, which he said was filled with copper wiring and other items he said were related to his two businesses, Redstone Electric Company and Redstone's Handyman Services.* Rothstein loaded the debris onto a trailer behind his van. He drove to the landfill, where he paid a $33.80 dumping fee.

Later in September, Rothstein and Diehl-Armstrong decided to cut up Roden's body into small pieces. The decision, according to Rothstein's version of events, involved some debate. She did not want to bury the body, for fear of its discovery in some hidden grave. He agreed. They settled on dismembering and scattering it. She regretted

---

*"Redstone" is English for the German Rothstein.

the body was frozen; having a thawed corpse would be easier. There was nothing they could do about that, he said. He made a list of what they needed: plastic tarp, a meat grinder, a bucket for washing their hands, an ice crusher. They went shopping the afternoon of September 20, 2003.

Their conversation that afternoon probably resembled that of two lovers quarreling and finally reaching an agreement. That's what Diehl-Armstrong and Rothstein had held themselves out as for years: lovers. They first dated in the early 1970s, when she was finishing at Mercyhurst College and after he had left the University of Toledo, in Ohio, where he studied electrical engineering between 1962 and 1967 but never graduated. Rothstein returned to his hometown of Erie, to work for his parents, who founded and owned the Rola Bottling Company, the home of a local soft drink called Rola Cola, on the city's lower east side, on East Third Street near Parade Street. One of Diehl-Armstrong's friends urged her not to be so much of a bookworm and introduced her to Rothstein. They went roller-skating on their first date.

Diehl-Armstrong (then the twenty-one-year-old svelte and sharp Marjorie Diehl) thought that Rothstein (then twenty-six years old) was built like a young Elvis, with his sturdy frame and dark hair. She would long remember how, when they were engaged in the early 1970s, he bought her a full-carat, flawless diamond ring—"a perfect ring" from New York City—and sent her twelve long-stemmed roses and the record album for *Love Story*. Diehl and Rothstein fell in love when *Love Story* packed movie theaters in late 1970 and into 1971. Diehl dreamed of Rothstein as her Oliver Barrett IV, her Ryan O'Neal; she dreamed of herself as his Jennifer Cavilleri, his Ali Mc-Graw, who was dying of cancer.

They seemed a perfect couple, with their matching oddities, obsessions and IQs. Rothstein helped his parents run Rola Cola; she worked in the deli in the bottling-company's building, selling bagels and lox, with Rothstein's mother. Diehl was into astrology and voodoo—she once told a psychologist she could put spells on people she disliked and they would drop dead. She always asked people their signs; as a Pisces, she was intuitive but temperamental. He was into numerology and liked to chart dates. He was in pursuit of the date with the best karma, the date when the planets were aligned. They had both gone to college, they both believed they were more intelligent than most other people and they both liked to talk.

Diehl and Rothstein did not just take over conversations. They commandeered them. She and Rothstein each talked so much and so fast that the verbiage could wear down the listener and frustrate any effort to respond or, God forbid, rebut. You ended up giving up rather than sorting through all those words, all those comments about how Rothstein and Diehl knew what they were doing and how everyone else was a fucking moron. Rothstein, who was Jewish, could tell you who was an asshole in three languages: English, French and Hebrew. When he got rolling, the one-sided conversation was like theater. It was a soliloquy.

Despite his arrogance, Rothstein, like Diehl-Armstrong, had plenty of acquaintances. Rothstein, like Diehl-Armstrong, could be fascinating; you never knew what he was going to say next. He made plenty of friends through his activities in amateur radio and amateur photography. He met all kinds of people in his electrician and handyman businesses and through his participation in Erie community-theater productions. Rothstein sang with a group at Erie's Siebenbuerger Club, founded by song-loving German immigrants in the late 1890s. In later years, he made more friends through his interest in computers and computer programming. He told those he knew, as if to validate his intelligence, that he was a member of Mensa, but the organization of geniuses said he was never on the roster.

Rothstein expanded his social circle to form his own groups. He was a founding member of what he called the Tall Club, a gathering of men and women who were at least six feet two inches tall (Rothstein's height; he set the standard) and who got together regularly to eat lunch and solve the world's problems. Rothstein led another group: the Fractured Intellectuals. He and five or six friends (Diehl-Armstrong was not among them) met at 6:00 P.M. on Friday nights at an Erie pizza parlor (not Mama Mia's) to eat pizza and other Italian food (Rothstein was a vegetarian who subsisted mainly on tofu, vegetarian pizza and Dr Pepper) and dissect the news. No one understood the Fractured Intellectuals except themselves. Rothstein held court as the most brilliant jester of them all.

Rothstein inherited his penchant for the unusual and

outlandish from his father. Matthias Rothstein died at age ninety in 1993, but when Bill Rothstein, the oldest of his three children, was dating Marjorie Diehl, in the early 1970s, Matthias Rothstein was nearing the end of a long and colorful connection to commercial Erie. His tireless promotions earned him the moniker "Mad Man Matty."

He was a former Pepsi distributor from Wilkes-Barre who owned and ran the Rola Bottling Company in Erie from 1945 to 1978. As his wife, and Bill Rothstein's mother, B. Virginia Rothstein, took on the duties of mixologist, Mad Matty Rothstein experimented in different cola flavorings and hawked the concoctions any way he could. He gave out free samples of Rola Cola. He held a promotion in winter in which the temperature set the price of his drinks—and Erie's winter temperatures sometimes dipped to zero or below. In the 1950s, as postwar Erie prospered, Mad Man Matty booked a downtown auditorium weekly for a local talent show that Rola sponsored. It was called the Hill Billy Jamboree. Bill Rothstein, born in 1944, grew up a child of the offbeat stage.

Life was a performance to Bill Rothstein; it was also like one big inside joke. You were either in on the joke, in on his intelligence and his ideas, or you were out. You either laughed with him or he laughed at you. Diehl-Armstrong remembered him having a sign on a wall at his house: "If you love someone, set them free, and if they come back, they loved you. And if they don't, go out and shoot them." He was always playing tricks. He secretly and illegally taped phone calls with his friends and others, including the utility companies; Pennsylvania law requires two-way consent to record such conversations. Rothstein, adept at diversion, adopted a code for his friends to find him, especially those friends who were returning to Erie after years away. If you were one of the initiated, you need not look under his name in the phone book. You looked under a different name, that of his alter ego, William D. Schmuck.* Under that name, you would find the phone number and address for the one and only William Ansel Rothstein.

Among Rothstein's friends, Diehl-Armstrong was a true insider, for a time. For all the people he knew, Rothstein associated with very few women, other than mainly his mother and Diehl-Armstrong. Rothstein was into pornography, a friend later told the FBI. Another friend told investigators he doubted Rothstein ever had sexual intercourse. Rothstein knew prostitutes, the friend said, but never used them for sex. There was always a question about whether Rothstein was gay or bisexual. Once, when the Rola Cola plant was still operating, Rothstein was in a booth, working a cash register for customers, and some of the guys sent a hooker into the booth. Nothing happened. Rothstein, who neither drank, smoked nor used drugs, sent the woman away. He kept working.

Rothstein was known to be loyal. One of his friends told the FBI, in the context of Rothstein cleaning up after Roden's death, that he could never say no—especially to Diehl-Armstrong.

---

*Rothstein would also write "Bill Schmuck" on the return address of envelopes he mailed.

After years of being a couple, after years of being in on each other's jokes, Bill Rothstein and Marjorie Diehl split, at least romantically. They had lived together with his parents at 8645 Peach Street, but they eventually wore each other out. Some said she could not get over his being Jewish, but the reasons for their split were surely deeper and as complicated as the two would-be spouses. Their engagement lasted nine months. More than thirty years after they met, she recalled him as "a devious piece of shit" and a "sicko" who was intensely jealous and manipulative. "Rothstein was a brilliant guy," Diehl-Armstrong would say later. "You fuck with the master, you fuck with disaster."

The feeling was mutual. Rothstein considered Diehl-Armstrong a manipulative nag who told him she relied on sex to get what she wanted from men. "She will use sex," he once said. "This is what she tells me. She thinks she's like somebody fantastic; well, she has very nice teeth, she probably has put a lot of money into them, and she does have nice fine-pored skin, but she hasn't taken a look at herself for a long time. But she thinks that all these guys are after her and they may be after her because she has large breasts. A lot of guys are into that kind of stuff, so she will say things to them to get what they want."

Rothstein wearied of her constantly saying she was always right. "Marjorie is a person who never makes a mistake," he said. "She is never wrong so therefore there is always somebody else. Everything is somebody else's fault; no matter when it was, no matter when it is, if it goes wrong, it's somebody else's fault."

———

Yet they stayed in touch. During her trial in the killing of Bob Thomas, he called her lawyer, told the lawyer how much he loved her and offered to help in any way he could. The lawyer declined the assistance. In the years after her acquittal in the Thomas case, she relied on Rothstein for odd jobs; he complied. She thought he loved her and cared for her like a big brother. Rothstein could not abide Jim Roden, but he answered Diehl-Armstrong's calls. Rothstein's jealousy annoyed her, but she looked him up constantly.

A sense of dread lurked in their relationship, but they remained friends. Neither knew what to expect from the other, but each knew what the other was capable of doing. Rothstein destroyed the murder weapon in the Louis Allessie case in 1977 and got away with it. Seven years later, Diehl opened fire on Bob Thomas and escaped a murder conviction and a possible life sentence. Their wariness of each other, and their understanding of each other's potential for criminality, joined them.

By the summer of 2003, Rothstein and Diehl-Armstrong had plenty to talk about, plenty of memories to reminisce about: friends they knew, crimes they had committed, problems they were facing, dreams they still had. That summer, both were entangled in protracted probate disputes.

His involved the estate of his mother, B. Virginia

Rothstein, who died at age eighty-five in August 2000, leaving him to live alone, with his German shepherd, Thunder, at 8645 Peach Street—the beloved family homestead, the only real home he had known since he was five years old. His mother's estate was unsettled. He was the executor. His sister had gone to court claiming he was delinquent in administering the estate and liquidating its assets, including the house. Rothstein reluctantly put the house up for sale; he would distribute the proceeds from the sale to his sister.

Rothstein insisted on listing the house for $250,000, despite his real estate agent telling him the price was too high. The house was appraised at $83,000; the most serious offer the real estate agent had received was for $125,000. Rothstein kept the price at $250,000. He had no money and nowhere else to stay. He was in no hurry to sell 8645 Peach Street.

Diehl-Armstrong's dispute involved the estate of her mother, Agnes Diehl, who died at age eighty-three in July 2000. Diehl-Armstrong had fought over the administration of the estate with her father, Harold, who was eighty-five years old in August 2003. Diehl-Armstrong said she wanted to ensure her father was safeguarding the money her mother had left him. Diehl-Armstrong believed that money would be her legacy one day.

In the summer of 2003, she was again livid at her father, this time because he was giving away his money: $100,000 to one neighbor, $50,000 to another, $100,000 to another, $1,000 to the mail carrier. His friends and neighbors had been good to him a long time, Harold

Diehl said. His only daughter and her violent tendencies were another story; he and his wife had done what they could and spent $60,000 on her lawyer in the Bob Thomas case, but that was a long time ago.

Diehl-Armstrong complained her father was squandering her inheritance. With the way things were going, she said, with him spreading money around to the vultures in his neighborhood, nothing would be left for her when he died.

———

Mental illness undoubtedly complicated Diehl-Armstrong's relationship with her father and with money, and mental illness surely stunted her career path. Rothstein suffered from no known mental illness. His outsize ego, his narcissism, made dealing with him difficult and made his keeping a full-time, nine-to-five, work-for-a-boss job more difficult still. It would not be until 1991 that Rothstein would earn a college degree, a bachelor's in education from Edinboro University of Pennsylvania, in southern Erie County. The degree allowed him to obtain his teaching certificate as an instructor in middle school and high school science.

Bill Rothstein, the smartest guy around, found work as a substitute shop and science teacher at area school districts, including the Erie School District, where he was so good with his hands that a principal and the district's athletic director hired him to do electrical work at their homes. At school, administrators reminded Rothstein to dress more professionally; he wore overalls to class. Shop class gave Rothstein a forum to show off his abilities. "He could build anything," one of his former students said.

————

In late September 2003, Bill Rothstein and Marjorie Diehl-Armstrong, both in their fifties, were no longer engaged, but together again, with another common bond: the body in the freezer. For most couples or close friends, alcoholism or infidelity or depression comprises the elephant in the room, the big issue everyone knows about but no one wants to address. Starting in mid-August 2003, when Diehl-Armstrong killed Jim Roden and Rothstein helped her afterward, the elephant in the room for the two of them was that body in the freezer. On September 20, 2003, they decided to act.

September 20 was a Saturday. By late afternoon, Rothstein was worried they would not be able to buy a suitable meat grinder or ice crusher to dismember Roden's body. Diehl-Armstrong's panic and paranoia had been heightened for weeks; she was all nerves. She was so worried about being caught in Roden's death that she still slept in her red Jeep in the parking lot of the Summit Township Walmart. On September 20, she and Rothstein purchased black plastic tarp; they would tape over the kitchen windows to prevent anyone from seeing them go to work on Roden's body. Their best chance at finding a meat grinder or ice crusher, they decided, was at A. Caplan Company, a restaurant- and kitchen-equipment store in Waterford, about ten minutes south of Rothstein's house. Caplan's advertised as kitchenware central: "If you cook, stop and look."

With Rothstein driving, he and Diehl-Armstrong got to Caplan's on September 20 at about 4:30 P.M., a half hour before closing. She waited in the van as he went inside to look for a meat grinder. He didn't find one he liked. He waited in the van as she went in; she smelled of cat urine, which made her a memorable customer. Diehl-Armstrong carried out an ice crusher, with the brand name Skier. It cost $94.34, including tax. The ice crusher was not large. It was designed to make crushed ice for cocktails; a chunk of ice deposited in the top went through a grinder and crushed ice came out the side. Diehl-Armstrong and Rothstein wondered how the thing could chip away at any large frozen object, let alone a frozen corpse. They would deal with that later. Diehl-Armstrong was to stay the night at Rothstein's—the first time he could remember her doing so in thirty years. They drove back to his house.

It was astonishing that the two of them were able to drive around so freely, to take shopping trips like they were newlyweds preparing for a party. Rothstein had a body in a freezer in his garage, and no one knew. Even with all the activity around his place because of the pizza bomber case, no one knew. Rothstein, employing his know-it-all attitude and his commanding way of dominating a conversation, had turned away the feds and the news media. Reporters had stopped by his house in the days after Brian Wells was killed to ask what Rothstein might have seen on the dirt road or near the TV tower. As he had done with the FBI, Rothstein told the reporters he saw nothing. He and

Diehl-Armstrong had hid the biggest scoop of all in his garage, but they were not telling.

As Rothstein had dismantled the gun in the Allessie case, as he had chopped up the shotgun his erstwhile fiancée had used on Roden, so he and Diehl-Armstrong would cut up Jim Roden's body and scatter the remains all over the county. They would be in on this secret until they died.

Unknown to Diehl-Armstrong, Rothstein that week had been making preparations if something went wrong. Maybe he was even hinting at suicide, though you never knew with Rothstein. That week, Rothstein had divided $68,370 of the $78,000 that Diehl-Armstrong had given him to dispose of Roden's body and sent it to two of Rothstein's friends and his brother. Rothstein spent the rest of the $78,000 on supplies. Diehl-Armstrong had some of the other remaining cash.

The three packages Rothstein mailed contained cash in denominations of $100, $50 and $20 bills, plus a note from Rothstein that suggested he wouldn't need the money, so the recipient should spend it. Of the $68,730, Rothstein sent his brother, who lived in Erie, $34,750. Rothstein sent one of his friends, D.M., who lived in Summit Township, $10,220; that note said the cash was "not hot." Rothstein mailed $23,400 and a note to an old Tall Club friend who was a college professor in New Jersey. Rothstein wrote:

> Things got really messed up. I never used any of your
> gloves. There are only 2 people who knew about you

getting this money. One of them is dead. Use it well. Thanx! Bill. Over, please.

Some of my more enjoyable days were ones spent with you guys. Please tell [two other people] I wish them well also.

———

Rothstein brought a saw with a disc-type blade into his kitchen the night of September 20. He and Diehl-Armstrong papered over the windows with the black tarp. They had the ice crusher. Rothstein said they needed a stapler to help hold the tarp in place. He said he had a stapler in his van. He went outside, got in his van, drove away and dialed his cell phone. It was 8:14 P.M. He called 911.

"What is your emergency?" the operator asked.

"Uh, ma'am, at 8645 Peach Street, there's a woman with green slacks, a blue shirt, a brown purse . . ."

"Well, what does she need? What's the problem?"

"Ah, there is, in the garage, in the freezer, a body. There is a woman there, she does not have a gun."

"Okay, she has a body in her freezer and she does not . . ."

"Nah, she doesn't have the body, the body's in *my* freezer. I'll be back later on. I just don't want anything to do with her. I'll tell you guys where to pick me up later on today."

The 911 operator connected Rothstein with the state police barracks that covered Summit Township.

"What is your emergency?" that operator asked.

Rothstein repeated his story about a body in a freezer at 8645 Peach Street.

"There's a woman there you might want to pick up and question," he said.

"How do you know that, sir?" the operator said, referring to the body in the freezer.

"Trust me, I know it."

"Who are you?"

"I'm the guy that lives there."

"You live there now?"

"Yes."

"And there's a body in the freezer?"

"In the garage, that is correct."

"And what is her name?"

"Marjorie Diehl. D-I-E-H-L. She's wearing green slacks, blue top, and she has a brown purse. I will be around, later, to see you guys after she's been picked up."

"Where's she at?"

"She's in the house."

"Who is this person in the, in the . . . Do you know who the person is in the freezer?"

"Uh, not sure."

"Male or female?"

"Male."

"What is your name, sir?"

"Bill Rothstein. I will contact you guys later."

"Okay, now Marjorie Diehl is at that residence now?"

"Yes."

"Who is she to you, sir?"

"Uh, I helped her do some stuff I shouldn't do, but I

never killed anybody, so I just want that known. I'll straighten. . . . I'll give you guys my story later on."

"Sir, we're going to have to question you."

"You'll see me later on tonight."

———————

Rothstein called back the state police at 9:10 P.M. He asked a trooper if Diehl-Armstrong had been picked up yet. The trooper said they were at work on it, that they had waited for Rothstein to call to get more information. Rothstein gave consent for the troopers to search his house. The troopers were putting together a search warrant anyway, just to be certain they got in properly.

"Until you guys get a hold of her and have her in your hands, I'm leery of the situation," Rothstein said. "I'm just cruisin' around Erie. When I call ya, and ya say, 'We got her, she's in here,' I'll just drive down to your place."

The trooper asked about Diehl-Armstrong's past. "Apparently Marjorie got away with this once before?" he said.

"I wouldn't say that," Rothstein said. "But let us say she had some problems before."

Rothstein told the trooper he had been considering suicide. When he drove to the barracks, Rothstein said, the troopers would find a revolver in his 1988 Ford van. He said he had planned to use the gun on himself.

"No, don't do that," the trooper said about suicide.

"No," Rothstein replied. "I said past tense, *was*, okay?"

Rothstein knew this trooper, Ronald Morgan; he was

acquainted with one of Morgan's relatives. Rothstein chatted with Morgan as if they were friends. Rothstein asked Morgan not to read him his rights.

"If you guys read me my rights, then I gotta shut up and say absolutely nothing," he said. "Right now, I can tell you things and it's like off the cuff, so to speak, okay? Although you can't use it in court."

"That's fine," Morgan said.

Already, Bill Rothstein was working on some kind of deal.

———

Rothstein called Morgan again, right before he pulled into the state police barracks. He described the filth in Diehl-Armstrong's house on East Seventh Street. Morgan asked if she was a transient.

"No, no, it's very difficult . . . ," Rothstein said. "She's extremely intelligent, extremely intelligent."

"She is?"

"Manipulates people; oh, yes. She's a manic. You know what manic-depressants [sic] are?"

"Yes."

"That's what she is: bipolar, swings very quickly, one way or the other."

"Wow."

Rothstein asked whether the troopers planned to arrest Diehl-Armstrong.

"Without a doubt, we will catch up with her," Morgan said. "I just wanted to make sure that you are safe, first of all."

Rothstein arrived at the barracks, located in Lawrence Park, shortly after 10:05 P.M. The troopers interviewed him. The troopers used the information to swear out a search warrant for 8645 Peach Street. The troopers got there at 3:00 A.M. on September 21. They found Diehl-Armstrong in the darkened house. They found Roden's body in the freezer.

Diehl-Armstrong went calmly. She sat on a bench at the barracks and briefly chatted with a trooper. Jim Roden had been shot, she muttered. Over the years, Diehl-Armstrong said, she had experienced "poor luck" with men.

One of those men, Rothstein, sat in another part of the barracks. He was still talking to the police. Police used his information to prepare the criminal complaint against Diehl-Armstrong for the killing of Jim Roden.

The ringing phone woke Jerry Clark in his bedroom at 6:30 A.M. on September 21, a Sunday. Bob Rudge was on the line.

"Come up to the tower site," Rudge said. "We have body number three."

Clark drove to Rothstein's house as the FBI's lead agent in the third interagency investigation since Brian Wells had been killed. State police were at Rothstein's house because it was located in Summit Township. The Erie police were at the house because Rothstein said Diehl-Armstrong shot Roden at her house on East

Seventh Street, in the city. The FBI was there to explore whether the whole affair might be linked to Wells' death.

Later in the day, the investigators got their first look inside Diehl-Armstrong's house. It repulsed them. The animal feces and urine and piles of garbage combined for such a health risk to the police that the Erie County Health Department declared the house unsafe to search. A city housing inspector declared the place uninhabitable. Not until the Health Department fumigated, or "bug-bombed," the house were the investigators allowed back in. When they resumed their search, the evidence specialists wore white hazmat "moon suits" and masks—the types of outfits usually donned by those cleaning up hazardous materials or environmental disasters.

Rothstein's house was not quite as bad as Diehl-Armstrong's, but it was close. Clark walked in the front door the morning of September 21 and marveled at the scope of the junk. It was everywhere, in every room, from floor to ceiling: junk. Large bags of dog food—Rothstein's German shepherd had died some time ago—filled a corner in one room, whose varnished pine walls suggested it might have been a study once. A used paint can sat on top of an upright piano. Papers were piled high on a desk. More papers were strewn about what appeared to be Rothstein's office; in one corner, papers and boxes and other stuff made a pile on the floor. In a bathroom, the upright part of the commode was detached from its base and sitting on the floor, in front of the tub, in which a metal pail was under the faucet. Dark brown splotches stained the sink and the toilet bowl. Chairs were piled atop each other in another room, where an open computer-processing unit, its wires hanging out, sat on a table, near a pair of pliers and set of screwdrivers. A box of old firecrackers, M-80s, sat on a table. A tower of stacked newspapers rested against one wall of the kitchen, where assorted pieces of junk were scattered, though the sink was visible and appeared to be clean. You couldn't tell, in the kitchen, whether it was night or day outside; black tarp shrouded the windows.

This is how Rothstein lived, in a house that looked like an indoor landfill. The agents and police officers and troopers saw the For Sale sign in the front yard. Good luck selling this place.

The mess shocked Jerry Clark. How were investigators to search through all this stuff? How would they know what was valuable to the criminal probes, and what was not? You could throw anything into this shithole and it would blend right in; a weapon or another key piece of evidence would be hiding in plain sight—just another piece of crap lost in an endless warren of garbage. The house went on forever. The search would take forever. The FBI agreed to help the state police.

Clark walked into the garage. It was jammed with debris, most of it from Diehl-Armstrong's house. Rothstein had not unloaded everything at the landfill. The bloody mattress was propped in between piles of boxes. The box springs from Roden's bed took up another space in the garage. An air-conditioning unit that had been in Roden's window was in the garage. So was Roden's ten-speed bike and his stereo. A wicker basket was in the garage; it too had come from Roden's apartment. Rothstein and Diehl-Armstrong had confiscated everything from the apartment they feared might have had blood on it.

A bucket of bloody paper towels sat near the rear of the garage, near a large white chest freezer. The Erie County coroner, Lyell Cook, checked the solidity of the body; no one could remove it from the freezer in its present state. A livery truck drove the freezer to the county morgue, where Roden's body would need four days to thaw.

Inside Rothstein's garage, the ice crusher turned up. In Rothstein's van, a set of two small blue and black Motorola walkie-talkies were found in the center console. On a seat of the van, just where Rothstein had said it would be, rested a .38-caliber, five-round Smith & Wesson revolver. Four of the bullets were unspent; the fifth had been fired. That chamber was empty of the bullet, but, this being a revolver, the shell casing was still inside the chamber. Wherever that gun had been fired, no evidence of the discharge would have been left at the scene. Investigators in the house discovered a light-blue collared work shirt whose front pocket contained two 12-gauge shotgun shells, one of which had been opened and emptied.

Another find emerged out of the house's grime. It appeared to be a suicide note. It was three pages, handwritten in large print and signed.

Police My body is in the bedroom on 1st floor in S.E. corner of the house.

1) This has nothing to do with the Wells case.

2) The body in the freezer in the garage is Jim Roden.

3) I did not kill him, nor participate in his death.

4) My apologies to those who cared for or about me. I am sorry that I let them down.

5) I am sorry to leave you this mess.

Bill Rothstein

———

At the state police barracks, Marjorie Diehl-Armstrong declined to make a formal statement. She blurted about Rothstein: "Hey, he's got a rapist living with him." She named the rapist: Floyd Stockton.

The remark about Stockton made its way to Clark, who was still at Rothstein's house. "Shit," he said, "I had a lead a year or so ago for this same guy."

Clark at that time had been helping find fugitives. The FBI in northern Washington State had sent word to the FBI in Erie to be on the lookout for Floyd Arthur Stockton Jr., known as Jay. He was a fifty-six-year-old registered sex offender wanted on charges that he raped a mentally disabled nineteen-year-old woman in Bellingham, Washington, in February 2002.

On September 21, 2003, Stockton was not at Rothstein's house. The FBI got information he was still in Erie County, somewhere. Jerry Clark started to investigate yet another person, Floyd Stockton, Rothstein's buddy. Clark hoped Stockton—unlike Wells, Pinetti and Roden—would be found alive.

PART II

INVESTIGATION

10

A Life on the Run

Three weeks after Brian Wells was killed, the Erie police, state police and the FBI had arrested a total of three people while investigating his death. Three arrests in such a short period of time would have ranked as a success, a shining example of a quickly closed case and the prowess of the FBI, except that none of the three suspects had been taken into custody on charges he or she was involved in Wells' slaying. Marjorie Diehl-Armstrong was accused of killing Jim Roden. Bill Rothstein was accused of, but not yet charged with, disposing of Roden's body. Jay Stockton was picked up on nothing more than a charge that he was a fugitive from justice.

Jerry Clark, who had been on Stockton's trail a year earlier, led the group of agents that found him later in the day on September 21, 2003, hours after Rothstein called

911 about Roden's body and hours after Diehl-Armstrong blew Stockton's cover to the police. Clark drove to Girard, a small town west of Erie. The FBI had traced the plate on a 1987 Ford Ranger pickup parked behind Rothstein's house to a woman who identified herself as K.W., Stockton's girlfriend. She told the FBI she and Stockton lived together at her apartment, near Girard.

At around 6:00 P.M. on September 21, Clark knocked on the door of the apartment. Stockton walked out.

Floyd "Jay" Stockton, so nicknamed because he was named after his father and, hence, a junior, was in a familiar spot—handcuffed and on the way to prison. He was fifty-six years old; was born in Jamestown, New York, just over the Pennsylvania line; had grown up in Erie; and had been incarcerated or drifted for much of his life. His lasting friendship with Bill Rothstein was intermittent. Stockton was always floating from place to place, away from one problem or another, away from one wife or another, when he wasn't behind bars. He looked up Rothstein whenever he could.

Stockton first got locked up in the early 1960s, when he was sixteen years old, for stealing a car. Years after he got out, in 1968, he met Rothstein; Stockton stopped by the Rola Bottling Company to buy beer, which Rola's sold, along with its homemade soda. Rothstein was at the register. The two talked; Stockton came to like Rothstein enough that he made a point of regularly buying his beer at Rola's. Rothstein was thin then—in the time he knew him, Stockton once estimated, Rothstein gained 150 pounds—but he had a weirdly funny sense of humor, including jokes based on sexual puns. Stockton liked those jokes.

Stockton and Rothstein, who shared the same birth date, though three years apart, spent their evenings hanging out in the cashier's booth at Rola's. They'd sometimes go to concerts or see friends. Stockton was the wilder one, the one with the eighth-grade education and the GED, the one into pot and booze. Rothstein was the teetotaling straight man, the college-educated intellectual who liked to watch other people get messed up but stayed sober himself. Rothstein counseled Stockton as the latter's first marriage collapsed. During the day, Stockton worked at foundries, and at night he played guitar in local rock bands. As best as he could, Rothstein made sure Stockton stayed out of trouble.

He was not always successful. Stockton got jammed up on marijuana charges in the mid-1970s. After a prison stint, he left Erie to work in oil fields out West. After a months-long stay in Erie to visit Rothstein, in 1980, Stockton again headed west, to Montana, where he was convicted of rape in 1983, was sentenced to ten years in prison, and was registered as a sex offender. Stockton, divorced again, stayed out west after his release, this time moving to Bellingham, Washington, near the Canadian border, where he lived with a woman and her family, including the woman's nineteen-year-old mentally disabled daughter. In May 2002, the Whatcom County Sheriff's Office charged Stockton with raping the nineteen-year-old and forcing her to perform oral sex on him in April 2002.

The prosecutor swore out two felony rape charges against Stockton on May 14, 2002. By then, he was already gone.

He had fled to Idaho and planned to go to Portland, Maine. He bought a Greyhound ticket and was headed that way, until he stopped in Erie to visit relatives. He asked Rothstein to drive him to the bus station, to resume his journey to Portland. Stockton stayed in Summit Township. Rothstein explained how he, as the oldest child, was the executor of his mother's estate. He said Stockton could help fix up the house at 8645 Peach Street and work for Rothstein's handyman business. Stockton, on the lam in the rape case, moved in with Rothstein in the spring of 2002.

They renewed their friendship. They woke up in the same house together, with Rothstein jokingly greeting Stockton with a "Hey, morning, pervert"—an example of Rothstein's odd and sexually charged humor. They worked together: Stockton, six feet tall, 190 pounds, with a lanky build, short brown hair and stubble for a beard; and Rothstein, with the full beard, the ubiquitous bib overalls, the body shaped like Santa Claus'. They ate together. They talked for hours. The two were around each other so much, and in Rothstein's junk-filled house together so often, that Marjorie Diehl-Armstrong would later tell Jerry Clark that she believed Stockton and Rothstein, her former fiancé, were lovers.

———————

The FBI talked to Stockton on September 21. He said he had stopped living with Rothstein and moved in with K.W., his girlfriend, two or three weeks before September 21, which put him at Rothstein's house when Wells was killed. The FBI gave Stockton a lie-detector test about his involvement in Wells' death. He passed.

Clark's bosses cleared Stockton as a suspect in the Wells case, but Clark thought the decision hasty. He disliked polygraphs partly because of the false sense of certainty he believed they conveyed. A polygraph could be beaten. Experienced criminals, especially those with antisocial traits, could fool lie detectors; they could control their emotions and even their breathing in ways that could outwit the machine and the polygrapher. Such criminals have no fear of lying, and they have lessened physiological response to fear. That is how polygraphs work: they pick up on increased heart rate and galvanic skin response, which are both bodily reactions to fear.

Stockton, with his scruffy beard and his backwoods, I'm-kind-of-slow demeanor, came off to many of the investigators as a dumb hick. Clark thought otherwise. This Stockton, he was sharp, and he was savvy. He knew how to answer pointed questions.

Other investigators shared Clark's suspicions that Stockton was playing ignorant. One of them was a state trooper, Mark Russo, who waited with Stockton in the lobby of the FBI office after Stockton took the polygraph test, on September 23. Stockton suddenly started talking to Russo about the Vietnam War, and how Stockton's greatest regret was that he never served in Vietnam, where he thought he could have honored his family's name. Stockton teared up as he spoke.

Russo reviewed the evidence: Stockton was living with Rothstein when Wells was killed; Rothstein's house was next to the site of the TV tower; the word *VIETNAM* was written on one of the pieces of orange tape that investigators found at the pickup spot near the McKean Township sign; and now Stockton, unprompted, was crying about not fighting in Vietnam. Stockton had waived extradition to Washington. He would be leaving soon. Russo asked to talk to Stockton one last time before he got on the plane and headed west.

The interview occurred on October 3. It lasted three hours and twenty minutes. Stockton said he was at Rothstein's house at the time Wells was killed. He said he had nothing to do with that case. The FBI, content with the polygraph, saw nothing in the interview to change the supervisors' stance that Stockton was not a person of interest in the Wells case.

On October 15, Stockton appeared before a judge in Whatcom County, Washington, to answer the rape charges. Stockton pleaded guilty in the rape case on December 11, 2003. He was sentenced to two years in prison and three to four years of probation.

Jay Stockton was incarcerated again and away once more from his good friend Bill Rothstein. But he was free, at this point, from getting grilled about Rothstein and Brian Wells.

11

Actor and Audience

The Erie police quickly charged Marjorie Diehl-Armstrong in the death of Jim Roden. Detectives swore out the criminal complaint on September 21. Bill Rothstein's statements provided the main evidence. The police said she shot Roden in the chest and neck, and they accused her of homicide, aggravated assault, possessing an instrument of crime, tampering with evidence, conspiring to tamper with evidence, abuse of a corpse and conspiring to abuse a corpse.*

---

*The Erie police in the criminal complaint against Diehl-Armstrong stated "full body X-rays of victim at Coroners [sic] office show wounds to the neck and chest." But the wounds were clearly to Roden's back. The autopsy report states Roden was shot twice in the midback; a video of the autopsy supports that finding. Eric Vey, MD, Erie County's forensic pathologist and an employee of the Erie County

Still she said nothing. She never admitted to killing Roden; Rothstein supplied the evidence against her, and she never objected.

To the police officers and prosecutors familiar with Diehl-Armstrong's past and her inclination toward garrulousness, her silence, though initially surprising, was understandable. Surely she wanted to say something. They also remembered she knew how the justice system worked. Just as she did when she killed Bob Thomas, Diehl-Armstrong exercised her Fifth Amendment right against self-incrimination and kept her mouth shut. If she intended to say anything, maybe she would wait until she took the witness stand at trial. Then she would talk and talk.

Diehl-Armstrong might have been quiet, but she once more had become the biggest story in town. Her arrest made the front page of the *Erie Times-News*, where the reporter on the story, Ed Palattella, who had been at the paper since 1990, had little problem piecing together her

---

Coroner's Office, performed the autopsy and concluded Roden "died as a result of two shotgun wounds to the right posterior thorax," according to the autopsy report. Some of the confusion over where Roden was shot might have been caused by the initial frozen state of his body or by a misreading of the coroner's report and the autopsy report. The coroner's report, which summarized Vey's findings, stated: "Two obvious shotgun wounds were noted in the right back, just below the scapula. X-rays that were taken after removal from the freezer showed the evidence of pellets in the thorax and neck." The autopsy showed the pellets traveled through Roden's body, after he was shot in the back. Vey, in an interview, said the trajectory of the shot showed Roden was facedown on the bed when he was killed. He said Roden might have been asleep.

background: the files in the newspaper's morgue bulged with yellowed clippings about Diehl's killing of Bob Thomas in 1984. Nineteen years later, the police were holding Diehl-Armstrong for fatally shooting another boyfriend. No one seemed shocked, including her father, Harold Diehl. He had stood by his daughter during the Thomas case, but Harold Diehl's patience had thinned since then. He sounded weary when Palattella telephoned him the night of September 21 and told him of his only child's latest legal woes.

"I don't want to hear anything about it," he said. "I'll worry about it when the time comes."

The Erie police drafted the criminal complaint against Diehl-Armstrong as she sat silently in a room at the state police barracks in Lawrence Park. The police were far from ready to charge Rothstein, who wanted to bargain with the prosecutors. He sat in a basement room in the barracks, chatting with any investigator who had a question.

He started with the Erie police and the state police; both agencies were investigating the Roden case. By now, Rothstein had an incentive to really open up. Brad Foulk, the district attorney, said he would give Rothstein consideration in the cover-up of Roden's slaying if he agreed to testify against Diehl-Armstrong in the killing. Rothstein accepted. Foulk had not eliminated the possibility of prosecuting Rothstein for something related to Roden's death, and he warned Rothstein he would rescind the offer if police caught Rothstein lying. Rothstein had put himself in a good spot. Not as good as his situation in the Louis Allessie case, in which he got immunity and avoided prosecution altogether, but still a nice place to be, if you had already confessed to stuffing a body in a freezer.

A state police trooper and two Erie police detectives, Sergeant Frank Kwitowski and John Holmes, joined Rothstein in the interrogation room at 7:07 A.M. on September 21. The interview lasted until 11:46 A.M.— four hours and thirty-nine minutes.

Rothstein, who had no lawyer present, appeared to be holding nothing back. He described how he carried Roden's body out of Diehl-Armstrong's house and put it in the freezer. He spoke little about Brian Wells; he said only that reporters and the FBI had asked him about Wells' death because his house was so close to the TV tower. The state trooper and the Erie police detectives moved on. They were not interested in Wells. Their focus was Roden.

The detectives and trooper accused Rothstein of smirking at them and providing nonsensical answers about Roden's death. They could not understand why Rothstein agreed to help Diehl-Armstrong and get himself in the middle of a homicide investigation.

"What motivates you to put yourself in this position?" one of the investigators asked. "Explain that to us."

"I try and help people," Rothstein replied.

"What does she have over you, Bill?"

"Nothing."

"So you would put yourself in jeopardy of being caught in this heinous crime just to help her out?"

"Probably," Rothstein said.

"You have feelings for her, don't you?"

"What kind of feelings are you referring to?" Rothstein said. "Romance feelings? No. I'd like to see her succeed. I'd like to see her make something of herself."

Rothstein said he had Diehl-Armstrong's best interests in mind but was frightened of her. He said he drove her to Caplan's, where she bought the ice crusher, as a ruse to stall her and prevent her from carrying out the plan to cut up Roden's body. Rothstein said he was worried Diehl-Armstrong would come after him with a knife if he confronted her.

"You're afraid of her?" one of the investigators said.

Rothstein laughed.

"Have you seen her?" he said.

The investigator asked Rothstein why, if he was so afraid of Diehl-Armstrong, he agreed to hide Roden's body when she came to his house. Why didn't he just call the police?

"Because I wanted to try and help her out," Rothstein said.

"Now you're in it. You put yourself in it."

"I know I did," Rothstein said. "I fucked up."

Rothstein told the trooper and the detectives he was glad he called 911 rather than kill himself.

"It's not that I wanted to harm myself, but I just wanted an easy out," Rothstein said. "And there was no easy out. This is the easiest one I could come up with for me."

The interview ended. The detectives and the trooper asked Rothstein if he wanted something to drink or eat.

"Let me see what I got here in my wallet," Rothstein said. "Maybe I could buy a pizza or something. Whoops! No money."

————

Jerry Clark also interviewed Rothstein on September 21, but about the Wells case. As he prepared for his interview, Clark thought Rothstein's purported suicide note alone could spur hours of questioning. Who writes a note like that, in which the would-be suicide denies being part of something, in this case, the bombing death of Wells? Why would anyone be so cryptic, and maybe deceitful, in a suicide note, the written equivalent of a deathbed confession?

Clark had to fight to get into the interrogation room at the state police barracks. The assistant Erie County district attorney handling the Roden homicide questioned why Clark needed to interview Rothstein.

"I have a homicide, too," Clark said.

Foulk, the district attorney, interceded. Clark got to go in.

Clark was ready to work over Rothstein, to draw him out and have him explain what he was doing on August 28 and what he knew about Wells. Clark had long ago learned to avoid open-ended questions; the subject would figure out what the interrogator wanted to hear and answer accordingly. Clark liked to let the subject talk as he guided the conversation.

Clark walked into the room. Rothstein, who had said in the 911 calls he had been set to shoot himself, showed no signs of despondency. Rothstein quickly turned the session into a mental battle between him and Clark. Rothstein was arrogant and condescending.

"Let me get this out of the way first," Rothstein told

Clark in the tone of teacher instructing a new pupil. "I'm smartest guy in this room."

Clark chuckled.

"Jeez, Bill," he said. "My wife says that to me all the time. So I think we are all right."

Rothstein stared blankly ahead. Clark thought Rothstein probably considered smiling a sign of weakness.

Rothstein moved from chair to chair, saying he could not get comfortable. He tried to take control of the conversation by asking Clark questions and refusing most of the time to talk in anything but hypothetical statements. Rothstein said he felt more comfortable talking hypothetically. That is the way, he said, this conversation is going to be.

Rothstein offered some specifics. He told Clark he knew neither Brian Wells nor Robert Pinetti. He said whatever he had learned about the Wells case he had read in the *Erie Times-News*. Rothstein said he had ordered pizza from Mama Mia's about ten years earlier. He said the pizza "sucked," so he never placed an order there again. On August 28, Rothstein said, he picked up Diehl-Armstrong at the Walmart in Summit Township and spent the day with her in North East, a town in eastern Erie County that is surrounded by vineyards and wineries. That must have been a sight, thought Clark, those two on a wine-tasting tour. Rothstein said he dropped off Diehl-Armstrong at the Walmart at 7:30 P.M. on August 28.

Clark asked Rothstein about the Shell station at the intersection of Peach Street and Robison Road, where, outside the station, stood the pay phone. Rothstein said he visited that Shell station almost daily, because it was so close to his house, and said he was probably there sometime on August 28. Rothstein told Clark he might have even used the pay phone that day; he said it was possible his fingerprints were on the receiver. If so, Rothstein said, it was because he had used the pay phone to call his cell phone, which he said he had given to Diehl-Armstrong.

Rothstein spoke confidently and firmly. Clark quickly felt that Rothstein was capable of building the collar bomb—he had the intelligence, the electrical and mechanical background, and he taught robotics. Rothstein had linked himself to the pay phone. Clark got Rothstein on the subject of Wells' death.

"Why," Clark asked, "would a guy who gets a bomb put around his neck not drive right to the police station?"

Rothstein launched into the hypothetical statements. The bombers, he said, may have put electrical charges in the collar to make sure Wells would stay on his directed route; they even might have shown him how he would get shocked if he veered off course. The bombers could have used a radio-controlled transmitter to detonate the bomb; they could have used a voltage charger with a solid-state transistor. Detonation, whether via remote control or a timer, would have been in a serial pattern. The bombers could have put ultrasonics or infrared devices in the cane-shaped gun Wells carried into the bank.

Rothstein mused about the bomb. Smokeless powder was a potential ingredient, Rothstein said. But, he said, the bombers probably decided to use powder emptied from shotgun shells, rather than powder purchased separately, because the commercially bought powder could contain taggants—chemical markers investigators can use to trace a box of smokeless powder to its point of purchase.* Rothstein, still speaking hypothetically, said *if* he were doing it, he would get the smokeless powder for a bomb by cutting off the tops of shotgun shells.

Clark tried to keep the conversation going. He and Rothstein bantered. Rothstein never got close to resuming a discussion about the Wells case.

"What's your birth date?" Rothstein asked Clark in his deep and gruff voice.

Rothstein wanted to talk about numerology. Clark told him the date he was born in November 1960. Rothstein paused and thought about the date. He said certain days were better than others.

The conversation had faded. Clark reluctantly ended it. He wanted to ask Rothstein more questions, but he had no leverage to force an admission. Clark had no evidence to threaten Rothstein with an indictment in the Wells case. Rothstein could have easily continued to sit there and pontificate about what he would have done, *if* this or *if* that. Clark believed this interview was only the beginning with Rothstein: he would talk to him again, probably soon. He would be ready to confront Rothstein with evidence then. Clark thought he had laid the foundation for making the case against this peculiar man sitting across from him.

Clark walked out into the hallway. He felt like beating his fists on his chest. He was ecstatic.

---

*The ATF has explored the use of these identification taggants in commercial explosives, but Congress has not approved the practice.

"This guy is in," Clark told himself. "This guy is in."

Rothstein had not confessed to being part of the Wells case, but he had come very close. He said he might have used the pay phone; that itself represented an admission. Instead of distancing himself from the Shell station, Rothstein had put himself there, probably because he was worried about fingerprints on the phone. The North East alibi would be easy to check.

"I was really dancing with him," Clark thought.

Clark talked to Bob Rudge.

"I think he is in, Bob," Clark said. "This guy is in. He was doing all this hypothetical stuff. Who does that?"

Clark remained alone in his position. The FBI was still treating as a priority the possibility that a black man had jumped Wells. The prevailing theory at the FBI was still that Rothstein would have been nuts to have a pizza delivered so close to his house, when he had a dead body in the freezer in his garage. Clark tried to explain that Rothstein was not rational. None of the agents should assume that he was thinking rationally on August 28. The guy stuck a body in his freezer, for Chrissakes, Clark said. Why wouldn't he get involved in something as bizarre as the Wells case?

Clark reminded Rudge and others that Rothstein believed he was smarter than everyone else. Rothstein had told Rudge, after Clark interviewed him, that Rothstein thought Clark was trying to get psychoanalytical with him, to "mind fuck" him. Rothstein said he did not appreciate the tone of Clark's questions. Rothstein, Clark said, was just the type of psychopath who would order the pizza despite having a body in his freezer. Rothstein believed that, no matter what happened, his intellect would rescue him; everyone else was stupid. To Rothstein, Clark said, this was all a game. He was playing with them.

———

Diehl-Armstrong, newly charged with homicide, was sent to the Erie County Prison at the end of the day on September 21. As was typical in homicide cases in Erie County, the magistrate who arraigned her ordered her held without bond. She was not getting out. Rothstein was free. The police had not charged him yet in the Roden case. The district attorney's office had him put up at a local Ramada Inn, where he slept in what was probably the cleanest room he had been in for quite some time.

Rothstein made the most of his freedom. The Erie police and state police asked him to take them on tours of Diehl-Armstrong's house and his house, to detail what he had done at each in the Roden case. Rothstein, still without a lawyer present, obliged; he would hold up his end of the bargain with Foulk. Rothstein consented to the Erie police videotaping both walk-throughs.

———

First stop: Diehl-Armstrong's newly fumigated house on East Seventh Street. The thirty-minute tour started the late evening of September 22. Rothstein wore blue-denim Carhartt bib overalls, a light-blue collared work shirt and boots. Three Erie police detectives, including Frank Kwitowski and John Holmes, followed him, and so did three members of the Erie police identification unit, including one operating the video camera.

Rothstein, wearing blue latex gloves, took control. He answered questions and made statements. He was Falstaffian in his girth and his loquaciousness. Rothstein explained how he rolled up Roden's body in the tarp, pulled it down the stairs, and cleaned up Roden's apartment with hydrogen peroxide. He added lines and markings to a sketch one of the evidence specialists had created of Roden's bedroom. Rothstein wanted to make sure everyone was clear about what happened and how Roden's body was curled into the fetal position on the bed.

"Go ahead," Rothstein said to the investigators in Roden's apartment. "Questions?"

The police crew and Rothstein crammed into the bedroom. Rothstein pointed to a spot on the floor he refinished with plywood; he said Diehl-Armstrong asked him to cover up blood there.

Rothstein recalled seeing some blood on Roden's sheets, probably from Roden's "thoracic cavity."

The group walked into Roden's kitchen. Rothstein held up a long, portable ultraviolet light. He said he and Diehl-Armstrong tried to use it to identify blood spots in the apartment so Rothstein would know where to scrub and paint. He said Diehl-Armstrong actually called the state police to ask how to best detect and erase bloodstains. The ultraviolet light did not work.

Rothstein walked down the stairs. He stopped at the door that led to Diehl-Armstrong's part of the house.

"This stuff here looks like dog shit I think on the door," he said. "But I'm not sure what that it is."

The group walked outside. Rothstein, still in the spotlight of the video camera, wrapped up the proceedings at this location.

"Anything else here?" he said. "Questions?"

"No, I think you did a great job," one of the investigators said. "Thank you very much for all your help."

"I wouldn't say I did a great job," Rothstein said. "I'd say I did bad stuff."

"I know, but you are at least helping us out," the investigator said. "You can make it better."

Rothstein stood on Diehl-Armstrong's lawn. He was set for more.

"Nobody has any questions?" he said. "Okay, we ready to roll to Peach Street?"

"Yep," an investigator said. "I think we are ready to go."

———

Next stop: Rothstein's house at 8645 Peach Street. The eighty-five-minute tour commenced at 9:30 P.M. The group had grown. It included three Erie police detectives, Kwitowski and Holmes among them; a state trooper; a state police evidence specialist; and an FBI evidence specialist. The FBI specialist was there only because the bureau had agreed to help the state police catalog the junk in Rothstein's house. Neither Clark nor any other FBI agents were on the scene.

Rothstein told the crowd to call him "Bill." A member of the police entourage asked Rothstein about what appeared to be a liver-shaped blood clot found in the kitchen trash can; the clot was contained in a small plastic bag. Rothstein referred to Diehl-Armstrong during the discussion.

"Somebody said there was a liver out here?" said Rothstein, the vegetarian. "If there's a liver, it's probably not a human liver; it's maybe she had like liver for her dogs or her cats, 'cause she had dogs and cats."

"It appeared that it was a bag of blood," the state police evidence specialist said.

Rothstein raised his right arm and held up his hand.

"That's me," he said. "OK? And a razor blade in the bottom of it. It was I."

"And what is that?" the evidence specialist said.

Rothstein again raised his right arm, as if to show off his wrist.

"Stupid attempt at suicide," he said. "You guys got my note?"*

"Yeah," an investigator said.

No one asked why Rothstein said he had tried to slice his wrists, when he said in the 911 calls he planned to shoot himself with the revolver that police later found in his van.

Rothstein explained how he destroyed Diehl-Armstrong's shotgun and melted it into small pieces he had strewn throughout the back roads of the county. He held up a pair of pants and said he had cut himself to drip blood on them to see if ultraviolet light would reveal the splotches.

"One of them," Rothstein said of a pair of pants, "I actually pissed on the pants, to see if I could detect urine."

---

*Investigators later determined the blood in the bag was Rothstein's, who did not explain why he initially said the clot was an animal liver.

The state trooper stopped Rothstein. He wanted to know about the suicide note.

"Why did you think to put in there that it wasn't related to Wells?" the trooper said.

Rothstein gave a Gallic shrug.

"So you wouldn't go off hog wild, saying this has to do with the Wells shit," Rothstein said. "There would be more shit in the newspaper and everything else. It kind of goes along with the last two things [in the suicide note], like, jeez, I'm sorry this shit happened. It is that kind of thing. But I wanted you guys to know, so you don't have to waste your time, trying to figure out, 'Is this part of the Wells situation or not?' Because you guys would have been for another couple of years looking on that shit with that."

The tour neared its end.

"How long have you lived here, Mr. Rothstein?" the state trooper asked.

"Maybe fifty-five years," Rothstein said.

"Is that right?" the trooper said.

Rothstein smiled.

"Wow," the trooper said. "You grew up here, huh?"

"Well, I never grew up," Rothstein said with another smile. "I've lived here all my life."

Rothstein soon walked out the front door. A siren blared and a spotlight illuminated the front yard as the FBI evidence crew set up its trailer. It was around 11:00 P.M. Rothstein was all done for the night.

———

Rothstein met with the FBI the next day, September 23, to take a polygraph test and to answer several more questions. Rothstein passed the test, which bolstered what by then had become the overriding theory at the Erie FBI office— that Rothstein was clear of any part in Wells' death. Clark remained skeptical. He was not surprised that Rothstein passed the lie-detector test; Rothstein was so calm during the exam, Clark had been told, he appeared to have been sleeping. Clark was convinced that Rothstein had prepared to beat that polygraph. Investigators had found literature in his house that explained how to outsmart lie-detection machines. First Stockton passed, and then his pal Rothstein; for Clark, the twin success was not a coincidence.

Clark was never overly impressed with polygraph results anyway. For Clark, the value of the polygraph was not in its administration, in its results, which were inadmissible in court; no, the polygraph was valuable because investigators could often get confessions simply by threatening an investigative target with a lie-detector test. A polygraph could be beaten; agents had to remember that truth when they reviewed the results of a lie-detector test.

———

Also on September 23, the FBI asked Rothstein about his storage habits. An agent wanted to know about the notice from a self-storage unit that was found in Rothstein's van. Rothstein explained how he had dumped a total of 1,040 pounds of debris at the landfill, including junk from the self-storage unit and his house. The agent wanted to know why, in one of Rothstein's shirt pockets, investigators had found the full shotgun shell and the opened shell. Rothstein said he had opened the shell—filled with 12-gauge shot, the most common kind—to examine the pellets, so he knew what to look for when he cleaned up the mess in Roden's bedroom. Rothstein said he did not want to leave any shot behind—a point he never made during his walking tour of Diehl-Armstrong's house.

———

Two days later, on September 25, the FBI announced a $50,000 reward for anyone who provided information that would lead to an arrest in the Wells case. The amount would later climb to $100,000. Since the FBI had set up its hotline, on August 29, the Erie office had received 800 calls on the Wells case. Bob Rudge, the head of the Erie office, said he hoped the $50,000 reward would prompt more people to pick up the phone.

Rudge, at this point, did not link the cases of Roden and Wells. He said the FBI had no evidence Rothstein had a part in the Wells case, despite the suicide note.

"All I can say at this time is that we have no evidence that would suggest Rothstein was associated with this crime," Rudge told reporters on September 26. "I don't mean to close the door on all possibilities."

A week later, more information had become public: Rothstein had told investigators he regularly used the Shell station pay phone from which someone had placed Wells' final order. The *Erie Times-News* asked Rudge if

Rothstein's use of the phone changed the FBI's perspective on whether he was in on the Wells case.

"It doesn't change our opinion," Rudge said. "We're hoping to follow the evidence we develop through the investigation. At this time, no evidence connects him or his situation to the Wells case."

The running joke at the *Erie Times-News* by now was that the FBI agents were getting skunked by Bill Rothstein, the weirdo handyman who looked like something out of central casting for the role of evil genius. What more did the FBI need from Rothstein, a sign around his neck that said "I did it"?

In a story on October 5, the *Erie Times-News* reported on Rothstein's career as a substitute teacher at the Erie School District and listed his skills in robotics and electrical work. A principal who had supervised Rothstein said he appeared to match the profile of the type of person the FBI was saying would carry out the Wells bomb plot.

"There's no doubt," the principal said of Rothstein, "that he fits everything they're looking for."

———

Marshall Piccinini, the assistant U.S. attorney, chafed at public criticism that the FBI was not interested in Rothstein. The FBI was; the body in his freezer made Rothstein hard to ignore. But in the hectic days after August 28 and September 21, 2003, the feds also had to sort through the flood of tips they were receiving on other people, such as J.J. Rothstein was just one person the FBI was looking at.

But the FBI, publicly, had distanced itself from

Rothstein in the fall of 2003. Ed Palattella, one of the *Erie Times-News* reporters on the Wells story, more than once gave the feds the benefit of the doubt. He believed that the FBI, which held itself out to be the best crime-fighting force in the land, knew what it was doing in publicly saying Rothstein wasn't a target. This careless, uncritical thinking damaged Palattella's reporting.

When the Erie police charged Diehl-Armstrong in Roden's death on September 21, the officers paraded her before the local television news cameras. Shortly thereafter, Palattella got a call from Tom Sedwick. He was the retired college professor who had called the FBI hotline on September 5 to report a woman driving the wrong way had passed him on I-79 on August 28, around the time Wells had been killed.

Sedwick was excited on the phone with Palattella. He said he finally knew the identity of the disheveled woman who had been behind the wheel of that wrong-way car. Sedwick said he had seen Marjorie Diehl-Armstrong on the local news. He said he was certain the woman in the car had been her. Those piercing blue eyes, Sedwick said: he would never forget Diehl-Armstrong looking straight at him with those eyes as the two cars passed on the highway, their driver's side windows across from each other.

Palattella did not pursue the tip. The FBI was giving no indication that Rothstein was part of the Wells case, so why would Diehl-Armstrong be involved? Sedwick had to be mistaken, Palattella thought. Diehl-Armstrong couldn't have been in that car on the highway. Why would she have been?

12

Team of Two

Among the edicts J. Edgar Hoover issued in his thirty-seven-year reign over the Federal Bureau of Investigation was that agents, if at all possible, should not get assignments in their hometowns. Hoover wanted his G-men to be objective and personally distant from the people they investigated. He feared that stationing an agent where the agent had grown up would open the FBI to corruption, to agents looking the other way.

Jerry Clark, who generally held Hoover and his legacy in high regard, disagreed with him on this point. It doesn't matter where you live, Clark said to his fellow agents: if you are crooked, you are crooked; corruption resides in a person's character, and that flaw will fester no matter how stiff the restrictions on where an agent can live and work. The FBI had softened its stance against hometown appointments by the time Clark returned to Erie in the spring of 2001.

Clark immediately realized the advantage of being "an Erie guy"—someone who went to high school at Cathedral Prep and college at Edinboro University. You went to the all-male Prep, it was like being in a brotherhood. So many men in Erie—lawyers, judges, politicians—went to Prep, stayed in Erie and remained connected. Jerry Clark knew a lot of people in Erie; a lot of people knew Jerry Clark. Erie was a different place, a little big city where the identities of many residents were tied up in whom they knew and how long they had known them. Grade-school reunions were not unheard of in Erie.

Clark had learned the importance of cultivating friendships from his father, Gerald C. Clark Sr., a former Millcreek cop who got to know those on his beat and met even more people in his second career as a landlord and builder of apartments. Gerald Clark Sr. died of stomach cancer at age seventy-two in January 2002, six months after Jerry Clark returned to Erie, partly to be with his mom and dad during his dad's final illness.

"It is all about connections," Gerald C. Clark Jr. liked to say about what his father taught him.

Clark figured he could rely on those connections and his familiarity with Erie in the Wells case, if not for tips then surely for an understanding of Erie—its neighborhoods, its residents, its criminals. Above all, being from Erie made Clark feel more committed to solving the Wells case. His wife and two children and extended family lived in Erie. He wanted his hometown to be safe and to be known for more than the pizza bomber case, which he knew would darken the city's reputation the longer it remained unsolved.

———

Probably because his father was a cop—one of the first police officers on the new force in Millcreek in the 1950s—Jerry Clark wanted to go into law enforcement as a kid. As soon as he made that choice, he decided he wanted to join the FBI, what he considered the country's premier law-enforcement agency, no matter what route he had to take.

Clark's passion for the FBI, particularly its emphasis on developing behavioral profiles and trying to understand the mind of the criminal, flourished in college, where he told one of his psychology professors he wanted to be an FBI profiler. Serial killers like the Son of Sam and Ted Bundy, especially Ted Bundy, enthralled Clark. He could not get Bundy out of his mind. How, Clark wondered, could a guy who went to law school kill people like that? The psychology professor suggested that Clark, after graduating from Edinboro University with a bachelor's degree in psychology, attend the City University of New York's John Jay College of Criminal Justice, which offered a graduate degree in the burgeoning field of forensic psychology.

While at John Jay, Clark in 1984 applied for an internship with the FBI's Behavioral Science Unit, which the bureau formed in the 1970s. He wanted to work with the agents who by then were acknowledged as the founders of behavioral science at the bureau, men (and, at that time, they were all men) such as Robert Ressler, Roy

Hazelwood, John Douglas and Roger Depue. The Behavioral Science Unit's public profile would increase with Thomas Harris' 1988 novel, *The Silence of the Lambs*, in which a novice FBI agent tracks a serial killer.

In 1984, Clark was a finalist for an internship as a research assistant with the Behavioral Science Unit. The FBI took someone else.

"Thank you for your interest in the FBI," Depue wrote to Clark on May 2, 1984, "and I hope you continue to consider the FBI as a future career."

That summer, while on break from John Jay, Clark got an internship at an Erie hospital, evaluating mental-health patients and performing psychological testing. He replied to Depue on May 11, 1984: "I hope that my goals of becoming a special agent and working for the Behavioral Science Unit as a psychological profiler can still someday be attained."

————

After three years at John Jay, Clark, then twenty-four, graduated with a master's degree in forensic psychology in 1985. A hiring freeze blocked Clark's plan to apply to the FBI at that time. He hoped to use other federal law-enforcement agencies as a path to the bureau. Clark joined the Naval Criminal Investigative Service, the NCIS, and was stationed in Philadelphia. Clark's job took on an international bent. He helped guard Israeli Prime Minister Yitzhak Rabin during his visits to the United Nations. Clark spent time in Italy as a bodyguard for U.S. Navy Admiral Frank Kelso, shortly after the ships under Kelso's

command bombed Libya's Colonel Mu'ammar al-Gad-
hafi, in April 1986.

Clark returned to Erie for his next jobs, as a probation
officer for Erie County and a forensic therapist at a
mental-health unit at a local hospital. He joined the DEA,
in Cleveland, in 1990. Five years later, he was studying at
the FBI Academy, in Quantico, to be an FBI agent.*

Clark became a special agent for the FBI in 1995. After six
years with the FBI in Dayton, chasing bank robbers and
fugitives, Clark, then forty years old, returned to Erie in
2000. He had his dream job in his dream location. On August
28, 2003, Clark got his dream assignment—he was the
case agent on a Major Case. Now all he had to do was solve it.

Clark, a churchgoing Roman Catholic, a second-
generation cop, for years carried on his key chain a lami-
nated prayer card to Saint Michael, the patron saint of
police officers; Michael was depicted casting Lucifer from
Paradise. With the way the Wells investigation was going
in the fall of 2003, Clark might have considered praying
to another saint—Saint Jude, the patron saint of lost causes.

———

The shape of the investigation changed in early 2004.
The large contingent of FBI agents and others disbanded

———

*By nature of his jobs with the FBI, DEA and NCIS, Clark achieved
the rare distinction of graduating from three major training
academies for federal law-enforcement agents: the FBI Academy at
Quantico, Virginia; the DEA Training Academy, also at Quantico;
and the Federal Law Enforcement Training Center, in Glynco,
Georgia, near Savannah, where the NCIS and other agencies train.

and went home to resume work on their own cases. The departures eventually left Clark as the only FBI agent assigned to the Wells case. Also still on the case was a representative from the state police and Jason Wick, an ATF special agent based in Pittsburgh. The two—Jerry and Jason—were on their way to becoming the faces of law enforcement in the pizza bomber probe.

Working like this, with just the two of them as the primary investigators, suited the pair. Wick, like Clark, had become frustrated. They worried the involvement of so many agencies over three jurisdictions risked the miring of the investigation in bureaucracy and confusion and missed signals between the feds and the police. With Wick and Clark in charge, they could review all the evidence and catalog everything themselves. When a lead developed, they could evaluate it quickly.

Wick, thirty-seven years old, liked the action. He had been an ATF agent since 1989. He did his job the way he had played strong safety for the football team at Indiana University of Pennsylvania, near Pittsburgh and north of Latrobe, Wick's hometown. Wick was all high impact, high speed on the field. Wick envisioned himself working on a SWAT team for a police department after he graduated with a degree in political science. Federal work appealed to him more. He got a job at the ATF, investigating drugs, guns, arsons and explosive devices, including pipe bombs.

Clark and Wick got along well, despite their agencies' different cultures: FBI agents showed up for an investigation wearing suits and ties; ATF agents showed up wearing jeans and T-shirts. Clark and Wick traded ideas easily and respected each other's skills and hard work. Clark shared Wick's investigative philosophy: "It's not what you know. It's what you can prove."

Both considered good interviewing techniques the telltale signs of a good investigator. Wick, six feet tall and 195 pounds, with short-cropped hair and the build of a former defensive back, looked like a jarhead when he walked into the interrogation room. He used his tough appearance to his advantage; he questioned people so calmly at times that he disarmed them, and they opened up. In the interrogation room, Wick liked to say to himself, "You get nowhere being a badass," though he was the first to acknowledge that he had a temper and was known to chew out suspects and fellow investigators alike. If the Clark-Wick partnership had a good cop and a bad cop, the former was Clark and the latter Wick. Clark rarely raised his voice; if anything, he sometimes seemed too deferential, too willing to let suspects say their piece before skewering them with their own inconsistencies.

It didn't matter that Clark and Wick exhibited different personas at the interview table. What was important is that they knew how to interview at all. Clark and Wick had seen lots of new agents or police officers arrive with stunning technological skills, new agents and officers who could tear apart a computer or navigate the Internet with their eyes closed. But these new agents and officers sometimes struggled with interviews; they sometimes lacked the social skills and perception to extract a confession or verbally massage a clue from a reluctant witness. Clark and Wick worried interviewing had become a lost art.

Wick blamed the *CSI* culture. The endless TV cop shows made everything seem so simple; case solved in an hour, including commercial breaks. Interviews are hard work. You must be organized. Wick and Clark knew that preparation, while time-consuming, determined an interview's success. They knew you must be persistent and direct to elicit information; you had to be willing to visit a witness or suspect repeatedly, to ask follow-up questions and to question inconsistent answers. The best interviewers knew when to challenge, and why.

As the Wells investigation wore on into early 2004, Clark and Wick realized how critical interviewing techniques would be. This was not a case, they said to each other, where the physical evidence would produce the important clues. They would have to make this case by getting someone to reveal a secret.

———

Clark and Wick narrowed their scope. Before the other agents cleared out and Clark and Wick took over, the investigators had broken into three groups; Clark had overseen each. Clark and Wick studied each group's findings.

One squad had explored the leads related to J.J.; investigators considered whether he could possibly be the "black guy" Wells mentioned. That probe finally fizzled after agents could uncover no evidence connecting J.J. to the bombing.*

Another group had pursued a tip that a former employee of Mama Mia's had left on poor terms with the owner, Tony Ditomo, and had threatened revenge. While he worked at the pizza shop, the employee had rented the house that Robert Pinetti owned in the city of Erie; the FBI also explored whether, as a high school student, the employee had known Rothstein. The theory of the disgruntled ex-worker looked promising until Clark confirmed the former employee's alibi: when Wells was killed, he had been interviewing for a job at a pet store near the Millcreek Mall.

The third of the three original groups had looked at Bill Rothstein. For Clark and Wick, in early 2004, he was their primary person of interest.

———

Finding the maker of the collar bomb was so difficult for Clark and Wick because the bomb and the collar were so devoid of productive clues. The components of the bomb—kitchen timers, batteries, a digital clock—were household goods so common that the FBI could not determine where they had been purchased.

Clark and Wick studied other evidence, excluding the bomb and its components:

———

*Neither J.J. nor his girlfriend, Angie, was charged in the Wells case. They later moved to Indiana, and J.J. continued to insist the FBI wronged him by investigating him and searching his apartment in Erie.

- A shoe impression the state police took from the clearing at the TV tower site. The impression was of a Crown Neolite rubber sole with a heel size of fifteen to sixteen, which corresponds to a shoe size of ten to eleven and one-half.

- A total of fourteen other shoe impressions, including three of the low-cut, Franklin-made sneaker that Wells wore. The eleven other impressions were not clear enough for the FBI and state police to identify the shoes that made them. All the shoe impressions were clustered around the fenced-in outbuildings in the clearing at the end of the dirt road, where vehicles could turn around, suggesting that a meeting or scuffle among a number of people had occurred there.

- Carpet fibers found on the piece of duct tape stuck on the garbage bag found under the collar bomb; the fibers were white, gold, green, red and gray. The notes had instructed Wells to put the money in the bag.

- Twelve tire impressions from the dirt road and the clearing. Five of the impressions were consistent with an Aurora Radial H710, the tires on Wells' Geo Metro. One impression was consistent with a General Ameri*G4S, which was the tire on a car of an employee for one of the local TV stations that used the site.

- DNA and fingerprints from the handset of the pay telephone at the Shell station.

- Indented writings the FBI lab found pressed into the paper of the "bomb-hostage" note that Wells gave the bank teller. The indentations were formed when someone wrote on a piece of paper that had been on top of the paper for the note. The indentations were of two telephone numbers, each of which had indented markings above them: "RC" read one; "Ryan" read the other.

———————

The indentations looked promising. Once Clark identified the corresponding residences of those indented phone numbers, that would be it: if those people knew Rothstein or anyone else connected to the case, then Marshall Piccinini, the prosecutor, might as well start drafting an indictment.

Clark identified the residents whose telephone numbers were indented into the notes. They lived in the area, but none of them knew Rothstein or anyone else the FBI thought might be connected to the case. None of them had any idea why their numbers would have been written on a piece of paper that most likely had been part of the tablet or sheaf that included the paper for the bomb-hostage note. Maybe, Clark thought, whoever wrote the note got the paper from a Staples or an OfficeMax, where a sheaf or tablet had been out in public so patrons or employees could jot notes.

None of the nine pages of notes the FBI collected in the case revealed their origins. The FBI concluded that whoever wrote the notes typed them first, then placed blank sheets of paper over the typewritten pages, and finally traced over the typeface by hand. The technique produced uniform lettering clean of handwriting tics that the FBI lab could have analyzed. Evidence specialists found seventy-nine fingerprints on the notes. Seventy-seven of them were Wells'; the other two belonged to a member of the Erie police's bomb squad who handled one piece of paper without gloves.

The other pieces of evidence came up short, too. The handset of the pay telephone was so dirty with fingerprints and DNA, as would be expected of a pay phone at a busy gas station, that the FBI lab could not link the DNA or fingerprints to anyone. The FBI had yet to match the carpet fibers to any evidence seized in the Wells case. The FBI could find no vehicle that matched tire impressions found at the tower site that were neither from Wells' car nor the car of the TV station employee.

———

The impression of the tread of the Crown Neolite sole teased Clark and Wick. The size of the tread corresponded with a shoe size of eleven and one-half, close to Rothstein's size twelve. Clark tried to link the impression to an actual boot or shoe. The FBI and state police found no matching footwear at Diehl-Armstrong's house or Rothstein's house; Rothstein told the investigators he tossed his bloody boots and overalls in the landfill as soon as he hid Roden's body in the freezer. Clark called shoe stores, shoe suppliers, shoe manufacturers, but found no information to lead him to the original shoe or boot. Lots of shoe manufacturers used Crown Neolite soles; trying to connect the markings on one sole to a specific shoe or boot would be folly.

Even the *GUESS* T-shirt's provenance remained inscrutable; the FBI determined it was a counterfeit, making its history impossible to trace. The T-shirt's message blared like a taunt, as if the person behind the bomb plot dared investigators to guess what had happened.

The inability of the investigators to find bomb-making materials at Rothstein's house or anywhere else also showed the bomber's professionalism. As Wick learned from his years of investigating pipe bombs and other IEDs, any good bomber knows that you leave behind nothing; and if you do, you bury it seven states away—or in the landfill.

Only Rothstein could explain more fully why he dumped so much of his stuff in the landfill so quickly after Diehl-Armstrong shot Roden. By early 2004, Rothstein had a lawyer and was no longer talking to the police or the FBI. When he did talk, it was in a courtroom, where he looked down from the witness box at Marjorie Diehl-Armstrong, who sat several feet away, at the defense table.

The state police charged Bill Rothstein with four crimes on October 9, 2003: abuse of a corpse, conspiring with Diehl-Armstrong to abuse a corpse, tampering with evidence and conspiring with Diehl-Armstrong to tamper with evidence. He was released on bond and waived his right to a preliminary hearing, where a magistrate decides whether enough evidence exists to send a case to trial. Rothstein, to hold up his part of the plea bargain, testified against Diehl-Armstrong at her preliminary hearing. It was the only time he would take the stand against her.

Rothstein was the second person to sit in the witness chair in a first-floor courtroom at the Erie County Court-house on January 20, 2004. He testified after Tom Rup-czewski, who sold Diehl-Armstrong the 12-gauge Remington shotgun through the classified ad.

Brad Foulk, the district attorney, called Rothstein to the stand. Rothstein testified Diehl-Armstrong told him she shot Roden.

"What was your response," Foulk said, "when she told you Roden was dead?"

"Basically I assumed that she was telling the truth, and I wanted to help her," Rothstein testified. "Because I thought maybe this will straighten her out, because she was going to give up on guys, because she kept going around with the wrong guys, she claimed."

Foulk asked Rothstein what Diehl-Armstrong told him about why she killed Roden. In one of his answers, Rothstein testified Diehl-Armstrong said she was upset at Roden because she felt he was not doing enough to find out who robbed her on May 30, 2003. Rothstein said Diehl-Armstrong told him Roden made some comment about not looking for this or that suspect any longer.

"And she said that she thought at that time, 'Well, for sure you aren't,' or something similar to that, like he would never do it again, and I believe that's when she shot him," Rothstein testified.

In another response, Rothstein said Diehl-Armstrong told him she was angry at Roden because she held him partly responsible for the break-in. Roden had introduced her to Ken Barnes, his fishing buddy, on the South Pier, Rothstein testified; Diehl-Armstrong believed Barnes robbed her.

"The reason that she gave for actually killing him," Rothstein said of Roden, "was because she thought he was responsible—not directly; it wasn't like he instigated anything to cause this—but it was because of the connections to it . . . that she was perturbed with Jim."

Rothstein spoke circuitously about why Diehl-Armstrong told him she wanted to hide Roden's body. He said Diehl-Armstrong was worried that a county judge was about to come over to her house on East Seventh Street to check on Roden because Roden "had some kind of, I believe, a judgment against him, or some kind of order; I don't know if it was a PFA or not." Rothstein was referring to a protection-from-abuse order, or a restraining order, like the one Diehl-Armstrong took out against Roden in 1994. That PFA had expired years earlier; no judge in Erie County had a policy of paying personal visits in PFA cases.

Questioned by the defense, Rothstein said he did not kill Roden.

The magistrate ordered Diehl-Armstrong held for trial on the homicide count and other charges. The preliminary hearing ended with no mention of Brian Wells. Everything Foulk and his assistant prosecutors did publicly in the Roden case—the evidence they presented in court, the documents they filed, the comments they made to the media—signaled they were treating the Roden and Wells cases as unconnected. Both were strange, and linked by geography, but that is where the similarities, from what the district attorney's office said, stopped.

———

Diehl-Armstrong said nothing in her defense at the preliminary hearing. After she left the courtroom in handcuffs, sheriff's deputies led her into a hall and a bank of elevators for the return trip to the Erie County Prison. Diehl-Armstrong, who wore prison-issued plastic shoes and a prison-issued denim shirt, her hair long and her piercing blue eyes peering out of her pale face, gazed directly into a television camera. She sounded like a deranged Cassandra, whose comments risked going unheeded.

"Rothstein is a filthy liar," Diehl-Armstrong snarled into the lens. "Rothstein should be charged with the death of Brian Wells and a lot of other charges."

13

Another Death (Part Two)

This would be the last time Jerry Clark would get to talk to Bill Rothstein. Clark formulated the questions in his mind as he drove to Millcreek Community Hospital, on Peach Street near Mama Mia's, on July 27, 2004. If Rothstein was going to say he did it, this would be the time; this would have to be the time.

Clark had not spoken to Rothstein since they tangled in that basement interrogation room in the state police barracks the morning of September 21, 2003. Rothstein's lawyer later barred any further questioning.

Since the time Clark had interviewed Rothstein, the circumstances had changed. Rothstein had no reason to decline to talk now, on July 27, 2004. Whatever he told Clark, in reality, could never be used against him. Bill Rothstein, who had turned sixty years old in January, was dying.

Clark got the call earlier in the day from Foulk, the district attorney, who had been monitoring the where-abouts of his star witness against his high-profile defendant, Diehl-Armstrong, who was awaiting trial in the Roden case. Rothstein on May 25, 2004, had sold his family's house at 8645 Peach Street for $115,000, considerably less than the $250,000 he had wanted. Even if the house had not sold, Rothstein would have been too ill to be living there now, in the summer of 2004.

"Bill Rothstein's in the hospital," Foulk told Clark.

Clark called Rothstein's lawyer, Gene Placidi.

"I have a few questions to ask him," Clark said.

Placidi consented. He agreed to the interview so the FBI could show Rothstein photos of people investigators believed might have been connected to the Wells case; at that point, the FBI wanted to be sure the case involved no students Rothstein had taught in high school

Clark and Placidi walked into the hospital room. Clark glanced at Rothstein, who was on his back on the bed. The doctors had diagnosed Rothstein with stage IV non-Hodgkin's lymphoma; the cancer had spread from the lymph nodes to other organs.

"My God," Clark said to himself, "he's been sick for a while."

Clark thought Rothstein had a month to live. Clark had seen the stomach cancer race through his father's body. Rothstein looked like his dad did toward the end. Rothstein, like his father had been, was heavily medicated.

Rothstein looked so bad, Clark thought his cancer had taken hold before August 28, 2003. If that were the case—and, as he studied Rothstein's thin and white face, Clark thought that *had* to be the case—Rothstein would have had nothing to lose by participating in the Wells plot. He knew he was dying on August 28, 2003.

Rothstein's life had been full of calculated misdirection and oddities and crime and theatrics and practical jokes. Rothstein would have wanted to spend his final time on earth using his vaunted intellect to concoct the ultimate feat of warped ingenuity—the staging of the death of another human being. While he was dying, Rothstein would want to play God with another person's life.

Clark had to get a deathbed confession.

He bent over Rothstein. Clark identified himself. He showed Rothstein the photos. Rothstein said some of the people looked vaguely familiar.

Clark asked Rothstein about August 28, 2003.

"Where were you that day?" he said.

Rothstein grunted.

"I don't remember," he said.

"You told me before, when I interviewed you," Clark said. "You told me you and Marjorie Diehl-Armstrong went to North East that day."

Clark countered as best he could, but this was tough. Rothstein was dying, and the drugs had fogged his mind. Clark asked Rothstein if, after hearing what he had said in September 2003, he remembered what he was doing on August 28, 2003.

"I met with Marge," Rothstein said haltingly. "We probably worked on her car and took it to a garage."

Rothstein had offered a different alibi than saying they had been on a day trip to North East. Clark had interviewed a lot of people but none who gave conflicting statements on a deathbed.

"Where did you work on the car?" Clark said. "What was the name of the repair shop?"

"I don't know," Rothstein said.

"You didn't tell me this before," Clark said.

Rothstein had no explanation for the difference.

"What else were you doing that day?" Clark said.

Rothstein said he might have been at the Shell station at Peach Street and Robison Road, but he was unsure. He said he might have used the pay telephone at the Shell station, but he could not be positive.

"Where did you and Marge go that day?" Clark said.

"I don't remember."

Clark had to get more.

"Were you involved in the Wells case?"

Rothstein grunted.

Placidi whispered to Clark. They stepped into the hall, where Placidi said he was concerned about the intensity of the questions.

"Gene," Clark said, his voice rising in a plea, "this guy's dying. You can't let him take it with him. My dad had cancer: this guy's dying."

Placidi said he had to protect his client. He said he wanted to make sure Rothstein understood he was not obligated to answer any questions.

Clark implored Placidi. Clark wielded no legal leverage;

a federal grand jury could not indict a dead man. His leverage bordered on the spiritual: Clark was giving Rothstein a final chance to unburden himself.

"Don't let this guy take it to his death," Clark said. "Let him tell me."

Placidi agreed to let Clark ask a few more questions. Placidi explained the situation to Rothstein, who assented to continuing the interview.

"Were you involved in the Wells case?" Clark said.

"No!" Rothstein mumbled, his voice rising. "Nooo!"

Rothstein raised an arm high above his head. He lifted his index finger and swept it through the air. He sketched two letters: *NO*.

"You're sicker than I knew," Clark said. "Tell me."

"No. Nooo!"

Clark never spoke to Rothstein again.

———

Clark rued yet another lost chance. Rothstein's fatal cancer was on its way to undermining the investigation. In the months before Rothstein ended up in the hospital, Clark and Jason Wick had gathered more evidence they believed linked Rothstein to the Wells case. They had little doubt, by the summer of 2004, that Rothstein had called in Wells' final order, helped make the collar bomb and helped plan the plot, even to the point of ordering a pizza with sausage and pepperoni on it. Rothstein was a vegetarian; who would ever suspect him of ordering a pie with meat?

With each day, Diehl-Armstrong, mainly because of

her relationship with Rothstein, had also emerged as a legitimate person of interest by the summer of 2004. So had Floyd Stockton.

As for Brian Wells, Clark and Wick remained unsure of whether he was an innocent victim or a willing participant. But from what they knew in the summer of 2004, before Clark interviewed Rothstein, they were certain they were getting closer to uncovering his true role.

———————

A major clue had come in March 2004 from Michael Douglas, a thirty-six-year-old draftsman for an Erie architectural firm. He had first visited the Erie FBI office in person, unprompted, in the weeks after Wells was killed.

Douglas told the FBI then that he was driving north on upper Peach Street between 12:30 and 1:00 P.M. on Wednesday, August 27, 2003, to go to a movie matinee with his wife. It was a rare day off for Douglas.

Douglas said he was driving near the New Motors auto dealership when he spotted Brian Wells' bluish-green Geo Metro. Douglas said it pulled out onto Peach Street from the dirt road to the TV tower next to Rothstein's house. Another car followed Wells' Geo. When that car pulled out onto Peach Street, it nearly cut off Douglas' car. Douglas slammed on the brakes.

Douglas said he knew Wells was driving the Geo. After August 28, 2003, he said, he saw a photo of the car in the *Erie Times-News* coverage of Wells' death. That recognition led Douglas to drive to the Erie FBI office.

Whomever Douglas spoke to at the FBI office in 2003 made a note of his visit, but no one talked to him and completed an FD-302, the form in which an agent summarizes the interview. No one followed up with Douglas. So he called the FBI office again on March 3, 2004.

Clark got on the line this time. Unlike before, when any number of agents handled calls on the Wells case, everyone at the Erie office knew to route all the inquiries to one agent: Clark.

"Hey," Douglas told Clark, "I think this is pretty important."

Clark listened.

"*What* did you see?" Clark said.

Douglas reiterated his sighting of Wells' Geo.

"We need to get you in right now," Clark said.

This information had immense importance. Based on what Douglas was saying, Brian Wells had been at the site of the TV tower the day before he was killed, a day Mama Mia's had no record of him delivering a pizza to that spot. Wells didn't need directions to the tower site when he got on the phone at Mama Mia's on August 28: he knew where he was going, but he never told Tony Ditomo, his boss. Why had Wells been there on August 27? Had he been in on a planning meeting at Rothstein's house?

Douglas' information thrilled Jason Wick, though he seethed about not getting it earlier. Wick imagined what he and Clark could have done with Douglas' information in 2003.

Wick interviewed Douglas on March 3, 2004. He dutifully completed an ATF "Report of Investigation" form, the equivalent of an FBI 302. The FBI brass, still leery about the Rothstein angle, ordered Douglas polygraphed. He passed.

In the days after Wells died, the state police had looked for evidence on Peach Street, near the intersection with the dirt road. Troopers had found skid marks on Peach Street. More than a year later, Clark and Wick realized the significance of those skid marks: Douglas had made them when he braked his car suddenly on August 27, 2003.

Douglas never wavered in his account: the first car, the Geo Metro, was Wells' car, and Wells had been behind the wheel.

"He just turned to his left and looked at me," Douglas would testify later. "He looked at the traffic coming down before he proceeded out, he just looked dead at our vehicle. And I could see it plain as day."

———

On March 3, 2004, the same day Wick interviewed Douglas, the *Erie Times-News* published a letter to the editor from one of Brian Wells' five siblings, a sister, Jean Heid, who lived in Erie. It was the first time Wells' family had expressed a lengthy opinion about Wells' fate and the investigation.

Heid, forty-four years old, urged Wells' killer or killers to turn themselves in. She believed her brother was innocent, though the FBI was telling the public agents had not discarded the possibility that Wells might have been involved. Heid thanked the agents working the case in the letter, titled "The death of Brian Wells":

I don't know who killed Brian so mercilessly and callously but I do know they meant to kill and that they are still present among us.

The grief and heartache they have caused is enormous. I am saddened that those responsible haven't come forward to confess their evil. I pray and fast for those involved to be brought to conversion, to unburden themselves, to look to God, to find peace, to be caught and brought to justice. . . .

Law enforcement can and will help you. Be not afraid. Listen to your heart, come forward confessing. Though your sins are as scarlet, Christ's blood can make them white as snow.

———

Around this time, in early 2004, Clark and Wick happened upon evidence that raised their suspicions about Stockton. As part of their review of all the information in the Wells case, they had read a transcript of Stockton's interview with the state trooper, Mark Russo, on October 3, 2003—the interview Russo arranged after Stockton passed the polygraph but then cried to Russo about not fighting in Vietnam.

In the October 3 interview, according to the transcript, Stockton consistently told Russo he did not know Wells and had no part in his death. Stockton said he was at Rothstein's house on August 28, 2003. Clark and Wick grew interested when they read what Stockton said happened at 3:00 P.M., eighteen minutes before Wells died. Stockton said he was alone in Rothstein's house, heard a knock on the door and looked out a window. Stockton did not answer the door. He said he saw a police cruiser idling on the dirt road, alongside Rothstein's garage.

The cruiser had been sent there after troopers learned the location of Wells' final delivery. The troopers had obtained that information by visiting Mama Mia's, which Wells had said was his employer, while Wells was handcuffed in the parking lot of Eyeglass World. Stockton did not know that, and Russo did not tell him.

Russo asked Stockton what his first thought was when he saw the cruiser on the dirt road.

"I thought something was going on," Stockton said.

He said he thought maybe the police had finally caught up with him, because he was on the run in the rape case. He said he realized he was not in trouble when no police officers called out his name.

"So I turned the TV on," Stockton said. "I figured, 'Well, maybe the news will have something about what was going on.' And they did, they had a bulletin come on, they started showing footage of Wells in front of the car."

Russo asked, "So the very first you ever heard of this incident is turning on the television because the police are knocking at your door?"

"Yeah, it was," Stockton said.

Stockton told Russo that, based on the presence of the cruiser, he thought the tower site or the dirt road had something to do with what was on TV.

"Why would you make that link?" Russo said.

"Huh?" Stockton said.

"Why would you make that connection?"

"Because of the location," Stockton said. "It's in the vicinity: freeway, close to the freeway, you know what I'm saying. So, I'm saying, 'Well, maybe there is some correlation to that; maybe it has something to do with it.' I'm just assuming."

Clark and Wick couldn't believe what they had read. Who turns on the local TV news in the middle of the afternoon to see why a police cruiser is parked outside his window? This wasn't the O. J. Simpson chase; Stockton would have had no reason to believe the local TV news would broadcast live coverage of a local crime on August 28, 2003—unless Stockton knew a big crime was occurring. Also, Stockton assumed the TV tower site was part of the Wells case, solely because a police cruiser was parked outside his window. Who thinks like that?

Clark and Wick wanted to talk to Stockton in early 2004, but he was incarcerated in Washington State. They wanted to talk to Rothstein, but his lawyer had said his client was granting no interviews. They wanted to talk to Marjorie Diehl-Armstrong, but she was off-limits as well in early 2004. She was in a mental institution.

———

On March 22, 2004, the Erie County judge presiding over the Roden case ordered Diehl-Armstrong to undergo a six-month psychiatric review at Mayview State Hospital, near Pittsburgh, where she had been sent during the Bob Thomas case. The defense requested the exam, which would determine whether Diehl-Armstrong was mentally competent to stand trial in the Roden case.

Diehl-Armstrong's court-appointed lawyer in the Roden case was well aware of her mental-health history. He said a psychiatric exam was warranted based on her "nonsensical" conversations with him and the number of psychotropic drugs investigators found at her East Seventh Street residence. The district attorney's office consented to the defense's request for the exam.

The FBI was prohibited from interviewing Diehl-Armstrong while she was at Mayview; doing so would risk a judge throwing out a statement because she gave it while housed at a mental institution. An unstable mental state would mean an unreliable interview.

Bill Rothstein turned and moaned. His visitors this time were two reporters from the *Erie Times-News*. It was July 30, 2004, three days after Clark's interview. The reporters, Ed Palattella and Tim Hahn, had gotten a tip earlier in the day that Rothstein was dying. They left the newspaper building quickly; they hoped to talk to Rothstein before he breathed his last.

Palattella and Hahn, the *Times-News*' police reporter, tracked Rothstein's whereabouts to Pleasant Ridge Manor East, the county-run nursing home for the indigent, where Rothstein had been transferred from Millcreek Community Hospital. Palattella and Hahn had no idea Clark had visited Rothstein at the hospital on July 27.

Rothstein's room was white and bare. He was alone; he had no photographs of family members, no get-well cards, none of the other trinkets of affection that often brighten the institutional rooms of the chronically ill and dying. What a way to go, Palattella thought; if Rothstein, the self-proclaimed genius, was indeed behind the Wells case, he had no one to brag to now. He was all by himself, his eyes sunken, his skin pallid, his wits unable to save him from every man's ultimate fate.

Palattella and Hahn bent over Rothstein's bed. They identified themselves as reporters.

"Uh," he said, indicating he was having a hard time hearing.

The reporters shouted questions about the Wells case. While lying on his side, his eyes rolling in his head, Rothstein responded by lifting one arm high and sketching the air with an index finger: *NO*.

"No!" Rothstein groaned. "Nooo!"

Palattella and Hahn were uneasy; they were unsure Rothstein was coherent. They left the room.

Several hours later, Bill Rothstein was dead.

14

A Deadly Profile

I n 1983, infuriated by the acquittal a year earlier of John Hinckley Jr., statehouses across the United States, including in Harrisburg, Pennsylvania, established a new verdict in criminal cases: guilty but mentally ill. Lawmakers were outraged that the jury had found Hinckley not guilty by reason of insanity in the attempted assassination of President Ronald Reagan in 1981. The nation's criminal insanity laws, based on the M'Naghten rule, from mid-nineteenth-century Great Britain, underwent modifications. A verdict of guilty but mentally ill was seen as supplementing what was the general M'Naghten standard: that a defendant is not guilty by reason of insanity if he or she cannot differentiate right from wrong.

A verdict of guilty but mentally ill carries the same punishment as a regular guilty verdict in Pennsylvania, except the defendant must get mental-health treatment while in prison; the defendant does not stay indefinitely in a mental institution. At trial, a jury can consider a verdict of guilty but mentally ill if the defense argues insanity; a defendant may also plead guilty but mentally ill.

Pennsylvania law defines a defendant who is guilty but mentally ill as "[o]ne who as a result of a mental disease or defect, lacks substantial capacity either to appreciate the wrongfulness of his conduct or to conform his conduct to the requirements of law."

———

At 8:34 A.M. on January 7, 2005, in a wood-paneled courtroom on the second floor of the Erie County Courthouse, the district attorney, Brad Foulk, stood next to Marjorie Diehl-Armstrong and, while in front of the judge's bench, asked her whether she understood the legal definition of guilty but mentally ill.

"Yes," she replied.

This plea hearing was to be followed by Diehl-Armstrong's sentencing for the death of Jim Roden.

For forty minutes, Diehl-Armstrong stood calmly in the courtroom and agreed she was suffering from a mental illness—a bipolar disorder—when she killed Roden. She acknowledged that the presiding judge, Shad Connelly, had agreed with the examining psychiatrist in September 2004 and found her mentally competent to stand trial, a ruling that prepared the way for this plea hearing.

The psychiatrist, in his report to the judge, said

Diehl-Armstrong had, by August 2004, received the maximum benefit from her hospitalization at Mayview State Hospital and no longer needed inpatient care. He said psychotropic drugs, including those for schizophrenia, had restored her to competency. The psychiatrist said Diehl-Armstrong's bipolar disorder went into remission while she was on the drugs. He warned that, without supervision, Diehl-Armstrong would likely go off her medications and regress to her manic state.

Four months after that diagnosis, on January 7, 2005, Diehl-Armstrong stood in front of Connelly and pleaded guilty but mentally ill to two counts: third-degree murder, or an unpremeditated killing with malice, and abuse of a corpse. In return, the Erie County District Attorney's Office dropped the other five charges against her. The abuse-of-a-corpse count pertained to the allegations she bought the ice crusher and conspired with Bill Rothstein to dismember Roden's body.

"I just want to say for the record that I'm pleading guilty because of the complicity aspect of this," Diehl-Armstrong told Connelly. "I'm not saying I had nothing to do with purchasing a freezer, putting the body in a freezer or anything like that, but I knew Mr. Rothstein was doing wrong and I didn't stop it so therefore I feel I was guilty of complicity."

She apologized to Roden's family.

Connelly said Diehl-Armstrong was in need of ongoing mental-health treatment. She is, he said, "severely mentally disabled." He accepted the guilty plea and prepared to sentence her.

"I'm not going to be in any more trouble, Your Honor," she said. "I've learned my lesson. And if I get another chance at life, I'm not going to lose it and I'm going to thank God and the people who gave it to me. I'm really going to appreciate it from the bottom of my heart. And this is the truth. I'm not a bad person, Your Honor."

Foulk spoke next. In another example of everyone in Erie seeming to be connected, he graduated from Erie's Academy High School in 1965, two years ahead of Diehl-Armstrong; she had been a sophomore his senior year. Like most any lawyer of his age in Erie County, Foulk remembered Diehl-Armstrong's acquittal in the Thomas case.

"I've known Marjorie for forty-some years, and I'm familiar with the prior conduct of Marjorie over the years and going all the way back to the mid-1980s," Foulk told Connelly. "I'm familiar with the charges. And I know the court cannot take into account an acquittal a number of years ago, but I think it's important to note that the conduct she engaged in during the late '80s was almost identical to this particular conduct.

"And I know she's pleading guilty but mentally ill today, and I think the psychiatric reports reflect a woman who is suffering from a mental disorder that without question, without question, if she were ever placed on the streets again she would kill another man."

Diehl-Armstrong interjected.

"Oh," she said, "how can he say that?"

Connelly recounted Diehl-Armstrong's mental problems, emphasized her intelligence and called Roden's death "a tragedy." He sentenced her to seven to twenty years in state prison for third-degree murder and two years of probation for abuse of a corpse.

The name of Brian Wells never came up.

Diehl-Armstrong's sentence could have been much longer. Under Pennsylvania law, the maximum sentence for third-degree murder is forty years; had she been convicted of first-degree murder, or a premeditated killing, she would have faced the death penalty or gotten life without parole. Pennsylvania requires a convict to serve at least the minimum sentence before being eligible for parole. For Diehl-Armstrong, then fifty-five years old and with a sentence of seven to twenty years, she would have to serve seven years before the Parole Board would even consider hearing her case.

Judge Connelly ordered Diehl-Armstrong incarcerated in the state prison system, which holds inmates whose sentences are at least two years. But because she pleaded guilty but mentally ill, and was "in need of immediate treatment," he directed her to start serving her sentence at Mayview State Hospital—the one place she would still be insulated from investigators. Diehl-Armstrong didn't mind being at Mayview rather than a regular state prison. Mayview, she said, had better food.

By early 2005, Jerry Clark was, on a day-to-day level, fully in charge of the Wells investigation. In August

2004—about two weeks before the first anniversary of Wells' death—the FBI promoted Bob Rudge, Clark's supervisor in Erie, to assistant special agent in charge of the FBI's Pittsburgh Field Office. The FBI offered Clark the job as supervisor of the Erie Resident Agency office, which answers to Pittsburgh. Clark turned it down. If his ideal job was to be an FBI agent in Erie, his hometown, Clark's ultimate ideal job was to be the supervisor of the Erie FBI office. If he took the supervisor's post, Clark would have had to relinquish the Wells case; the FBI prohibits supervisors from handling investigations. Clark could not accept the trade-off.

"I am not giving this case up," he told his superiors. "I want to be the supervisor here more than anything you know, but I am not giving this case up."

In early 2005, Clark still had the Wells case—and he supervised the Erie office. The FBI had yet to pick Rudge's successor, so Clark served as the interim supervisor. He oversaw the administration of the office, but, as an interim boss, he was allowed to work the Wells case on top of everything else. Those above him in the FBI continued to doubt a Rothstein–Diehl-Armstrong angle, but Clark and Jason Wick in early 2005 were in a better position to pursue their theory than at any time since Wells' death.

Clark let the public in on his plans. On February 12, 2005, in a front-page article in the *Erie Times-News*, Clark told reporter Tim Hahn that the FBI was moving ahead in the Wells investigation. As Hahn reported, based on his interview with Clark:

No individual previously identified by themselves or by investigators as persons of interest in the case have been ruled out as being involved in the crime. They include Marjorie Diehl-Armstrong . . . ; the late William Rothstein . . . ; Robert Pinetti, Wells' co-worker who died of a drug overdose days after Wells was killed; and Wells himself.

Clark heard from his supervisors as soon as the story was published. Clark had insisted to them, based on his deathbed interview with Rothstein, in which he changed his alibi, that Rothstein had to have been part of the Wells plot. If Rothstein was in, Clark said, so was Diehl-Armstrong. As for Pinetti and Wells, Clark had told his supervisors he had no reason to conclude they were not involved.

"What are you doing, putting these people in?" was the message Clark got from Pittsburgh.

"Because," Clark replied, "they are still in."

———

Clark's tactic—saying who was in the investigation, not saying anyone was out—differed from the approach that Rudge had taken when he supervised Clark in the Wells case in 2003.

"All I can say at this time is that we have no evidence that would suggest Rothstein was associated with this crime," Rudge said of the Wells case on September 26, 2003. "I don't mean to close the door on all possibilities."

Rudge retired from the FBI in 2011, after twenty-five years of service. Looking back, he said, the lack of physical evidence against Rothstein, as well as Wells' dying comments about the black men, influenced the FBI's reluctance to zero in on Rothstein exclusively, at least at first. Rudge said the FBI had to explore the possibility that J.J. could have been involved. He said that Rothstein's not failing the polygraph test complicated the FBI's consideration of whether to make Rothstein an early target.

"I don't think at any time we ever completely ruled any person in or out," Rudge said. "There were some very strong coincidences that led us in the wrong direction for some time. With all the stones we were overturning, we weren't finding the hidden jewel that would convince us we were 100 percent on the right track."

———

In March 2005, Clark was still feeling resistance from his superiors on the Rothstein angle. He got exasperated when the internal questions continued after the FBI's Behavioral Analysis Unit completed its long-awaited final profile on the person or persons behind the bombing and bank robbery.

The seven-page report, dated March 11, 2005, was by Mary Ellen O'Toole, one of the FBI's most senior profilers.* Clark read the report as a biography of Rothstein—a

———

*O'Toole retired in 2009 after twenty-eight years with the FBI. Her other cases included those on the Green River killer, the Zodiac killer, the Unabomber and the Columbine killings.

Svengali-like fiend who manipulated a semicomplicit Wells. Clark was struck by the section of the report, near the end, when O'Toole theorized why the bomber chose the PNC Bank in the Summit Towne Centre. O'Toole wrote, in part:

> This is a complex crime and most likely involves more than one person. However, it is the opinion of the BAU that there is one "mastermind" who authored the notes/instructions and built both the collar-bomb and the shotgun, then oversaw the design and implementation of the crime, and orchestrated it on August 28, 2003.
>
> It is the opinion of the BAU that this crime is much more than an elaborate bank robbery and money was probably not the primary motive.
>
> It is the opinion of the BAU that Brian Wells was not a random victim, and he was not kidnaped [sic] and forced to wear the collar-bomb. . . .
>
> It is also the opinion of the BAU that Wells was complicit in this crime only in so far as he allowed the collar-bomb to be placed on him. However, we opine that he was duped in terms of what he was told about the bomb's functionality, what could happen to him and the real motive for the crime. . . .
>
> Wells had the time and the ability to alert someone that he was in trouble—if he believed he was. . . . Wells did not draw attention to himself by evidencing obvious signs of fear, concerns, dread, panic, etc., despite the fact he was wearing a fully functional explosive device strapped to his neck which he was incapable of

extracting. This is totally contrary to Wells' personality as described by those who knew him. They characterized him as somewhat meek, a little naïve, a low-key individual who was non-confrontational and fearful of situations he perceived as threatening. . . .

This offender shows an inclination towards "shop-type" projects or projects typically seen in a "VO-TECH" class . . .

The use of scrap items as well as inexpensive store-bought materials suggest this offender is a frugal person—probably described by those who know him as a pack-rat—someone who saves scraps of various and sundry materials in order to reuse them in various projects, and supplements with pieces readily available in discount stores. . . .

The instructions/notes are very cumbersome to read and understand, particularly if the reader were under a great deal of stress and pressured to comprehend their content. They require repeated reviews in order to understand the offender's specific instructions. It is the opinion of the BAU that Wells was familiar with his particular instructions prior to August 28, 2003. . . .

There seems to be a significant shift in the offender's affect when he writes about the violence to the bank, its customers and employees. He implies that he and his group have followed certain employees and customers, and know the location of their residences. The offender threatens that these people will either be shot or their residences bombed if the offender and his group do not receive the money. . . .

These threats go far beyond what is traditionally seen in a bank robbery note. This degree of anger as evidenced by these exaggerated threats of near Armageddon are not even realistic—and suggest this offender has a personal problem with the bank. Consideration that the victim bank/PNC was specifically selected as a target may be important. Historical letters sent to that bank or its headquarters containing similar threats for real or perceived wrongs should be investigated.

15

Breakthrough

All women sentenced to state prison in Pennsylvania eventually go to the State Correctional Institution (SCI) at Muncy, one of Pennsylvania's two state prisons for women. SCI Muncy, near Williamsport, is the classification center for the state's female inmates; Muncy's staff decides whether an inmate will stay at Muncy or head to the minimum-security SCI Cambridge Springs, in the county just south of Erie. SCI Cambridge Springs typically houses inmates whose sentences are about to expire.

SCI Cambridge Springs opened in 1993. SCI Muncy opened in the 1920s as the Muncy Industrial Home, a training school for female convicts between the ages of sixteen and thirty. SCI Muncy's main brick building looks like a cross between a castle and Independence Hall in Philadelphia.

Clark picked up on the age of SCI Muncy as soon as he and Wick walked into the main building after the four-hour drive from Erie on April 27, 2005. As he and Wick headed to a basement room, they seemed to be wandering into a dungeon. The brick-lined halls were dark. Clark thought of the scene in the movie *The Silence of the Lambs*, when FBI trainee Clarice Starling interviews Hannibal Lecter at the dank Baltimore State Hospital for the Criminally Insane. Lecter, Clark thought, was a serial killer, too, just like he believed Marjorie Diehl-Armstrong was turning out to be.

Clark and Wick turned into a cramped, hot room. Clark, who had done thousands of interviews, was nervous. He tried to calm down by reminding himself that he was prepared, that, having lived in Erie and studied her past, he knew all kinds of things about Diehl-Armstrong.

Diehl-Armstrong sat down at the interview table. Clark looked at her. Her dark blue eyes stared right through him. She was just frightening.

Mayview State Hospital, after treating Diehl-Armstrong, had transferred her to SCI Muncy about a month earlier, on March 16. As Clark and Wick prepared to arrange an interview, a state police investigator, David Gluth, who was part of the Wells team, visited Diehl-Armstrong at Muncy on another case. Gluth, then a corporal, was the state police's specialist on cold-case homicides in Erie. In the interview with Gluth, Diehl-Armstrong said she had information on the Wells case, that Rothstein and Stockton were involved, that the case consumed Rothstein's attention. She said she was willing to talk. The state police, much to Clark's appreciation, from the start of the Wells case believed Rothstein was involved. Gluth relayed the information to the FBI.

Clark sat across the small table from Diehl-Armstrong, with Wick to the side. They were not treating her as a suspect; they did not have to read her Miranda rights. In any case, she did not ask for a lawyer. She was unmedicated.

After she returned to Mayview following her sentence in the Roden case, in January 2005, Diehl-Armstrong had been prescribed the drug Abilify, used to treat schizophrenia. It was the last psychotropic drug she was known to take. She had accepted Abilify, her psychiatrist at Mayview said, because it was the only medication she had not yet tried and because it gave her no significant side effects. Diehl-Armstrong went off Abilify not long after she was prescribed it. She said it made her dizzy and caused her to shake and rock.

Clark opened his interview with Diehl-Armstrong by recalling her fixation on her teeth. He had read about that in her file.

"Marge," Clark said, "you have a million-dollar smile."

Diehl-Armstrong seemed pleased, but she kept her distance. She swore like a trucker: she used *fuck* as a noun, verb, adjective, even a conjunction. She spoke calmly, but loudly, and a lot. She said she was not involved in the Wells case, but Rothstein was. She said he needed the money to make the payments on his mother's house at 8645 Peach Street, and that he would be evicted if he didn't come up with cash soon. Rothstein and Floyd

Stockton were lovers, she said, who used to work on cars in the garage of Rothstein's friend, D.M., whom Rothstein had mailed $10,220 at the time Rothstein said he was contemplating suicide in September 2003. Diehl-Armstrong said Rothstein knew Wells, and that Rothstein talked Wells into wearing the bomb and robbing the bank. Wells, she said, was "a flunky pizza delivery driver" who needed money. She said Rothstein told her he was involved in the Wells case, but did not elaborate.

Clark slowed the conversation. He told Diehl-Armstrong that Rothstein said she was with him in North East on August 28, 2003.

"If he said that," she said, "he was lying."

Diehl-Armstrong volunteered where she was on the afternoon of August 28, 2003: at the Barnes & Noble bookstore on upper Peach Street, near the Millcreek Mall and about a mile south of the Summit Towne Centre. She said she ate lunch at the KFC restaurant next to Barnes & Noble, then drove to Rothstein's house, where she found no one home.

"Why was Jim Roden killed?" Clark said.

"I can't answer that," Diehl-Armstrong said.

She said she had more information, but that she would say no more for now. For her to talk again, she said, the FBI would have to move her to SCI Cambridge Springs.

Clark and Wick made their way out of the basement. They had bits and pieces of information—not enough to implicate Diehl-Armstrong, but a start. Her answer to the question about Roden lingered with them. Why wouldn't she say why she killed him, even after she pleaded guilty?

"Now I've got to do my homework," Clark said to himself.

About a month later, on May 23, 2005, Clark and Wick again interviewed Diehl-Armstrong at SCI Muncy. She talked at length about Rothstein, how he read books by 1960s activist Abbie Hoffman, subscribed to *Soldier of Fortune* magazine and kept *The Anarchist Cookbook* around his house. She spoke much less about the Wells case. She would not respond to questions about the components she believed Rothstein used to make the collar bomb. Clark asked her specifically about timers. She rebuffed him. First, she said, get me to Cambridge Springs.

No lawyer was present at this interview, though Diehl-Armstrong had been getting legal advice. It had been coming from her personal attorney in Erie, Larry D'Ambrosio. He had been prodding Diehl-Armstrong to talk to Clark.

"Don't forget to let me know if you know anything about a timer," D'Ambrosio wrote to her at SCI Muncy on June 21, 2005. "Did Bill buy one or did he ask you for one, etc. We're still trying to get you into Cambridge Springs. We need input from you."

———

Diehl-Armstrong might have been reticent with Clark and Wick, but she was talking a lot to others in prison. Her friendships with fellow inmates developed first at the Erie County Prison in the days after September 21, 2003, when she was jailed without bond on the charges she killed Roden and put his body in a freezer—charges the other inmates noticed. Diehl-Armstrong's coterie included a fellow prisoner by the name of Gloria Bishop.* She became friends with Diehl-Armstrong when she stood up to her. Bishop, thirty-six years old, was sitting at a table with someone Diehl-Armstrong did not like. Diehl-Armstrong asked Bishop how she could sit next to the woman.

"When I saw her in the med line," Diehl-Armstrong spewed, according to Bishop, "I wanted to smash her head like a watermelon and watch the seeds pop out."

"Yeah," Bishop replied, with mock concern. "You know, it doesn't pay to piss off the Freezer Queen—you end up an entrée."

Diehl-Armstrong thought Bishop's rejoinder hilarious: the Freezer Queen tag was funny. Diehl-Armstrong laughed and pointed across the table.

"I really like you," she said.

The generally social nature of the women in prison soon combined with two factors: Diehl-Armstrong's incessant talking and the general truism that most prisoners will do whatever they can to get out—including informing on their fellow inmates. Many of the inmates, after listening day in and day out to Diehl-Armstrong's surge of words, went to the FBI to report what she said.

In Bishop's case, she got no breaks for her help, which she would later testify she offered out of "a moral

---

*All of Diehl-Armstrong's fellow inmates who spoke to investigators in her case were convicted of far less serious crimes than third-degree murder, and each, based on testimony, turned her life around in prison.

obligation." She said Diehl-Armstrong told her she killed Jim Roden. Bishop wrote a letter to a relative about what Diehl-Armstrong confided to her in prison, and the relative contacted Foulk at the district attorney's office. Soon the Erie police were interviewing Bishop about Diehl-Armstrong's admission to her that she murdered Roden.

Clark, in reviewing the Roden case, became interested in Bishop. He asked Gluth to interview her. On June 6, 2005, Bishop recounted to Gluth the things she said Diehl-Armstrong told her—including the things about Wells' death.

"She had stated that she measured him for the collar," Bishop would testify later. "She did state that she measured Brian for the collar."

Regarding Rothstein, Bishop testified Diehl-Armstrong told her "he was stupid for using the pay phone by his house."

The bank robbery "was all about the money," Bishop testified of Diehl-Armstrong's comments. She said Diehl-Armstrong told her she was angry at her father.

"She didn't like her father very much," Bishop said. "She felt that he had squandered her inheritance. And she was angry because he wouldn't get her a lawyer for the Roden trial; she had to have a public defender."

———

Gloria Bishop was one of many inmates to come forward. Through them, Clark finally established what frequently stands as the cornerstone of any major FBI case but that had been lacking so far in this investigation—informants.

With so many of the persons of interest in the Wells case dead, informants had been hard to come by. Not now, not with Diehl-Armstrong behind bars and unable or unwilling to keep her mouth shut.

The tips had come from SCI Muncy shortly after Clark and Wick drove back to Erie from their interview on May 23, 2005. Diehl-Armstrong was shooting her mouth off about the FBI coming to talk to her, and one of the inmates contacted the guards and said she had something she herself wanted to tell the FBI. With each woman, with each informant, that is how it would work—a female inmate would hear Diehl-Armstrong, the woman would speak to an authority at the prison, that person would contact Clark. He and Wick would conduct an interview they tried to keep secret from Diehl-Armstrong.

The clues flooded in.

16

"She Killed Him to Keep Him Quiet"

Inmate Lisa Kastle said she went to the FBI as a matter of conscience. Kastle said she felt morally compelled to divulge the atrocities Diehl-Armstrong was admitting to her and other inmates on a daily basis at the Erie County Prison and at SCI Muncy. Clark and Wick interviewed Kastle on June 3, 2005.

She was a thirty-eight-year-old Erie resident who had grown up in Pittsburgh and had a degree in business. Kastle said Diehl-Armstrong, speaking in the context of the Wells case, told her why she killed Roden.

"He was going to go to the police," Kastle said, "to basically tell them about the plan they had."

Diehl-Armstrong told her she was part of the Wells plot "to get money," Kastle said. Diehl-Armstrong, she said, wished her father "was dead."

Kastle, though friendly with Diehl-Armstrong, existed on the fringes of her inner circle of inmates. At the center of that circle, Kastle said, resided an inmate by the name of Kelly Makela. Kastle said Makela would sit beside Diehl-Armstrong daily at the Erie County Prison and write furiously as Diehl-Armstrong chattered about the Wells case. Kastle said Makela, writing in blue ink on yellow legal paper, took notes of just about every conversation, starting right after Diehl-Armstrong's arrest on September 21, 2003.

———

Kelly Makela was serving time after pleading no contest to firing seventeen rounds in the air near her then husband in 1997, eight days after their wedding—she had married, she said, the devil himself. Makela jumped bond in 1998, fled to South Carolina and was picked up in July 2003, when a judge ordered her to await prosecution at the Erie County Prison.

Makela, like Diehl-Armstrong, had been caught up in domestic violence. Makela had worked as a security guard and aspired to be a police officer. Makela said Diehl-Armstrong was drawn to her because of their domestic-violence cases and because Diehl-Armstrong thought she could use Makela's understanding of police procedure to help her get out of the Roden mess. Makela and Diehl-Armstrong had plenty of time to talk, at the Erie County Prison and later at SCI Muncy.

Clark and Wick interviewed the thirty-seven-year-old Makela at SCI Muncy on June 8, 2005. She said Diehl-Armstrong told her Roden was part of the Wells plot, that he was supposed to drive Wells to the PNC Bank branch in the Summit Towne Centre, but that Roden, for whatever reason, wanted to back out in the summer of 2003. So, Makela said, recounting her conversations, Diehl-Armstrong shot him to death with a shotgun she bought out of the newspaper for $450.

"She killed him to keep him quiet and from going to the police," Makela said of her conversations.

"You have got to be kidding me," Clark said to himself. Finally.

Finally, Clark and Wick had hit on solid evidence of the link, first from Lisa Kastle and now, even better, from the note-taking Kelly Makela. As they had long suspected, Roden's death was related to the Wells case. Diehl-Armstrong, based on what these women were telling them, killed Roden to keep the conspiracy intact, to prevent him from turning her and Rothstein in to the police and dismantling their plan to get lots of cash from the bank robbery, cash Rothstein needed to keep from getting kicked out of the family homestead, cash she needed right then, for some reason or another—maybe because she simply craved money, maybe because she believed her father was cheating her out of her inheritance. This was like a confession, what Diehl-Armstrong had told Makela, her closest confidante behind bars.

Diehl-Armstrong told Makela more, much more, enough to fill what Makela recalled as at least twenty-four pages of notes, notes she took during what she estimated as her "thousands of hours" with Diehl-Armstrong in prison, notes composed of scribbles she scrambled to get on paper, to keep pace with Diehl-Armstrong's chattering. "Slow down," Makela would tell her. "I can't write that fast."

Rothstein called in the pizza order from the pay phone at the Shell station, Makela said Diehl-Armstrong told her. Diehl-Armstrong helped measure Wells' neck for the bomb. They were just "toying with" Wells, who was going to die anyway. Rothstein was a "cheap son of a bitch" for not buying an upright freezer, which would have made storing Roden's body easier. Rothstein built the collar bomb with scraps of metal and other junk from the shuttered Rola Bottling plant and with stuff from his house and with items he bought at RadioShack. Wells was to rob the bank and give the money to Stockton, who was to give the money to Rothstein, who would use rubbing alcohol to clean the bills of fingerprints. Diehl-Armstrong and Rothstein and Stockton knew Wells, but when Wells got to the site of the TV tower, "he didn't want to go through with it."

To force Wells to comply, "they locked the bomb on his neck and they ended up shooting at him," Makela said Diehl-Armstrong told her.

Everyone—Diehl-Armstrong, Rothstein, Roden, Stockton, Wells—pledged to work together on August 28, 2003, and afterward, Makela said. No one, Makela said Diehl-Armstrong told her, was to dime out anyone else: that's why Diehl-Armstrong killed Roden.

But why did Rothstein break the pact and call 911 about Roden's body, leading to Diehl-Armstrong's arrest? "Because," Makela said Diehl-Armstrong told her, "it would take the heat off the Wells case if they found the body in the freezer."

Someone else was in on the Wells plot, Makela said Diehl-Armstrong told her, someone else who, in the end, could not be trusted—Robert Pinetti, Wells' co-worker. Diehl-Armstrong said Pinetti knew about the robbery, but "they killed him." They "shot him up" with some kind of undetectable drug, Makela said Diehl-Armstrong told her, to make his death look like an overdose.

Diehl-Armstrong and Rothstein reveled in their ability to stay clear of the FBI for so long in the Wells case, Makela said. The two heard about the FBI trying to find the black man seen hurdling the cement divider near the Millcreek Mall on August 28, 2003, the black man who turned out to be a construction worker from New Jersey. Makela said Diehl-Armstrong told her she and Rothstein broke into laughter when they heard that news.

All this information, Makela said, was in her notes, which she no longer had. She said Diehl-Armstrong one day grabbed a bunch of the notes and never returned them. She said the rest of the notes, twenty-four pages, she had given to the Erie police, to help in the prosecution of the Roden case.

Makela said Gloria Bishop told Brad Foulk that she had the notes. Makela said she gave the notes to the Erie police on February 10, 2004, at Foulk's direction, and while Foulk was prosecuting Diehl-Armstrong for Roden's death. Foulk had the Erie police interview Makela as well.

Makela did not want to relinquish the notes at first. Marge was her friend; she did not want to betray her. Makela thought more about what Diehl-Armstrong told her, about killing Roden and helping to kill Wells, and changed her mind.*

"It was the right thing to do," Makela would testify later. "If she got out, she'd kill again."

At Foulk's direction, Erie detectives interviewed Makela several times while she was in prison in 2004, but only about the Roden case. Makela said she tried to give the detectives information on the Wells case, but they always responded the same way: we'll get to that later.

They never did.

———

Neither Clark nor Wick knew why Diehl-Armstrong specifically wanted the transfer to SCI Cambridge Springs, about forty miles south of Erie. She mentioned being closer to her father, though he was not expected to be a frequent visitor, with his only child apparently wanting him dead over her inheritance. As a minimum-security prison, SCI Cambridge Springs was newer and more relaxed than SCI Muncy. For whatever reason, Diehl-Armstrong fixated on getting to SCI Cambridge Springs, a request Clark and Wick welcomed. If they could satisfy one of her many obsessions, she would feel indebted to

———

*Makela also tried to get a break on her prison sentence in exchange for turning over the notes in the Roden case, but court records show she never got a deal, though Foulk, the district attorney, spoke on her behalf at sentencing and wrote to the state Parole Board. She pleaded no contest to aggravated assault and other charges, and was sentenced in Erie County Common Pleas Court on March 8, 2004, to twenty-one months to ten years in state prison.

them. If Diehl-Armstrong wanted to use them, that was fine. They'd oblige her. Maybe she would talk more.

And she did talk—with her lawyer present. Usually, an attorney at a prison rankled Clark and Wick; an attorney almost always wants the client to say as little as possible, if anything at all. But not Larry D'Ambrosio, Armstrong's personal attorney, a seventy-three-year-old sole practitioner whom she had known since she rented an apartment from him in the early 1970s.

When Clark and Wick met with Diehl-Armstrong and D'Ambrosio on July 5, 2005, at SCI Cambridge Springs, where she had been transferred, D'Ambrosio encouraged her to reveal what she knew: he said Margie—D'Ambrosio always called her Margie, as if she were a child—wanted to help the FBI solve the Wells case.

Diehl-Armstrong seemed to trust D'Ambrosio. While incarcerated, she had named him her personal power of attorney, which put him in charge of all her finances and real estate, including the house on East Seventh Street and a lakefront lot on Carter Beach Road, east of Erie, where her cottage stood until a fire destroyed it in January 2004. The job occupied D'Ambrosio. Roden's mother and two sons sued Diehl-Armstrong and Rothstein in a wrongful death claim in Erie County Common Pleas Court in February 2005. Rothstein's estate paid $5,000. Another of Diehl-Armstrong's lawyers reached a settlement in which she paid the Rodens $55,000. D'Ambrosio, as her personal attorney, helped on that case.

Diehl-Armstrong repeatedly relied on D'Ambrosio's advice in the meeting room at SCI Cambridge Springs. As

The Erie police's bomb squad examines the dead body of Brian Wells after the collar bomb that was locked to his neck exploded.

Marjorie Diehl-Armstrong, in the mug shot Erie police took of her after she was arrested in the shooting death of her live-in boyfriend, Jim Roden, whose body was found in a freezer on September 21, 2003. Nearly four years later, a federal grand jury would indict her in the Brian Wells pizza bomber case and allege she killed Roden to keep him quiet about the bank-robbery plot in which Wells participated.

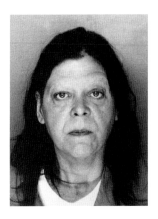

ERIE TIMES-NEWS, VIA ERIE BUREAU OF POLICE

Brian Wells, in one of the few photographs of him that was made public after his bombing death on August 28, 2003. This is from his driver's license.   RICH FORSGREN/ERIE TIMES-NEWS

Brian Wells heads out of the PNC Bank in the Summit Towne Centre after robbing it of $8,702. Wells is carrying the cash in a white canvas bag. In his left hand is a homemade cane-shaped shotgun. He is sucking on a lollipop he grabbed while in the bank. The collar bomb is protruding from under his white T-shirt. He had demanded $250,000 from the chief teller, but left with whatever money she could give him.

ERIE TIMES-NEWS, VIA FBI

The FBI built this model of the collar and the box that contained the bomb; the box is empty of components. The collar is attached backward here. Wells wore the bomb with the open section away from his chest, rather than against it.   ERIE TIMES-NEWS, VIA FBI

The second page of the note found in Wells' car. The drawing showed him where to find another note, which was taped to the bottom of a rock at the base of a McDonald's drive-through sign near the bank.

At 1:30 P.M. on August 28, 2003, an order phoned in to this pizza parlor sent Brian Wells on his way in the bank-robbery plot that would end in his bombing death at 3:18 P.M. Wells, forty-six years old, had worked at Mama Mia's for nearly a decade.   ISAAC BREKKEN/ERIE TIMES-NEWS

Brian Wells delivered his pizza order by driving his Geo Metro down a dirt road to this clearing, the location of the transmission tower for WSEE-TV; the CBS affiliate in Erie, Pennsylvania. He had the collar bomb locked to his neck in the clearing.   RICH FORSGREN/ERIE TIMES-NEWS

Robert Pinetti, Brian Wells' friend and fellow pizza deliveryman. His death of a drug overdose three days after Wells' slaying complicated the pizza bomber case.   ERIE TIMES-NEWS

Jim Roden, Marjorie Diehl-Armstrong's boyfriend, whose body was found in a freezer in Bill Rothstein's garage on September 21, 2003. When Diehl-Armstrong and Roden started living together in 1993, she said she was fated to love him. Ten years later, to cover up the pizza bomber plot, she shot Roden twice in the back with a 12-gauge shotgun she bought out of the newspaper, the FBI said.   ERIE TIMES-NEWS

Jessica Hoopsick, a prostitute whom Brian Wells frequented, became a key witness for the FBI in unraveling the pizza bomber case.

Bill Rothstein on September 23, 2003, in front of Marjorie Diehl-Armstrong's house, where a month earlier she shot and killed Jim Roden, her live-in boyfriend. Rothstein, who had helped remove Roden's body from the house in a tarp, helped Erie police go through the house after they discovered Roden's body in Rothstein's freezer on September 21, 2003.

Ken Barnes is led into the FBI office in Erie, Pennsylvania, on July 12, 2007, three days after his indictment in the pizza bomber case. From left to right is ATF Special Agent Jason Wick and, lead investigator in the case, FBI Special Agent Jerry Clark.   JACK HANRAHAN/ERIE TIMES-NEWS

Ken Barnes' house was in worse condition than those of Marjorie Diehl-Armstrong and Bill Rothstein. Barnes ran a crack house amid the trash. Prostitutes turned tricks for drugs in a squalid bedroom upstairs, where Brian Wells spent time with prostitute Jessica Hoopsick.   FBI PHOTO

soon as she walked in, and saw Clark and Wick, she turned to D'Ambrosio and asked if she needed an immunity letter from the feds; without such a letter, she said, she was worried about getting charged with conspiracy or as an accessory. Diehl-Armstrong's request got Clark thinking: who asks for immunity if he or she is innocent?

"I don't want to hang myself," Diehl-Armstrong said in the interview room.

D'Ambrosio advised Margie not to worry.

She told Clark and Wick about Roden and Rothstein, two men she said coveted her. Using the passive voice, she said Roden was killed over an argument between him and Rothstein about the Wells plot. She said Roden threatened to reveal the plot to someone she did not name, so Roden was killed, with Rothstein present. Diehl-Armstrong balked at discussing more about Roden's death. She said she did not want to risk getting pulled into the Wells investigation.

Clark and Wick guided the conversation to their earlier questions about the timers in the collar bomb. Diehl-Armstrong first said Rothstein probably got the timers at RadioShack or Circuit City, but she did not know the type. Clark pressed her. What about the timers? Where did Rothstein get them?

Diehl-Armstrong turned to D'Ambrosio.

"Should I tell them, Larry?"

"Yes," D'Ambrosio said.

She said Rothstein wanted kitchen timers. Sometime in June 2003, she gave them to him—two relatively new kitchen timers she owned. Diehl-Armstrong reached into the air in the interview room and made a motion with her hand as if she was turning the dial of an egg timer. Clark and Wick asked her why she never mentioned the timers to them at the previous interview, at SCI Muncy.

"I did not want to hurt myself," she said.

Clark asked Diehl-Armstrong about the nine pages of notes in the Wells case. She said she would have to see the notes to know who wrote them, but said Rothstein had been typing a note instead of using his computer. She said she went with Rothstein when he made copies of documents at Kinko's, Staples and the post office. She said she had no idea what Rothstein was copying.

The words flowed. She said she saw Rothstein cut open and empty shotgun shells. She said she was at Barnes & Noble and KFC the afternoon Wells was killed. She said she drove to Rothstein's house afterward, and no one was home.

Diehl-Armstrong stopped the interview.

"If I say any more, I'm dead," she said. "I've hung myself already."

A prison's ability to elicit conversation from even the most taciturn of inmates—the chattiness due to the inmate's boredom, braggadocio, bitterness or a combination thereof—also benefited Clark and Wick in their dealings with Floyd Stockton.

In the summer of 2005, Stockton was locked up in the Airway Heights Correctional Facility in Spokane, Washington, serving his two-year sentence for raping the mentally disabled nineteen-year-old woman in Bellingham. Stockton never lost touch with what was happening across the country, in Erie, Pennsylvania. Twice a day he used the prison telephone to place collect calls to his girlfriend, K.W., who was still in Erie County.

As a prerecorded message tells the caller and the listener, telephone calls from prison are taped. Stockton and his girlfriend knew this, but they chatted anyway. In an attempt to tweak the conversations and steer them toward the Wells case, Clark and Wick regularly met with K.W. "Tickling the wire," the technique is called—an investigator plants an idea in someone's mind, and that person soon is bringing up the topic while talking to the target of the investigation in a taped conversation. The technique worked with K.W.

"We have been investigating this thing," Clark told her during one meeting, "and it appears that the Roden case and the Wells case are connected."

Sure enough, Clark and Wick's visit came up when Stockton called K.W. later that day.

"Did anybody talk to you today?" she asked him.

"No."

"Well, I had a couple of visitors."

"Oh yeah?"

"Yeah. They think the two things are related."

"Oh yeah?" Stockton replied.

He did not ask K.W. to specify the "two things"; to Clark, that omission showed Stockton knew what she was talking about.

Rothstein, Stockton's old friend, had implicated Stockton, too, though indirectly and with an ambiguity that Clark believed complemented Rothstein's evasiveness. K.W. gave Clark and Wick a two-page typewritten letter dated October

26, 2003. Rothstein wrote it to Stockton while Stockton was in the Whatcom County Jail, where he was being held after his extradition in the rape case. Part of the letter read:

Jay Stocktonian:

I'm sorry all this shit hit the fan. Partly the Well's [sic] situation and partly my own stupidity. Now we're both going to be paying and Well's [sic] accomplice will probably get away with murder. I know, bad pun. I hope you are doing well otherwise.

———————

Clark and Wick sat across from Stockton in a prisoner meeting room at the Airway Heights Correctional Facility on July 19, 2005. They had traveled there with David Gluth, the state police investigator, who rotated with Wick in the interview room. Clark and Wick brought up the Rothstein letter and Stockton's taped phone conversation with K.W. This information indicates you knew what was going on, Clark told him, even that you were involved. Stockton dug in: I had nothing to do with the Wells case, he said.

Stockton started crying, just as he had done in the hallway at the Erie FBI office, after he took the polygraph test. This is like handling a baby, Clark thought. Stockton repeated that he had no part of the Wells case.

"You know, Floyd," Clark said, without raising his voice, "that just doesn't seem right."

Wick was more direct. He shook his head and looked at Stockton.

"Floyd," Wick said, "that's bullshit."

This was yet another interview in which Wick and Clark clicked. They were thinking in tandem. Clark was getting ready to confront Stockton just as Wick interjected. Clark and Wick had become so comfortable with each other, they instinctively knew which role to play in an interview and when: Wick the aggressor and Clark the confessor; Clark the aggressor and Wick the confessor. They knew how to play the interview subjects off each other.

Their technique worked again here.

Stockton decided to talk some more.

He said he did not participate in the Wells plot, and didn't even know about it beforehand, but he spoke theoretically: what he would have done *if* this happened or *if* that happened. Stockton sounded like Rothstein in that interview room with Clark in late September 2003.

"Why was Roden killed?" Clark asked Stockton.

"Because of the collar bomb plot," he said.

Stockton, while distancing himself from the Wells case, readily said Diehl-Armstrong and Rothstein hatched the plot and carried it out because they needed money. Stockton was done talking—for now. Clark tried to establish trust so Stockton would talk more later. Stockton asked Clark to tell everyone that he had "done the right thing" and told the truth.

Clark hugged Stockton and left the room.

———

Later that day, Stockton telephoned his girlfriend.

"They were out here," he said.

She asked Stockton if the Wells plot and Roden's murder were related.

"Yes," he said.

Stockton said Rothstein had told him that Rothstein was involved in the "tower site" incident and "all that shit" around Rothstein's house.

The next day, July 20, 2005, Clark, Wick and Gluth interviewed Stockton again. He repeated what he had said in the phone conversation with K.W. He also said Diehl-Armstrong would leave messages on Rothstein's answering machine, saying Roden was a problem "that needed taken care of."

Stockton did not go further, and he did not implicate himself. But Clark, Wick and Gluth left the second interview feeling they had connected with Stockton, who was unpredictable in what he would say and when. The investigators believed he would be willing to talk more later.

Stockton seemed impressed.

In a parting gesture, he called Wick "a pit bull with a heart." He called Clark "a devil in sheep's clothing."

On August 19, 2005, Wick interviewed an inmate at Cambridge Springs, L.B., who said Diehl-Armstrong told her Roden was killed for "running his mouth," that Wells was "stupid" and "slow," and that Diehl-Armstrong held an abiding dislike for an unnamed Erie bank. The inmate said Diehl-Armstrong told her she was furious at the bank for freezing an account or taking money that belonged to her.

On August 30, 2005, Kelly Makela forwarded a letter to the FBI. Diehl-Armstrong, Makela wrote, said she and Rothstein used walkie-talkies to communicate during the bank-robbery plot.

On October 13, 2005, Clark interviewed a PNC Bank official who in 2000 managed the bank branch closest to Diehl-Armstrong's house on East Seventh Street. The interview revealed that on July 17, 2000, Harold Diehl, Diehl-Armstrong's father, came to the bank and got access to the safe-deposit box that was in the name of his wife, Agnes Diehl—who, unknown to the bank manager, had died the previous day, July 16, 2000. Within days after Harold Diehl's visit, the bank manager said, Diehl-Armstrong arrived at the bank with Larry D'Ambrosio, her personal attorney, and started screaming. The bank, Diehl-Armstrong said, improperly allowed her father to get into her mother's safe-deposit box. Diehl-Armstrong threatened to sue.

By the fall of 2005, Clark had gotten all the evidence the state police had gathered in its investigation of Roden's death. He had gone searching for it after talking to Makela and the other inmates, to see if what the state police had collected corroborated the inmates' stories.

Among the items the boxes contained: the five-round revolver that troopers found in Rothstein's van, with one bullet fired and the other chambers full; the set of two small blue-and-black Motorola walkie-talkies troopers found in the van; a CD of the video police shot of the inside of Rothstein's house; and a letter Diehl-Armstrong wrote to an investigator with the state Department of Revenue, complaining about her treatment by PNC Bank.

While watching the video of Rothstein's house, Clark spotted, on a desk, a diagram with an arrow written on it. Clark paused the video. He sat back in his chair. He struggled to recall where he had seen that kind of arrow before. Then he remembered: an arrow of the same design had been drawn on the front of the collar bomb, in red marker.

Also on the video, Clark saw long bars of angle iron hanging out of shelves near the ceiling of Rothstein's junk-jumbled garage. Clark and Wick stopped the video and studied the image, and agreed the angle iron in the garage looked like the same kind of angle iron that had been used to fashion the collar bomb's box. By then, however, in the fall of 2005—two years after the bombing, in August 2003, and a year and a half after the Rothstein homestead had sold, in May 2004—the angle iron in the garage was gone.

Clark turned to the three-page handwritten letter Diehl-Armstrong wrote to the Department of Revenue on September 6, 2000. Diehl-Armstrong's rage at PNC Bank was stoked by the fact that she had a legitimate point: because her mother had died, her father should not have been allowed access to the safe-deposit box. Diehl-Armstrong demanded in her letter that the Department of Revenue prosecute her father and the bank manager. She wrote, in closing: "Please see attached laws and penalties which I thank you for enforcing."

17

Belated Discovery

Clark could have walked the several blocks from the FBI office to the Erie County Courthouse on November 10, 2005. He drove instead. He had a feeling he might have too much to carry on foot.

The district attorney, Brad Foulk, had agreed to let Clark look through all the materials the district attorney's office had compiled in the Roden case. The district attorney's office had kept that information close while Diehl-Armstrong's prosecution was open, but the secrecy was no longer necessary. The Roden case had ended with Diehl-Armstrong's plea of guilty but mentally ill and her sentence of seven to twenty years.

Clark walked into the conference room at the district attorney's office. On the table in front of him sat five banker's boxes full of papers on the Roden case. Clark was mainly looking for Kelly Makela's notes. He opened one of the boxes. Clark noticed the label on one file: "Snitch Letters." Foulk let Clark sign out the boxes and carry them to his car. Clark drove to the FBI office.

———

Inside the "Snitch Letters" file were Makela's notes— twenty-four yellow legal pages covered in handwriting penned in blue ink. The notes were not dated, though based on what Makela said, she started taking them in late September 2003 and turned them over to the Erie police, at Foulk's direction, on February 10, 2004. That is when the police interviewed her, too.

The notes detailed Roden's death. On one page appeared a hand-drawn diagram of Roden's bedroom to illustrate where Diehl-Armstrong told Makela she shot him. Diehl-Armstrong, according to the notes, said she shot Roden from five to seven feet away—the same distance from which she said she fired upon Bob Thomas—and that she held the shotgun "waist high & that the recoil hurt her arm and shoulder & she did it." Makela also wrote, "She told me James was shot in the neck once and once in the chest."*

Robert Pinetti was in the notes, described as "the other pizza guy." The twenty-four pages, replete with fractured

———

*Diehl-Armstrong has never wavered from her contention that she shot Roden in the chest and neck; she told Ed Palattella in late 2011 that she shot Roden there. If she admitted to shooting a sleeping Roden in the back, the actual location of the wounds, she would have negated a self-defense claim.

syntax and misspellings and run-on sentences that signaled
a hasty transcription, read like a flurry of admissions.

Marge stated It's not like we didn't measure his neck
for the collar! And kept laughing. Lisa Kastle also
heard her make this statement to me, we were all
shocked at her statement and her laughing. . . . I
thought to myself nobody would make a statement
like that unless they were there, I also thought maybe
she made a deal with Rothstein He helps her/she helps
him/like the Hitchcock movie.

She also said Rothsteine needed money and Jay
owed him a favor. Jay's real name is Floyd Stockard &
he was for rape in Seattle Wash. by the FBI That Bill
harbored him for 2 years. She believes Bill Rothsteine
detonated the bomb on Wells and also built it. She
believes Floyd was the bushy hair or guy w/hair sticking out that ran from the woods. . . .

Marge told me that Bill, James, Floyd, the other
pizza guy and Wells planned the robbery. That Wells
was a little off he wasn't playing with a full deck. That
Bill made the bomb measured it for Wells at bill's
house he made it in the garage and in the house he
had wires and parts scattered here & there. Bill and
James didn't get along but the money was the main
factor to all of them & this wouldn't be the last bank.

James was supposed to drive Wells to the bank and
be the getaway driver. Bill and Floyd or the other pizza
guy would wait if anything went wrong then Bill
would detonated it then give the can gun to Floyd who

would get rid of it or the pizza guy, he'd just look like he was making another pizza delivery and would pass through any road blocks or questions. Bill waited and wasn't that far away and was at the gas station & used the pay phone earlier just a minute before the call for the pizza then parked in some parking lot.

James got into it with Marge and fought with him that fateful night and was going to leave, he had another girl and also was going to tell about the robbery & that's when she flipped and killed him. . . . Bill convinced Wells to do it himself or he'd blow him to bits right there. They held him at gunpoint at Bill's house and placed the collar on him and locked it. Then the robbery occurred and went wrong they killed Wells and the other pizza guy they shot him up with something at his apt.

Floyd was taken into custody for being wanted. Floyd and Bill are lovers thats why Floyd won't talk. Marge won't for she'll get the death penalty for the other killings for her knowledge and envolvement and Bill won't talk for he'll get the death penalty also. He gave up Marge because he knew she wouldn't talk and it would take the heat off Wells if she gave up the body and he'd walk away with only a few charges instead of murder because he's covered his tracks and go rid of the only people who knew and the evidence.

Marge is the only one who's left who could talk but won't and he said who would believe her anyway cuz of her past & this killing & murder and she told me he's very stupid but very, very intelligent and dangerous.

Clark sat in silence with the notes spread on his desk. He had considered Foulk, the keeper of these notes, a close friend. Foulk had quickly offered the assistance of the Erie County District Attorney's Office in the early stages of the Wells case. Clark could not get over that he had not seen these notes earlier.

Jason Wick believed the lack of disclosure exemplified the tension that could develop between the local cops and the feds. Clark, with his congenial manner and his network of friends in and outside law enforcement, worked to blunt that tension; he thought he had succeeded in the Wells case—until now. Clark hoped neither rivalry nor petulance drove the Erie police and then the district attorney's office to keep this treasure trove of evidence from the FBI.

Clark and Foulk discussed the matter. Foulk said he had to make the Roden case a priority. He had to get a guilty plea out of Diehl-Armstrong. He told Clark he feared that intertwining the Roden case and the Wells case would backfire. It would complicate the Roden case and prompt the unpredictable Diehl-Armstrong to back out of a plea and go to trial, particularly in light of Rothstein's death.

Foulk died of lung cancer at sixty-one years old in 2009, before the existence of the twenty-four pages of notes became public, in February 2004. Years later, Frank Kwitowski, the Erie police detective sergeant who had led the investigation of the Roden case, said he got the notes from Makela and gave them all to Foulk, at the district attorney's request. Kwitowski said Foulk ordered the Erie police to investigate only the Roden case, and not the Wells case, because of jurisdictional issues.

"Her notes were forwarded to the DA's office," Kwitowski, now captain of detectives for the Erie police, told the *Erie Times-News* in 2010. "Whether the DA's office provided that to the feds, or when, I can't answer that.

"As far as we were concerned, we were directed from the get-go to investigate the homicide, not question on the Wells case," Kwitowski said. "But certainly any information was to be turned over to the DA's office, to disseminate to the feds."

Bob Rudge, Clark's supervisor in the early stages of the Wells case, was also a close friend of Foulk. Rudge said he never knew about Makela's notes until Clark got them in November 2005. Rudge, looking back, said he believed an "overburdened" Erie police department, rather than Foulk, led to the late disclosure of the notes to the FBI.

"I was extremely close to Brad," Rudge said. "I would not for a minute believe that he would keep information from being presented that would solve the case."

Makela years later recalled asking Foulk about the fate of the notes about the same time she handed them over to the Erie police, in February 2004. What happened to the notes interested her greatly: the more use law enforcement got out of the notes, the better chance Makela had of getting a sentencing break, though a judge never granted her one.

Makela said she asked Foulk if he was going to turn over the notes to the FBI.

She said Foulk brushed her off.

"The FBI is a different department," he said.

––––––

Clark was left to speculate as to why he never got the notes. Maybe Foulk and the police watched the FBI going after the J.J. angle in the Wells case and thought Makela's notes would be an unwelcome diversion. Or perhaps the police really were in Foulk's thrall. Or maybe Foulk was worried about not getting a guilty plea, of losing the Roden case, of being the second district attorney to lose to Diehl-Armstrong.

––––––

The belated discovery of Makela's notes aside, the Wells investigation had turned out to be productive in 2005. The interviews with the inmates and the talks with Diehl-Armstrong had moved the investigation forward significantly.

Clark still would have liked to have had Makela's notes while Rothstein had been alive. As Assistant U.S. Attorney Marshall Piccinini told Clark, however, Diehl-Armstrong would have been at Mayview State Hospital and out of reach even if Makela's notes had been available to them in February 2004. By the time Clark got the notes, in late 2005, Piccinini said, Diehl-Armstrong had helped their case and deepened her problems by talking to all those inmates, often repeating what was in Makela's notes.

Without that kind of corroboration, Piccinini said, Makela would be open to accusations that she made up the notes' contents, and the notes' value as evidence would diminish. As you would expect from a transcription of Diehl-Armstrong's chatter, the twenty-four pages of notes were scattered with blather; at one point, according to the notes, Diehl-Armstrong said Rothstein used the cane gun to detonate the bomb, which did not happen. No matter when Clark and Wick would have received the notes, Piccinini said, they would have needed to gather evidence to separate the gibberish from the truth.

Time had ended up working in their favor with the notes, Piccinini said, and time was still with them: Diehl-Armstrong and Stockton were in prison. They were not going anywhere.

With the contents of the notes in hand, Clark and Wick set out to close the gaps in the investigation. They wanted to find out how Wells knew Rothstein and Diehl-Armstrong. In late 2005, Clark and Wick put the pressure on Diehl-Armstrong's fishing buddy, Ken Barnes.

18

The Hobo

Parade Street, the oldest thoroughfare in Erie, originates on a bluff that overlooks Presque Isle Bay. At the foot of the street stands a historical marker that commemorates the spot of the Erie Stone and Fort Presque Isle. When the French occupied the fort, the troops performed their military exercises by parading on what was then the wide dirt lot that fronted the fort. The road to the fort was named Parade Street.

Shoddy bars dot some sections of Parade Street today. So do run-down houses and vacant storefronts. Lower Parade Street, near the bay front, has improved through the vigilance of its Neighborhood Watch group and with the help of the Erie Redevelopment Authority, but many of the other blocks on Parade Street remain synonymous in Erie with blight and crime and poverty.

The railroad underpass at East Fifteenth and Parade streets long has been a pickup spot for prostitutes.

During the summer of 2005, when Jerry Clark and Jason Wick first interviewed Ken Barnes, they often drove along Parade Street and the other roads that cut through Erie's lower east side. He frequented Parade Street, to chat with the prostitutes, to deal in crack, to visit neighborhood food pantries. Barnes, then fifty-one years old, received $152 a month in food stamps and $630 a month in Social Security disability benefits, which he got for injuries he suffered in an automobile accident in 1998. Before that, Barnes, who had a GED, worked for fourteen years as a television repairman; he took apart and reassembled sets quickly. He also fixed computers, VCRs, stereos, microphones, remote controllers, vacuum cleaners—whatever the customers brought in.

In the summer of 2005, Barnes, unmarried and childless, was operating a crack house at his rented house at 617 Perry Street, on the lower east side. Barnes had developed a nice business by letting whores use his house to turn tricks; the johns or the whores paid Barnes in cash or crack.

Marjorie Diehl-Armstrong said she abhorred illegal drugs, yet she and Ken Barnes had been friends since the mid-1990s, after she met him through Roden's introduction via fishing. Barnes' friendship with Diehl-Armstrong extended beyond the South Pier. Barnes was not known, like Diehl-Armstrong, to have an interest in astrology and the occult, though he once took a trip with her to Lily Dale, the spiritualist enclave in nearby Chautauqua

County, New York. Barnes said Diehl-Armstrong wanted him to visit a psychic to see whether Barnes was "psychically in tune with her realm of reality," referring to Diehl-Armstrong's state of mind. They could not find a psychic. They walked around in the woods, looked at the animals and went home.

In the summer of 2005, with Diehl-Armstrong serving time for Roden's death, Clark and Wick wanted to ask Barnes about his excitable and erstwhile fishing buddy. They had gotten his name from the private criminal complaint Diehl-Armstrong filed over the burglary of her house on May 30, 2003. They knew little else about Barnes, other than he was a drug dealer. Clark first visited Barnes' place at 617 Perry Street, on August 11, 2005. He went with David Gluth, the state police investigator.

Computer parts, computer monitors, printers and other electronic components cluttered Barnes' front porch. Barnes said little to Clark and Gluth. He was fidgety; Clark thought the drugs had addled his nerves. Clark and Gluth asked Barnes if he knew Brian Wells. Barnes said he did not know Wells, but had heard of his death. The day after the bombing, Barnes said, he was having sex with a whore and she brought up Wells' name. She said she knew him as a client.

Barnes identified the prostitute—Jessica Hoopsick, whose name and number Clark had found in Wells' notebook.

With that bit of information, Barnes had turned into the critical link in the Wells case: Diehl-Armstrong knew Rothstein and Barnes, and Barnes knew Wells through

Hoopsick. Barnes connected Wells to Diehl-Armstrong and Rothstein.

––––––––

Clark and Wick kept following Barnes, kept stopping him on the street, to try to persuade him to talk more about Diehl-Armstrong. Wick referred to Barnes, with his scraggly beard and resemblance to a homeless person, as the hobo. Barnes, squat at five feet eight inches tall and 185 pounds, never moved too quickly. The drug use had deteriorated his health. He suffered from high blood pressure, coronary artery disease and diabetes.

"Let's go find Ken today," Wick frequently said to Clark in the summer of 2005. "I know he's out walking."

They would drive Parade Street. There, more often than not, they'd find Barnes, wearing secondhand wingtip shoes with no socks, shuffling down the sidewalk. He would keep walking.

"What do you guys want?" he would say.

––––––––

Barnes gradually let on that he knew plenty, though he frustrated Clark and Wick and Gluth by revealing tidbits of information here and there, indicating he had more, but saying the talk would have to wait.

In his first substantial interview, with Wick and Gluth, Barnes on August 18, 2005, said Diehl-Armstrong in the summer of 2003 started soliciting him to kill her father, an offer he said he declined; he said he had reported the request to Erie police in 2003. Barnes said she hinted in the summer of 2003 that she wanted Roden killed as well, and that she wanted Barnes to drive the getaway car when she robbed a bank.

Wick and Gluth, this time joined by Clark, interviewed Barnes again on September 13, 2005. Barnes said Diehl-Armstrong in May 2003 inquired about whether Barnes knew how to make a bomb with a timer. Barnes denied making any bombs or having a role in the Wells case.

————

Clark and Wick and Gluth were not the first investigators to talk to Barnes. As with Makela, the Erie police had interviewed him years earlier.

The first time the Erie police interviewed Barnes was on June 3, 2003. Detectives asked him about Diehl-Armstrong's claim that he robbed her on May 30, 2003; the police, at that time, had no way of knowing about the Wells plot. Barnes denied robbing Diehl-Armstrong.

————

Nearly four months later, on September 23, 2003, the Erie police interviewed Barnes again. The detectives were investigating Roden's death. They thought Barnes might know something because Diehl-Armstrong had accused him of robbing her.

Detective Sergeant Frank Kwitowski and his partner on the Roden case, Detective John Holmes, questioned Barnes about the Roden case for thirty-six minutes. The night before, on September 22, Kwitowski and Holmes had been among the detectives who had taken the guided tours with Rothstein of his and Diehl-Armstrong's houses. Also on September 22, Kwitowski and Holmes had interviewed Stockton and his girlfriend, K.W., and asked them only about the Roden case. The FBI and state police had spoken to them previously.

In his interview, Barnes explained that he did not know how or why Roden died. He detailed Diehl-Armstrong's anger at her father.

"She used to tell him she'd kill him right in front of him, right to his face," Barnes said. "She'd say, 'You son of a bitch, I'll have you knocked off.'"

Diehl-Armstrong, Barnes said, talked constantly about her father squandering her inheritance of as much as $12 million and how she wanted him committed to a nursing home or killed. Barnes said she asked him to murder her father and tried to offer Barnes a layout of her father's house.

"She told me he was eighty-four years old and she said if he got murdered, it would have to look like it was an accident. He can't have any marks on his body or nothing like that.

"Of course, I was just joking with her. I said, 'Well, Marge, that will cost you.'

"And she goes, 'How much?'" Barnes said.

"And I said quarter of a million. And, of course, I didn't tell her at that time, half up front."

Barnes said Diehl-Armstrong called him several days later to renew her request that he kill her father. He said he told Diehl-Armstrong he would need $100,000 up front.

"Of course," Barnes told the detectives, "I was just playing with her at the time, because I wouldn't kill nobody."

Barnes said he never got the money. He said he would not have killed Harold Diehl if he had received it.

"I've never killed a person in my life and never would," he said. "Hell, I hate to kill bugs. I don't like to kill flies. Hell, I cry when people shoot deers."

The detectives asked Barnes why Diehl-Armstrong would want Roden dead.

"He had something over her," Barnes said. "I never really knew what it was. But when he threatened her back that he would go to the cops, then she would shut up for a while."

Barnes never mentioned Wells or Rothstein. The detectives asked him about neither.

———————

By the time Clark and Wick and Gluth started interviewing Barnes, in the summer and fall of 2005, Clark had learned of the videotaped statement the Erie police had taken from Barnes two years earlier. As he had done upon learning about Makela's notes, Clark grumbled about not getting the information about Barnes sooner, and about the Erie detectives not raising the Wells case with Barnes. As he had done before, Clark then shifted to the other evidence he and Wick had developed against Diehl-Armstrong and the hobo.

Some of that evidence came from Tom Sedwick, who forced the FBI to listen to him in the summer of 2005.

Sedwick, the retired college professor, had not forgotten about the wrong-way car that passed him on I-79 on August 28, 2003. His irritation at the FBI persisted: why had no one followed up with him after he had phoned the authorities and said Marjorie Diehl-Armstrong had been behind the wheel of that car?

Sedwick found an opening for getting his story out in the summer of 2005. He read a piece in the *Erie Times-News* that Geraldo Rivera, the Fox News correspondent, was coming to Erie in July 2005 for a segment on the Wells case. Sedwick called Rivera's producers, who booked him for an interview for Rivera's special one-hour report, "The Pizza Bomber Mystery," scheduled to air on August 27, 2005, the day before the second anniversary of Wells' death. Sedwick, with his white hair and precise manner, was shaping up to be the star.

Clark got word that Sedwick was talking to Rivera. Clark interviewed Sedwick on August 8, 2005. Clark reviewed the report that an FBI agent had made of Sedwick's first call about the wrong-way car, on September 5, 2003. Clark could find no record that Sedwick had called the FBI or any other police agency later in September 2003, to identify Diehl-Armstrong as the driver.

None of that mattered now. Clark was talking to Sedwick, who reiterated his account: Marjorie Diehl-Armstrong passed him on I-79, driving a large gold-colored car the wrong way at regular highway speed on August 28, 2003. When he saw Diehl-Armstrong on the highway, Sedwick said, the time was about 1:45 P.M. Sedwick, driving a black Jeep Laredo, said he came to a dead stop on the highway while he watched Diehl-Armstrong drive by. He thought he might have pointed his finger at the car, because that was a gesture he was prone to using. He saw only Diehl-Armstrong in the car.

On August 10, 2005, the *Erie Times-News* published a story on Sedwick's sighting of Diehl-Armstrong on the highway. Ed Palattella had heard about Sedwick's interview with Rivera. He contacted Sedwick for an interview of his own. Sedwick reminded a sheepish Palattella that he had called him in late September 2003 and identified Diehl-Armstrong as the driver.

Sedwick's 1:45 P.M. sighting indicated Diehl-Armstrong drove I-79 before the bombing, perhaps to drop off the notes Wells was supposed to pick up later. Another motorist provided information that suggested she drove the highway after the bombing as well.

The *Times-News* account about Sedwick prompted a call to the paper from that second motorist, a retired mail carrier by the name of Tom Bolan. He also contacted the FBI. Bolan said he witnessed a car take an unusual route on I-79 on August 28, 2003. Bolan, seventy-seven years old in 2005, said he was in his car between 3:00 and 3:30 P.M., stopped at a red light on the bridge over I-79, near Exit 180, for the Millcreek Mall. Bolan, who was facing west, said he looked south and saw a southbound car turn onto the grassy median just below the overpass, and do a U-turn and head north. The median is directly across from the off ramp for Exit 180—where Wells was supposed to make his first stop off the highway and pick up a note in the woods.

Bolan was too far away to identify the driver of the car. The U-turn happened so fast, he barely saw the vehicle's color. He described it as large, about twenty years old and yellow or red.

Bolan's comments fit with what an inmate, Melissa Parker Kump, had told Clark and Wick. Kump, thirty-three years old, said she would walk the yard with Diehl-Armstrong while at SCI Cambridge Springs. She said Diehl-Armstrong told her she made "an illegal U-turn" on August 28, 2003. Kump said Diehl-Armstrong told her Roden was killed "because he was going to run his mouth and he was kind of greedy," and that Wells was "weak, a lackey, and she was afraid he would talk."

Another motorist, Charles Brandt, saw no wayward cars on I-79 on August 28, 2003. But he said he definitely saw Diehl-Armstrong. In an interview on August 17, 2005, after he called the FBI, Brandt told Clark he watched her straddle a guardrail along the on-ramp to I-90 westbound, to Cleveland, from southbound I-79. The spot is several yards south of the McKean Township sign on I-79—what was supposed to have been another stopping point for Wells.

Brandt, sixty-two years old, had finished his shift at 3:25 P.M. at a medical-supply plant outside Erie. He got on I-79 southbound to head home. He estimated he drove by the person on the guardrail at 40 mph about 3:45 P.M. on August 28, 2003. He observed a large person wearing a baseball cap, a flannel shirt and baggy jeans. Brandt said he and the person made eye contact.

Brandt soon realized the "man" was Diehl-Armstrong. He was watching the local television news in late September 2003, after Diehl-Armstrong's arrest in the Roden case, and he saw her. He concluded that the person he had come across on the highway was really this woman, whose long hair must have been tucked underneath the baseball cap.

Brandt said he was so sure of himself in late September 2003 that, after seeing Diehl-Armstrong on television, he called the FBI the next day. When Clark interviewed Brandt on August 17, 2005, he had never heard of him before.

———

Geraldo Rivera found the pizza bomber case interesting enough to make it the subject of a one-hour broadcast.* *America's Most Wanted*, also on Fox, highlighted the case as well; since the day Wells was killed, the show repeatedly asked viewers to call in tips. The night of September 17, 2005, to mark the second anniversary of the murder, *America's Most Wanted* recounted the "Erie collar bomber" case.

At a house in Summit Township, Michael Vogt, a delivery-truck driver for the United Parcel Service (UPS) for nineteen years, was watching the *America's Most*

———

*Rivera's special report, which mentioned Diehl-Armstrong's violent past and which strongly suggested she killed Wells, upset Diehl-Armstrong. She had Larry D'Ambrosio, her personal lawyer, sue Fox News for defamation in Erie County Common Pleas Court in February 2007. D'Ambrosio filed the initial writ but no other documents, and the suit went nowhere. He said Diehl-Armstrong had a more pressing legal concern—the Wells investigation.

Wanted episode with his family. Growing up, Vogt, now thirty-eight years old, had lived five doors down from the Rothstein homestead. Vogt had seen Bill Rothstein over the years. Vogt heard the *America's Most Wanted* announcer mention the 1:30 P.M. call made from the pay phone on August 28, 2003. Vogt was familiar with what the announcer was talking about.

Vogt was making deliveries for UPS on August 28, 2003. He drove by the pay phone at the Shell station at Peach Street and Robison Road at around 1:30 P.M. Vogt saw a man in bib overalls at the phone kiosk, holding the receiver to his ear; he was a large guy with a long white beard, thick glasses and pens sticking out of the front pocket of his overalls. Behind the phone, near the large man, was a car with two men inside. Vogt did not recognize them. Vogt thought the guy in the overalls must be frying in the seventy-five-degree heat.

"Nice bibs," Vogt said to himself.

Vogt continued to drive west on Robison Road to make another delivery. About fifteen minutes later, he retraced his route east on Robison Road and drove past the Shell station. The man in the overalls was still on the phone, with the receiver to his ear. Vogt saw a woman with dark hair standing near the man.

Later that day, Vogt heard the police sirens, saw the police helicopters overhead and heard about the bank robbery. He never connected the scene at the pay phone to the robbery until several weeks later, when the local media reported that Wells' final order was placed from that pay phone. Vogt thought the FBI already had the information about the phone, so he stayed quiet.

He stayed quiet again several more weeks later, when the news broke about Roden's body being found in Rothstein's freezer. Vogt saw the photos of Rothstein and Diehl-Armstrong in the *Erie Times-News* and on the local TV broadcasts. He recognized them as the same people he saw at the pay phone. Vogt had no doubt the guy in the bib overalls was Rothstein—he had seen him many times, as a kid, and even more recently, as he drove by Rothstein's house to visit his elderly parents, who still lived on upper Peach Street, near the Rothstein homestead.

Fear influenced Vogt to say nothing, at first. His house in Summit Township was a mile from Rothstein's back door; his parents' house was even closer. He worried what Rothstein and Diehl-Armstrong would do to his family or his parents if they discovered Vogt had reported them to the FBI. Besides, Vogt thought in the fall of 2003, the FBI by now surely had gathered all the information they needed on the pay phone.

In late August 2005, Vogt saw an *Erie Times-News* report about the Wells case. He read the article aloud to his son. He told him what he had seen that day while he was behind the wheel of his UPS truck. On September 17, 2005, as he watched *America's Most Wanted*, Vogt told the story to his family again, how he saw Bill Rothstein at the pay phone at around 1:30 P.M.

Vogt's son looked up at him.

"Dad," he said, "you got to call it in."

Vogt did not call *America's Most Wanted*, as host John Walsh asked. Vogt did not want the notoriety. He called the FBI, and Clark interviewed him on September 20, 2005. They met at the parking lot of the Shell station.

Vogt's information confirmed beyond all doubt to Clark that Rothstein had made the phone call and that Diehl-Armstrong had been with him at the time. Vogt was a perfect witness. He knew what Rothstein looked like from living near him. Vogt's job required scrupulous records, both electronically and on paper; those records showed, indisputably, that when Vogt's delivery truck passed the pay phone the first time on August 28, 2003, it was 1:30 P.M.

Both times he drove by, at 1:30 P.M. and 1:45 P.M., Vogt would later testify, he saw Rothstein holding the telephone receiver to his ear. While the 1:30 P.M. call corresponded with the pizza order, Clark reasoned Rothstein was on the phone at 1:45 P.M. to be certain that Wells drove by to deliver the order to the tower site. The second time he drove by the gas station, Vogt testified, the woman with the long hair—the woman he said was Marjorie Diehl-Armstrong—was initially looking at Rothstein.

"As I approached slowly," Vogt would later testify, "she turned and looked at me. We made eye contact."

Of all the witnesses Clark and Wick had interviewed up to this point, Vogt did the most for Marshall Piccinini, the prosecutor. With Vogt, the facts were indisputable: Rothstein and Diehl-Armstrong had been at that pay phone. Vogt, for Piccinini, moved the case forward the most.

Too bad Bill Rothstein was dead. The U.S. Attorney's Office could have easily proved that he made that phone call, and that he most likely had a hand in making the bomb. In 2005, in between trying to reinterview Barnes and reviewing their sessions with people like Vogt, Clark and Wick heard more about Rothstein:

How he had been seen with a cane-shaped gun years earlier; how he used to refer to himself and a friend as "The Troubleshooters," the same moniker that appeared in the bank-robbery notes; how, in June or July 2003, he had visited an Erie locksmith shop, where he shopped regularly, and asked to buy a lock in which the numbers rolled, like the kind of lock later found on the collar bomb, and how he had left the store because no such lock was in stock; how, in the summer of 2003, before Wells was killed, Rothstein asked a close friend for kitchen timers and metal supplies, including a metal screen, as well as plastic tubing and locks; how that friend, who lived above an abandoned hardware store in Erie, had no timers and none of the other items, and told Rothstein to visit a metal-supply store; how Rothstein in the summer of 2003, before Wells was killed, told that friend, who also cut the grass at Rothstein's house, not to come around anymore, because Rothstein said "he was busy on a big project," and that Jay Stockton would cut the grass instead; how that friend, an Erie resident named Ronald Levey, whom Stockton described as "slow" and who was fifty-one years old in 2005, said he had overheard

Stockton and Rothstein talk about building a bomb because they needed money; how, on August 28, 2003, after
Wells was killed, Levey stopped by Rothstein's house, and
saw Rothstein and Stockton acting nervous and "freaking
out," in Levey's words; how Rothstein, Levey said, told
him the "shit hit the fan" and "We have to lay low and
make ourselves scarce"; how Rothstein told Levey that
Wells would have needed a combination lock to have removed the bomb from his neck; how Levey said Rothstein
told him that Rothstein knew Wells, and that Wells probably thought the bomb was a fake; and, finally, how Levey
said Rothstein told him Wells "was probably killed so he
would not be a witness."

———————

The name of D.M., perhaps Rothstein's closest friend
besides Stockton, had come up throughout the investigation. The Summit Township resident was sixty-two years
old in the summer of 2005, five years after he retired as
a machinist at GE. D.M. was one of the three people to
whom Rothstein had sent thousands of dollars in cash in
September 2003; he belonged to Rothstein's Tall Club.
Clark wondered if Rothstein had tried to buy D.M.'s silence by sending him the money.

Diehl-Armstrong, in her first interview with Clark,
Wick and Gluth, in March 2005, had mentioned D.M.;
Stockton mentioned him as well. Clark and Wick interviewed D.M. on August 3, 2005. He confirmed he had
given Rothstein one of the few keys to D.M.'s large detached garage. D.M. said Rothstein often worked alone

in the garage. D.M. denied knowing anything about the Wells case. He said Rothstein told him that he was with Diehl-Armstrong in North East on August 28, 2003.

The FBI executed a search warrant on D.M.'s house and detached garage on August 3, 2005. The agents took, among other things, 18 screwdrivers, 638 drill bits, 8 gripping tools, 2 rivet guns, 11 cans of spray paint and 3 samples of green carpet, two from the house and one from the garage. The FBI lab in Quantico examined the tools and other evidence; it could not make definitive links to the collar bomb.

The lab compared the carpet samples to the green carpet fibers that had been stuck to the piece of duct tape that had been found on the garbage bag underneath the device. The lab found similarities between the carpet fibers and the carpet samples, but needed larger carpet samples to perform a more thorough exam and reach a more solid conclusion. When the FBI went back to D.M.'s place to cut more samples, all the green carpeting was gone.

19

"At That Point He Realized This Thing Was Real"

This was one of those days when Clark and Wick knew Ken Barnes would be out walking, probably to a food pantry. On this day in early December 2005, they found him on the street and asked if he wanted a ride. Wick was driving; Barnes got in the front seat. Clark got in the backseat, and settled behind Barnes. The three talked. Barnes had been helpful, Clark and Wick told him, but they were hoping he could provide more information. Barnes persisted in his equivocation.

Barnes pulled out a pocketknife. He opened the three-inch blade.

Wick looked over.

"Ken," he said, "what are you doing?"

Wick lifted his right arm and shielded the right side of his face; he feared Barnes would slash him. Wick thought

Barnes was trying to show him and Clark that he was not afraid of them, that he would not hesitate to hurt them if they treated him badly. Barnes, most of all, was nervous.

Wick stayed calm.

"Ken, you might want to put that thing away," he said. "You are doing a good job. You have nothing to worry about. Relax."

Clark removed his .40-caliber Glock from his holster. He held the nose of the barrel up against the back of the seat; if Barnes even moved slightly toward Wick, Clark would fire a bullet into Barnes' back.

"Fold that and give it to me," Clark said.

Barnes hesitated. He slowly turned over the knife. He never knew how close he had been to getting shot.

———

Several days later, on December 9, 2005, Marshall Piccinini was preparing Barnes to appear before a grand jury that had been hearing evidence in the Wells case for two years. Piccinini would call Barnes as a witness in the case against Diehl-Armstrong. Clark and Wick drove Barnes to Piccinini's office at the federal courthouse so Piccinini could review Barnes' previous statements to Clark, Wick and Gluth.

Piccinini did most of the talking. He sat at a conference table with Clark and Wick and Barnes, who was saying nothing new. Barnes reiterated that Diehl-Armstrong had solicited him to kill her father and to drive a getaway car, and had asked him about making a bomb. But that was all, Barnes said.

At the end of the interview, Piccinini remembered where Diehl-Armstrong had told Clark and Wick she had been on August 28, 2003.

"Were you with her at Barnes & Noble and Kentucky Fried Chicken?" Piccinini asked Barnes.

"Well, yeah," he said.

The interview concluded.

Wick left to drive Barnes home. Piccinini and Clark discussed what had just happened: Barnes, for the first time, had linked himself to Diehl-Armstrong and, most likely, the Wells case.

Clark, still at Piccinini's office, called Wick.

"He's fucking lying," Clark said of Barnes. "He's in. Did you drop him off yet?"

"Yeah, I dropped him off," Wick said.

Clark said they would have to wait the next day to reinterview Barnes.

Wick paused.

"Screw this," he said. "I'm going to get him right now."

Wick did a U-turn on State Street, in the middle of the city, drove back to 617 Perry Street and knocked on the door. Barnes surprised him by answering it.

"Get back in the car," Wick said. "You have to come downtown with me again."

Wick called Clark.

"Ken's in the car," he said. "He's coming back."

Wick drove Barnes to the FBI office. As Clark and Wick listened, Barnes gave his version of events. Barnes, the insider, provided what no one else had up to that point: an explanation of what happened before, during and after Brian Wells drove down the road to the TV tower on the afternoon of August 28, 2003.

———

It was the spring of 2003, Barnes would later testify. The construction of Jim Roden's apartment was going well. Barnes, whom Diehl-Armstrong paid $175 for his labor, was doing the wiring and plumbing. He and Roden had installed a partition and put in a sink, a stove and a toilet.

One day during a break in the construction, Diehl-Armstrong asked Barnes whether he wanted to help her rob a bank.

Barnes declined the request.

She asked him if he wanted to be the getaway driver.

Barnes declined.

Diehl-Armstrong asked Barnes if he knew Bill Rothstein. He had helped her in the past, she said; he was very trustworthy.

Diehl-Armstrong asked another question.

"Do you know how to make a bomb?"

"I know how to make one, but I don't want to make one for you," Barnes said.

"If you were to make a bomb, what would it be, what kind?" she said.

"A pipe bomb," Barnes said. "That would be the easiest kind to make."

"How would that work?"

"Get about a five-inch piece of nipple," Barnes said, referring to a piece of galvanized black pipe. "Get about a five-inch piece of nipple, and get an end cap. Put it on there and drill a hole down through it, smaller than a pencil. Take a piece of steel wool, roll it up and stick it inside the hole.

"Take shotgun shells, cut them open, take the powder out, put it down in the pipe and pack it down in there. Put in wadding; it will be either plastic or paper. Then you can fill it up with shrapnel. Gunpowder would make a bigger explosion than just plain old black powder that they used to use for musket loaders."

Diehl-Armstrong asked Barnes whether he could build a timer or a countdown device.

"Like a binary timer?" he asked. "It depends on what you want."

"What kind is there?" she said.

"I can give you some LEDs, like crystal, just like liquid crystal displays," Barnes said. "I could give you a circuit board from a power supply off a VCR, which has a switching power supply in it. I got a radio electronics magazine I'll let you use. It has the diagram in there on how to build one."

Barnes later gave Diehl-Armstrong all those things.

Diehl-Armstrong told him she had the bank selected that she wanted to rob: PNC Bank. They had hit her with too many finance charges, she said, and she had an argument with them about the money in the estate of her deceased mother.

Diehl-Armstrong talked about her father, who she said was spending her inheritance.

"Will you kill my father for me?" she asked. "How much would you charge? Have you ever killed anybody?"

Barnes lied.

"Yeah," he said, "I killed a guy a long time ago."

"How much will you charge me?"

Barnes decided to joke with Diehl-Armstrong.

"A quarter of a million dollars, $250,000," he said.

"Well," she said, referring to the murder of her father, "how would you do it?"

"I don't know."

"You'd have to make it look like an accident," she said. "I got an idea. Why don't you go into his house, hit him over the head while he's in bed, take him down the stairs into the kitchen area. Open the cellar door and throw him down so it looks like he broke his neck. Be careful; there's a dog down there."

Diehl-Armstrong said she would use the money from the bank robbery to give Barnes a down payment for the murder of the father. The amount of the down payment, she said, would be $100,000.

A short time later, Barnes met Rothstein. Barnes and Roden had spent a week working on the apartment, and they were done. That night, they went on a pizza run with Diehl-Armstrong. The three of them piled into Diehl-Armstrong's orange Camaro to get pizza somewhere on upper Peach Street. The Camaro stalled; Diehl-Armstrong pulled into the parking lot of a car dealer.

Roden and Diehl-Armstrong argued over what to do.

"I'm going to call Bill," she said.

She called from a pay phone.

Rothstein soon pulled up in a gold-colored Mercury Marquis, a big boat of a car that was popular in the 1970s, when gas was cheap. He wore overalls; Barnes thought he was dressed like a pig farmer. Rothstein tried to jump-start the Camaro, but it wouldn't start. Rothstein and Diehl-Armstrong talked.

"Well," she said, "let's call for a pizza."

Ten minutes later, a bluish-green Geo Metro pulled up. Brian Wells was driving. Jessica Hoopsick was next to him. Wells got out and delivered the pizza right there in the parking lot.

Barnes knew Hoopsick. They had met three years earlier through a mutual friend, a drug dealer. She regularly rented a room from Barnes at 617 Perry Street for $20 and used it to have sex with Wells, in exchange for money and crack, which Wells would get for her. Barnes also paid for sex with Hoopsick. Barnes knew Wells through Hoopsick. Barnes thought Wells looked mentally disabled.

Barnes, Roden and Diehl-Armstrong got in Rothstein's car. Rothstein said he would drive to his house to find a part to fix the Camaro. He drove a short distance to the house, at 8645 Peach Street. Wells and Hoopsick pulled in a few minutes later. They all drove down the dirt road to the site of the TV tower.

Wells got out and talked to Diehl-Armstrong and Rothstein. Barnes got in Wells' car, with Hoopsick still inside. The two smoked a joint and drank beer.

Later that night, Diehl-Armstrong got the Camaro started. She, Roden and Barnes climbed back in. She pulled out onto I-79, far from her house on East Seventh Street.

"Where are we going?" Barnes said.

"We're taking the scenic route," Diehl-Armstrong said. She stopped the Camaro along the highway. She and

Roden got out. Barnes said later that she probably had been scouting sites for the bank-robbery notes.

Barnes saw Rothstein again soon. It was the middle of June 2003. Barnes was having a party at his crack house at 2:30 A.M. A crowd had assembled on the front porch: Barnes, Wells, Jessica Hoopsick, Diehl-Armstrong, Roden and Rothstein. Barnes and Diehl-Armstrong were getting along. They had "buried the hatchet," Barnes said, despite her believing Barnes had robbed her on May 30, 2003. Diehl-Armstrong asked Barnes if he was still in "cahoots" for the bank robbery. Barnes said he did not want any part of it, but that he would go along.

"I want to get the money you promised me," he said.

"If you kill my father, I'll give you the money from the bank robbery," she said. "I'll show you the money."

Around this time, Barnes sold Diehl-Armstrong a pair of used Motorola walkie-talkies for $20. He had bought them at a flea market or garage sale.

More than two months later, on August 27, 2003, the penultimate "powwow" occurred, Barnes said. It was between 2:30 and 3:00 P.M. at the tower site near Rothstein's house.

Barnes drove to the TV tower site with Diehl-Armstrong in her red Jeep Cherokee. When they arrived, Rothstein was there. Wells pulled up moments later. Barnes smoked a cigarette while he leaned against Diehl-Armstrong's Jeep. Diehl-Armstrong vouched for Barnes' trustworthiness. A need for money had drawn Barnes and Diehl-Armstrong and Rothstein to this meeting. As far as Barnes knew, the promise of money had prodded Wells to be there, too. Barnes had heard Wells was short on money himself and needed to cover for Hoopsick and other women he was having sex with.

"I know that he was part of it," Barnes would testify later, "and he was a willing part of it because he owed drug money to the dealer; he got so much stuff on credit for the woman he was with and he couldn't pay."

Wells, Rothstein and Diehl-Armstrong huddled near the tower. Barnes stood fifteen feet away. He heard Diehl-Armstrong and Rothstein tell Wells the bomb was fake and that his wearing it would intimidate the tellers into giving him the money. They told Wells to give the notes to the tellers, leave the bank with the money and give the money to Rothstein, who would be waiting outside the bank. Rothstein then would give the money to Jay Stockton, who would divvy up the loot when things cooled off. Diehl-Armstrong and Rothstein told Wells he would have no money when the police stopped him, so he could say he wasn't involved.

"Bill went and got the device and brought it out," Barnes would testify later. "And at the same time, a few minutes later, Mr. Stockton came out and looked around and Bill got mad and told him to get back in the house. Then Marjorie and Bill continued to speak amongst them. And Marjorie was measuring his neck to see how the collar was going to fit.

"And Bill was monkeying with the straps on it, trying to figure out how they were going to do it. After five or ten minutes, Brian got back in his car and left. And Marge says to me, 'Come on; let's go.'"

Before he left, Barnes spoke to Rothstein about the

metal collar, which had an empty box hanging on the front. It was devoid of a bomb mechanism. Barnes didn't think the device looked real. Rothstein asked Barnes what Barnes would do to make it look like it held a genuine explosive mechanism.

"Put some wires in it from the collar down. Put them in the box but don't have them go anywhere," Barnes said. "Make it like a guessing game."

That night, at 11:30 P.M., Barnes was walking down Parade Street, trying to score crack for another party. The bluish-green Geo Metro pulled up. Wells was driving. Hoopsick was riding along.

She introduced Wells to Barnes.

"I know him," Barnes replied.

"Can you get us something?" Hoopsick said.

"Yeah," Barnes said. "But I need the money first."

Hoopsick wouldn't give Barnes money. The Geo Metro drove away.

The following day, August 28, 2003, Barnes would meet Wells again.

Between 10:30 and 11:00 A.M., Diehl-Armstrong picked up Barnes at 617 Perry Street in her red Jeep Cherokee, in which she was still living. They drove to the Barnes & Noble bookstore on upper Peach Street and ordered Starbucks coffee—the best coffee Barnes said he ever had. Diehl-Armstrong bought a book. The two of them sat in her Jeep in the parking lot.

"Do you remember what I talked with you about before, robbing a bank? It's going down today," Diehl-Armstrong said. "Today's the day."

Rothstein was supposed to meet them in the parking lot. He never arrived. Rothstein did show up a little later at the Shell station at Peach Street and Robison Road. Barnes and Diehl-Armstrong drove there in her Jeep. Rothstein pulled in driving the Mercury Marquis. He gave Diehl-Armstrong a $10 bill to fill the tank of the Jeep; she gave the cash to Barnes. He put gas in the Jeep—he used Pump 7, and did not have to prepay—while Rothstein and Diehl-Armstrong stood by the pay phone and talked. Barnes walked into the Shell station. He used the bathroom. He paid for the gas.

Everyone left for the site of the TV tower. Barnes drove with Diehl-Armstrong. Her Jeep headed down the dirt road. Two other people were already milling around the tower site: Rothstein and Robert Pinetti. Rothstein's van was pulled to the left, near the cluster of satellite dishes and outbuildings.

"As we got back there," Barnes would testify later, "Bill's van was here, there was another car here, who I think it was Mr. Pinetti's, and Marjorie pulled in this way, just in front and across from Bill's van. And then a few minutes later Brian came up, pulled up behind Marjorie's car.

"When he came, he brought the pizza out they had ordered, and he set it on the hood of Bill's van. And then Mr. Stockton came out from behind the one building that was down there, carrying this device. And he brought it up like towards Bill, and while Brian was looking at it, he got a look on his face; I think at that point he realized this thing was real. Because as far as I knew, it wasn't supposed to be. It was supposed to be just a gag to get the teller to give him some money."

Stockton was carrying the device in a white shirt so he would leave no fingerprints. It was the same device Rothstein and Diehl-Armstrong handled the day before, but it looked different. The contraption Rothstein and Diehl-Armstrong had put on Wells the day before had that hollow box on the front. This device had a full box hanging off the front—the box that contained the pipe bombs. Wells didn't want anything to do with this device. It looked like it held a real bomb.

"He turned to run, and when he went to run, Bill fired a pistol up in the air," Barnes would testify later. "At the same time Mr. Pinetti and Mr. Stockton tackled him, and got him down on the ground and was scuffling around with him a little bit. Then they come up holding him up. By then Marjorie and Bill were over there; Marjorie was helping hold the device while Bill was strapping it on. And he was yelling he didn't want to be a part of it anymore. I walked over and punched him in the face, not real hard, but just light."

"Quit being such a chicken," Barnes told Wells. "Go ahead and go through with it."

Barnes wanted his money. He wanted Wells to rob the bank.

Diehl-Armstrong and Rothstein put padding between the bomb and Wells' chest; the padding was a black garbage bag. Rothstein went to his van, got the cane gun and gave it to Wells. Diehl-Armstrong told him to use the gun if the tellers didn't believe he had a real bomb.

"Raise it up and say, 'This is a holdup,'" she said.

Barnes was impressed. He thought the cane gun was an ingenious touch.

Diehl-Armstrong pulled a white T-shirt out of her red purse: *GUESS Jeans*, it said on it. Barnes liked the twist: the shirt seemed to say, "Guess whether or not this bomb will go off." Diehl-Armstrong put the shirt on Wells.

She gave him some parting advice: if the police pull you over, tell them someone put the bomb on you and told you they would kill you if you didn't do it.

Wells waited around with the bomb on his neck. Barnes waited as well. So did Rothstein, Pinetti, Stockton and Diehl-Armstrong. They ate pizza. Barnes had a piece; Diehl-Armstrong had a piece. They put the insulated pizza bag in Rothstein's car.

Diehl-Armstrong and Barnes got in her Jeep. They drove away. Wells was still waiting.

"Let's go watch the bank get robbed," she said.

Diehl-Armstrong turned right on upper Peach Street, heading north, toward the Summit Towne Centre.

"Where are we going?" Barnes said.

"I want to get another book," she said.

They pulled into a strip mall set back from the east side of Peach Street, across the road from the Summit Towne Centre. Diehl-Armstrong and Barnes walked into what was then a Media Play store, not far from the Walmart. They separated. Barnes looked at CDs. Diehl-Armstrong looked for a book. Fifteen minutes later, Diehl-Armstrong looked at the clock.

"Let's go," she said to Barnes.

They got back in the Jeep. She zigzagged through the

parking lots and roads connecting the parking lots and parked in the front of the Eat'n Park restaurant, directly across upper Peach Street from the Summit Towne Centre entrance that led to the PNC Bank. She parked in the seventh space from the north driveway that emptied into the Eat'n Park lot. The parking lot was on a rise. Barnes sat in the Jeep with Diehl-Armstrong and looked west, across Peach Street. They could see everything: Summit Towne Centre, Eyeglass World, McDonald's, the PNC Bank.

Wells' Geo Metro drove by, heading north on Peach Street. Barnes tracked him through a pair of binoculars. Rothstein was following Wells in the Mercury Marquis. Wells turned into the Summit Towne Centre and drove to the bank. Rothstein pulled his car into the parking lot for Eyeglass World. Rothstein got out.

Wells walked into the bank.

Diehl-Armstrong looked through the binoculars.

"I think he's robbing the bank," she said.

Barnes grabbed the binoculars and put them to his eyes.

"I don't really see him," he said.

Diehl-Armstrong took back the binoculars. She looked through them.

"Yeah," she said. "He did."

State police cruisers covered the scene. Diehl-Armstrong and Barnes saw the troopers stop Wells.

"Looks like the bank was robbed. Ha, ha," she said.

"Let's get the hell out of here," he said.

They left before the explosion.

Diehl-Armstrong pulled up to a traffic light to turn south on upper Peach Street, toward Rothstein's house.

She squealed the tires and ran a red light. The Jeep almost got hit.

Diehl-Armstrong drove nearly two miles past Rothstein's house. She turned into the parking lot of an auto-auction business on upper Peach Street. Rothstein pulled in moments later, driving the Mercury Marquis. She and Rothstein talked in the parking lot. She walked over to her Jeep.

"Let's take Bill's car," Diehl-Armstrong said.

"Why?" Barnes said.

"I'm thinking of selling mine," she said. "I don't want it anymore. I need a different car."

They jumped into Rothstein's car. She drove along Peach Street to I-79. She got on the highway going the wrong way.

A tractor-trailer headed toward them. Barnes saw a sign warning that this route was the wrong way.

Barnes saw another motorist, an older guy with white hair, driving what looked like a gray-colored car in the correct direction. The guy shook his finger at them for driving the wrong way.

"Hey," Barnes said to Diehl-Armstrong. "We're going the wrong way down here."

Diehl-Armstrong said nothing. Barnes thought she looked like she was in a panic.

Diehl-Armstrong pulled into the median, did a U-turn and drove in the right direction, south on I-79. About halfway between the spot of the U-turn and the place where she had entered the highway, she pulled the Mercury Marquis to the side of the road and got out.

"I've got to take a piss," she said.

She walked around the back of the car, climbed over a guardrail, and walked down an embankment. She was gone several minutes. When she returned, she opened the back door of the car and threw something onto the backseat—something wrapped in a white shirt. Barnes did not see what it was.

Diehl-Armstrong jumped into the front seat. She drove back to the auto-auction business near Rothstein's house. He was waiting for her. She and Rothstein talked in the parking lot. She and Barnes got back into her Jeep.

"He couldn't sell it," she said.

"Give me the money," Barnes said.

"We didn't get no money."

"Then why am I here?" Barnes said. "The whole reason for me to come along was to get that money."

"I don't have it now," she said. "You'll have to do the job and I'll give you the money later."

"No," Barnes said. "That wasn't the deal. I was supposed to get half down."

Diehl-Armstrong headed to the lower east side and dropped off Barnes at 617 Perry Street at between 3:30 and 4:00 P.M.

"You better not tell anyone what you saw today," she said.

Barnes had reason to stay quiet. He had a crack house to keep in business. He didn't need any heat from the police.

Barnes sat at his kitchen table. He turned on the local TV news. He watched the footage of Wells, handcuffed in the parking lot, before and after the bomb detonated.

20

Trifecta of Trash

Marshall Piccinini set aside the subpoena for Barnes to appear before the grand jury as a witness. After he gave his statements to the investigators, Barnes had elevated his status to that of a person of interest. Eventually, Clark said to himself, Barnes would be indicted. Barnes had admitted he was with Diehl-Armstrong on August 28, 2003.

On December 12, 2005, three days after he had laid out what he knew, Barnes had gone so far as to drive with Wick and Clark and Gluth on the route he said he and Diehl-Armstrong had driven on August 28, 2003. Barnes & Noble, the TV tower site, the Eat'n Park parking lot: Barnes directed Clark and Wick and Gluth to stop at each. When Barnes got to the site of the TV tower, he pointed out the spot where he said Pinetti and Stockton tackled

Wells, and where he had punched Wells (lightly) in the face. The location matched where the state police had found the cluster of shoeprints.

The car ride and the other visits with Barnes bordered on the comical. Clark annoyed Wick by laughing along with the joke-telling Barnes. Clark tried to use Barnes' display of crude humor to get him laughing, to try to loosen him up. Clark never felt otherwise that Barnes' behavior—running the crack house, soliciting prostitutes, aiding in the death of Wells—could be classified only as abhorrent. But if indulging Barnes in his off-color musings drew out more admissions, Clark was willing to play along.

"How're things going, Ken?" Clark would say.

Barnes would retort with an X-rated bon mot.

"My life's like a sore dick," was one of his favorites. "You just can't beat it."

Even Diehl-Armstrong, she of the four-letter-word vocabulary, imperious manner and murderous past, said she could not stomach Barnes and what she characterized as his sick proclivities. She considered him a degenerate. Particularly galling, she said, was when he told her he saw nothing wrong with having sex with mentally disabled women.

"Her pussy is not retarded," Diehl-Armstrong said Barnes proclaimed.

"It is always a bad day when I cross Ken Barnes," she once said. "He is like a skunk."

————

Clark and Wick set out to make sure what Barnes had told them was accurate. They looked for Jessica Hoopsick. One day, they spotted her sitting on a concrete wall underneath the railroad underpass at East Fifteenth and Parade streets.

"Jess," Clark said. "Jess, what are you doing?"

Like Barnes, Hoopsick gave up little at first. Starting with an interview on January 11, 2006, she finally detailed her sexual relationship with Wells—she said he never used crack—and her drug-related relationship with Barnes. She said she felt guilty about Wells' death because she believed she was the link between Wells and Barnes. Hoopsick had known Wells for fifteen years. They had become friends.

"He took me and my mother grocery shopping," Hoopsick would testify later. "He took me to my doctor's appointments, my OB/GYN appointments."

Hoopsick told Clark and Wick she had been at a meeting on Barnes' front porch that included Wells, Barnes and another woman and a man whose names she said she did not know. Hoopsick said the group discussed a bank robbery. She said the conversation interested her because, as a crack addict, "you constantly need more money." She said she did not participate in the bank robbery.

The night of August 27, 2003, Hoopsick said, she and Wells were driving Parade Street, looking for crack, when they saw Barnes. Hoopsick said she introduced Wells to Barnes.

"This is Brian," Hoopsick said she told Barnes.

"Yeah," Barnes said. "I know."

Hoopsick said she found it odd that neither Barnes nor Wells said anything else.

Clark thought Hoopsick had to know more. She

probably spent more time with Wells than anyone, outside of Mama Mia's; she said they had a genuine friendship that went beyond him paying her in crack for sex. Wells had to have discussed the bank robbery with her. Hadn't she said she was interested in money? Hadn't Barnes said Wells and Hoopsick were in hock over drugs? Hoopsick said she had told Clark all she remembered. She might have met Diehl-Armstrong, she said, but she could not be sure. In the summer of 2003, she said, she had been high on crack much of the time.

———

Eight months had passed since Clark and Wick had last interviewed Diehl-Armstrong, at SCI Cambridge Springs on July 5, 2005. At the urging of her personal attorney, Larry D'Ambrosio, she had spoken of providing Rothstein with kitchen timers.

When Clark and Wick next met with Diehl-Armstrong, on February 10, 2006, Clark read her Miranda rights to her and D'Ambrosio. Clark told her he and Wick had developed more information since they had last spoken with her; Clark did not tell her they had spoken to Barnes. The new information, Clark told Diehl-Armstrong, could lead to her getting indicted. Wick told her she could get the death penalty. She grew agitated.

"Go ahead and indict me," Diehl-Armstrong shouted. "I've done research and know that you can indict a ham sandwich."

Diehl-Armstrong shouted at D'Ambrosio, who tried to intervene.

"Shut up, Larry," she said.

She told Clark and Wick that she was at the Barnes & Noble, KFC and Shell station on August 28, 2003, but only because Rothstein had directed her to be at those places so she would be associated with the Wells case. She had never said that before; now threatened with an indictment, she was saying Rothstein had framed her.

She said Rothstein directed her to be at certain places to ensure that if he were caught in the Wells case, she would be, too. She said Rothstein loved her and wanted no one else to have her.

"Now I know why you think I may have been involved," she said, "because Rothstein had me seen at locations associated to Wells."

The investigators asked her if she knew Wells.

"I didn't know Brian like that," she said.

She quickly clarified that she did not know Wells at all. Diehl-Armstrong denied being with Barnes on August 28, 2003.

"Why would I be with Barnes if he robbed me?" she said.

———

Four days later, on February 14, 2006, Clark and Wick met with Barnes and told him what Diehl-Armstrong had said about not being with him on August 28, 2003.

"That's bullshit," he said.

Barnes said Diehl-Armstrong in August 2003 was still upset with him over the robbery allegations but that the two of them were indeed together on August 28, 2003.

He got angry as he recounted what he and Diehl-Armstrong had done that day.

"How else would I know all I know unless I was with her?" Barnes said. "Diehl is lying to you."

———————

In early March 2006, Diehl-Armstrong's demeanor had changed. She was frantic, a fellow inmate, Jennifer Brininger, told a prison official, who relayed the information to Clark.

Brininger, twenty-eight years old and in for theft, had befriended Diehl-Armstrong first at SCI Cambridge Springs and then at SCI Muncy. She became convinced that Diehl-Armstrong had her wits about her, that she did the "Thorazine shuffle," referring to the antipsychotic medication, to try to dupe the prison staff into believing she suffered from a debilitating mental illness. She listened as Diehl-Armstrong told her that the investigators wanted her to give up information on the Wells case. Diehl-Armstrong said she hoped to get the $100,000 reward and fame.

"Do you think I'm going to be famous?" she asked Brininger. "They told me I have a million-dollar smile."

Brininger said it's a shame you have to commit a murder to become famous. Diehl-Armstrong laughed, but she seemed scared. She believed the Wells plot was a death-penalty case.

Diehl-Armstrong mentioned Barnes and Stockton.

"I hope that Ken didn't tell them anything," Brininger

said Diehl-Armstrong told her. "I won't tell on Ken and Floyd."

Diehl-Armstrong told Brininger she had become suspicious of Kelly Makela, who had been temporarily removed from the state prison system and transferred to the Erie County Prison on a federal hold—a sure sign, Diehl-Armstrong said, that Makela was up in Erie to testify before the federal grand jury in the Wells case. She would be found guilty, Diehl-Armstrong told Brininger, if Makela testified against her.

Diehl-Armstrong talked about how Makela might die. Makela already had suffered two brain aneurysms, Diehl-Armstrong said. All she had to do is scare Makela. Then she would die, of natural causes, from a third.

Brininger later reported, also in March 2006, that Diehl-Armstrong's anxiety about Barnes remained unabated. Diehl-Armstrong, Brininger said, was reading a book called *The History of Murder*, an encyclopedia of slayings through the ages, and was trying to get another book, called *The Temptress*, a pulp romance about an heiress who fends off two men who kidnap her. Diehl-Armstrong no longer referred to herself as the "Freezer Queen," Brininger said. She called herself the "Black Widow."

———

Finding Barnes no longer required Clark and Wick to drive Parade Street. On March 9, 2006, the state police charged him with selling an eighth of an ounce of powder cocaine—an "eight ball"—to an undercover trooper and a confidential informant. A magistrate set bond at

$25,000 cash, well beyond what Barnes could afford. The Erie County Prison was his new home.

Barnes later pleaded guilty to unlawful delivery, a felony, and was sentenced to eleven and one-half to twenty-three months in the Erie County Prison in August 2006. While behind bars, he continued to talk to Clark and Wick. He kept trying to project an image of a hot-headed thug. In one meeting, in a prison conference room, Clark and Wick listened as Barnes spoke about the shot fired at the TV tower site.

"Did you fire that shot?" Wick asked Barnes.

"That's it," Barnes said. "The interview's over."

Barnes got up to leave. He waited for the guards to arrive.

"I hit a nerve, didn't I?" Wick said. "We know you did this, and we know you did a lot of other bad things in your life, too."

Barnes snarled and made a fist. He cocked his arm at Wick.

Wick got into a boxer's crouch.

"Go ahead, Ken," he said. "Take your best shot."

Clark lunged and grabbed Barnes.

"Don't do it," Clark said. "You're going to lose this one, Ken."

Two prison guards arrived. Barnes returned to his cell.

———

Jerry Clark had sidestepped his way through Diehl-Armstrong's piles of garbage. He had maneuvered around

Rothstein's loads of debris. But Clark had never seen anything like this.

Search warrant in hand, he stood at the entrance to Barnes' house, at 617 Perry Street, the night of March 21, 2006, twelve days after Barnes' arrest on drug charges. Diehl-Armstrong's house, Rothstein's house, Barnes' house—they formed a trifecta of trash. Barnes' house, by far, ranked as the worst of the three. It was a jackpot of junk and squalor.

Garbage filled each of the seven rooms, including the four bedrooms, of the eighty-year-old two-story brick house, which Barnes had been renting from a woman by the name of A.O., his onetime girlfriend, for $500 a month. Swaths of the floors oozed with a half-inch layer of dog excrement—the leavings of Barnes' pets, a cairn terrier and a fox terrier, one named Gizmo and the other named Peanut. The dogs never went outside; the house stank of their feces and urine.

Computer components—motherboards, monitors, CPUs—made up much of the junk. In one room, hedge trimmers sat upon a pile of boxes and computer equipment that reached halfway to the ceiling. An avalanche of detritus spilled through a passage that, in a typical house, would connect the dining room and the living room: more computer equipment, more boxes, a folding beach chair.

Cans of Alpo dog food covered a round table in the kitchen, where Mason jars were cluttered near the sink, next to pots and pans caked with food. Blankets and clothing covered the kitchen floor, along with dog bowls.

Barnes had been sleeping in the kitchen, on a sleeping bag stretched across two hard chairs. When the house still had natural-gas service, Barnes would turn on the stove, open its door and get warm. When Clark executed the search warrant, the house had no gas service, no electricity and no water. The utility companies had shut them off. Barnes had been warding off the cold by running a space heater off a car battery; jumper cables connected the battery to the heater. The battery would last two days; Barnes would take it to A.O.'s house to recharge it. Barnes had powered his television set the same way.

Boxes and bags full of junk jammed Barnes' basement. "Worms," read the outside of one box, signaling that an angler lived in the house. Plastic bags covered whatever of the basement floor was clear of boxes. A freezer, unpowered for who knew how long because of the house's lack of electricity, reeked of rotting meat.

Upstairs, the grouting in the bathroom was falling out, as were several tiles. Deep brown stains made the sink and the toilet look like they were corroded by crap. In one bedroom, a bed frame without a mattress stood against a blue wall that was chipping paint. Above the bed, built into the corner of the wall, was a bookshelf. Looking out from it was a picture of Jesus Christ.

The walls of another bedroom were chipped and painted a tomato-colored red. A white bureau, which, when clean, would have brightened the room of a girl or young woman, had become the final resting place for a can of vegetable soup, a jar of grape jelly, an old box of cigars and a car battery. In one corner of the room, on the floor, without a frame, rested a mattress atop a set of box springs. At the head of the mattress was a window and a window screen. A dirty fitted plastic sheet that once fully covered the mattress was torn across the center, with the remnants of the sheet clinging to the mattress's sides. On top of the mattress were piled dirty blankets and a pink comforter. This was the bed where Brian Wells and Jessica Hoopsick had sex.

Clark, concerned about the health risks from so much filth, called Erie firefighters and arranged for the delivery of white hazmat "moon suits" like those the evidence specialists wore when they searched Diehl-Armstrong's house on East Seventh Street. Clark and the other agents put on the suits, complete with surgical masks, as they made their way through Barnes' house.

The agents had nowhere to turn. Usually in a search, Clark liked to store the collected materials in a room that was largely vacant of furniture. No such rooms existed in Barnes' house. Clark, Wick and the other agents created a bucket brigade for junk—the agents passed box after box to each other, from room to room, through the hall, down the staircase and out the front door, where an agent stacked the boxes and other debris inside a large portable storage unit known as a Conex box, which looked like a huge Dumpster with a door. It was parked in Barnes' driveway.

The agents focused on certain things: grinding wheels, screwdrivers, pliers, vises and other tools, as well as carpet samples, steel wool and a .12-gauge Winchester shotgun shell. The FBI lab would link none of the seized items to the making of the collar bomb.

The search of Barnes' house produced some valuable finds. In one room, right where Barnes said they would be located, was a stack of old electronics magazines. Barnes said he had gone to this stack to give Diehl-Armstrong a magazine that contained a diagram on how to build an electrical circuit for a bomb. Clark and Wick paged through the remaining magazines. The spring 1983 issue of *Electronics Special Projects* featured an article on how to build an automatic countdown timer that was "accurate to the second." The 1982 edition of *Integrated Circuit Projects* contained an article and diagram on how to build a sequential timer. On page 92 of the December 1974 issue of *Popular Electronics* was an article and diagram on how to build "the executive digital temper countdowner."

Clark and Wick and the other federal agents cleared Barnes' house of most everything, including his two dogs, Gizmo and Peanut. Parasites had infested both of them. The FBI delivered the dogs to the local Humane Society, which determined their health to be so poor that veterinarians put both down. Barnes went into a frenzy when Clark explained the dogs' fate. The conversation ended with Barnes crying. It was the only time Clark saw Barnes express concern for anyone or anything.

———

Ken Barnes had few friends. Even his closest relative in Erie, Ricky Barnes, his half brother, despised him.

At forty-nine years old in March 2006, Ricky Barnes

was three years younger than Ken, his oldest brother; they shared the same father, Harry Barnes Sr., who lived in another Pennsylvania county and who would die at age seventy-eight in 2011, after a life in which he was in trouble with the law. The middle of the three Barnes boys, Harry Barnes Jr., fifty-one years old in March 2006, was serving a life sentence for breaking into the house of a seventy-four-year-old woman in 1990 in a county south of Erie and killing her by setting her house on fire.

After Ken Barnes' arrest on the drug charges, Ricky Barnes stopped by the Erie FBI office to sign for his half brother's wallet and the $81 inside. Ricky wanted Ken to stay in prison. He said Ken had mistreated him and other relatives for a long time. He said Ken's name was on the deed to the title of the house where Ricky Barnes was living. If Ken left prison, Ricky feared Ken would kick him out.

Clark asked Ricky Barnes if he wanted to help build a case against his half brother. Ricky quickly said yes.

The cold lingers well into the spring in Erie, where snow is known to fall on Easter. When Ricky Barnes walked into the Erie County Prison on March 27, 2006, he wore a knit ski cap. Clark liked that the weather was stubbornly chilly. He liked that no one at the prison, particularly the inmates, would wonder why Ricky Barnes was wearing a ski cap. The FBI had hidden a microphone inside it.

Ricky Barnes had agreed to become an informant for the FBI; Clark gave him the source name Gizmo, after one of Ken's two pet terriers.* Under Clark's direction, Ricky regularly stopped by to see his half brother at the prison's visitors' area. Ricky and Ken would sit across from each other, a glass wall dividing them, and talk on the interconnected telephone handsets. Ricky Barnes after each chat would meet with Clark and relate what Ken had said.

To make the evidence against Ken Barnes even more airtight, the FBI put the hidden microphone in Ricky's ski cap. The prison's concerns for the privacy of the other inmates and their visitors precluded the FBI from bugging the entire visitors' area. The hidden microphone offered a way to pick up only the Barneses' conversations.

The bug almost worked. The visitors' area got crowded and the din drowned out the Barneses' discussions. The hidden microphone captured all the noise in the room, making what the Barneses were saying indistinguishable from any other conversation. The bugged chatter between Ricky and Ken was incomprehensible.

Ricky Barnes still turned out to be a productive source, because of his briefings with Clark. Ricky Barnes said Ken told him: Wells was forced to wear the bomb; Barnes was solicited to kill Diehl-Armstrong's father; no one would find evidence at Ken's house because the bomb wasn't built there; there was no black man involved, as claimed by Wells; Ken's only worry was that Diehl-Armstrong would testify against him, but if she didn't talk he would be okay; Diehl-Armstrong had two murders under her

---

*Ricky Barnes told the *Erie Times-News* he informed on his half brother.

belt and no one would believe her anyway; all the bomb-making materials were dumped at the landfill.

If you had been driving on upper Peach Street on the sunny morning of May 10, 2006, you might have passed it—a dark blue Ford Crown Victoria filled with five people. You probably would have recognized the Crown Vic as an unmarked police car. You probably would have guessed, correctly, that three of the five people in the car—the three clean-shaven men with short-cropped hair—were in law enforcement. Driving by, you would not have been able to see the hands of the long-haired woman who was sitting in the middle of the backseat, next to a bald man. Her hands were cuffed in front of her and locked to a leather belt cinched around her waist. She was wearing a tan jumpsuit—a typical uniform of female inmates at the Erie County Prison, where the inmates also wore green or orange.

Marjorie Diehl-Armstrong was seated in the middle of the backseat of the Pennsylvania State Police's unmarked Crown Vic. The bald Larry D'Ambrosio was to her right and Jerry Clark to her left. Behind the wheel sat David Gluth, the state police investigator. Jason Wick sat in the passenger seat. Diehl-Armstrong was talking a lot.

Diehl-Armstrong had agreed to go on this ride, just as Barnes—unbeknownst to Diehl-Armstrong—previously took the investigators on a guided tour of his whereabouts on August 28, 2003. To get more information out of Diehl-Armstrong, to get her to agree to a similar tour, Clark and Wick had been contacting her constantly. On May 5, 2006, she told Clark and Wick that she was not with Barnes on August 28, 2003. She said she has poor eyesight; she said someone could have been with her in a vehicle without her seeing the person.

On May 9, 2006, the day before the tour, Clark and Wick again met with Diehl-Armstrong at the Erie County Prison, where she was being held after refusing to comply with a federal grand jury subpoena for her fingerprints and samples of her handwriting and head hair. Diehl-Armstrong reiterated to Clark and Wick that Rothstein had set her up in the Wells case, by directing her to be at certain locations. She said he probably knew he was dying of cancer. She said he framed her so no one else could have her. She confirmed that she had been angry at PNC Bank over her mother's estate. She said Barnes wanted to push her father down the stairs. "It's not like I gave him the plans for the house," Diehl-Armstrong said.

She told Clark and Wick, also on May 9, 2006, that she might have been at the TV tower site the day Wells was killed. Then she said she was there, but she did not see anything.

The next day, on May 10, 2006, the TV tower site was one of several spots where the Crown Vic stopped after Gluth drove away from the Erie County Prison. Before driving to the tower site, the car stopped at the Barnes & Noble, where Diehl-Armstrong said she bought a book, coffee and a stuffed animal; the KFC parking lot; and the Shell station, where Diehl-Armstrong said Rothstein made a phone call, and where, she said, her red Jeep Cherokee was parked in the spot for Pump 6 or 7. Diehl-Armstrong said she had been at each place—at Rothstein's direction.

Gluth drove the Crown Vic down the dirt road and to the tower site. Clark and Wick let Diehl-Armstrong get out of the car at the secluded spot; she stayed in the car, and out of the sight of the public, throughout the rest of the tour. With her lawyer listening, Diehl-Armstrong said she did not go all the way back to the tower site on August 28, 2003, but had parked near the front of the dirt road. She said she saw Rothstein, Stockton, Barnes and Wells walk all the way back to the tower site; she said she heard what she thought was a gunshot. She said Rothstein told her a car had backfired.

The Crown Vic headed to Media Play on upper Peach Street, where Diehl-Armstrong said she had been as well. Then, at her direction, Gluth drove to the Eat'n Park parking lot. She pointed out where she had parked that day. It was the same space—the seventh slot from the north driveway—where Barnes, on his tour, had said he and Diehl-Armstrong had parked to watch Wells rob the bank.

Clark suggested that Diehl-Armstrong take a break. Clark bought her a Diet Coke and pretzels at a convenience store near Eyeglass World. She snacked as Gluth resumed the tour. After leaving the Eat'n Park, Diehl-Armstrong told Clark, she met Rothstein and they swapped vehicles— her red Jeep Cherokee for an older model car that she said might have belonged to one of Rothstein's friends.

Next stop: I-79. Diehl-Armstrong said she might have driven on the highway after the bank robbery, so Gluth offered to retrace that route. The Crown Vic drove along different stretches of I-79. Diehl-Armstrong said the stretches looked familiar, but said she could not be sure. Gluth stopped the Crown Vic in a police turnaround near Exit 180, for the Millcreek Mall. Clark asked her if she recognized the spot.

Diehl-Armstrong refused to say anything more. First, she said, she wanted immunity, just like the immunity Rothstein got in the Roden case. She didn't want to "screw herself" by revealing any more information without immunity.

"I've put my head in the lion's mouth," she said.

The Crown Vic returned to the Erie County Prison.

———

The guided tour marked the last of the eight interviews Wick and Clark would have with Diehl-Armstrong. Fed up with D'Ambrosio—she said he wasn't "worth shit" as a criminal lawyer—she got the federal magistrate judge in Erie to declare her indigent and appoint her an assistant federal public defender on September 26, 2006. Diehl-Armstrong wanted a different lawyer, a well-known Erie attorney by the name of Leonard Ambrose, who had won her the acquittal in the shooting of Bob Thomas, but Ambrose declined to represent her. One case with Marjorie Diehl-Armstrong was enough.

The assistant federal public defender, Tom Patton, immediately succeeded on one point. He got Diehl-Armstrong to stop meeting with Clark and Wick.

Clark and Wick moved on. They filled their time sorting through what other people had told them in the Wells case. One of them was Floyd Stockton.

21

Queen for a Day

I f Floyd Stockton possessed any secrets about the pizza
bomber case, they very well might soon vanish into
eternity, with the way Stockton looked at this moment. He was sprawled on a hotel room floor, pale and
lifeless, his pants soaked in his own urine.

His lawyer had come to this hotel room, in Seattle,
Washington, to interview Stockton about his knowledge
of Brian Wells. It was late 2006. The lawyers were getting
impatient with Stockton; he had complicated his case by
previously talking to the investigators without representa-
tion. Jerry Clark and Jason Wick and David Gluth had
questioned Stockton over those two days in July 2005 at
the Airway Heights Correctional Facility in Spokane. The
most recent interview had been on January 31, 2006;
Clark and Wick, this time with Marshall Piccinini joining

them, had met with Stockton at his probation officer's office in Bellingham; Stockton's two-year prison sentence in the rape case had ended in December 2005.

As he had done in previous interviews, Stockton on January 31, 2006, indicated he knew something about what happened on August 28, 2003. Stockton went so far as to say he had been inside Rothstein's house on August 27, 2003. He said he looked out a window and saw Wells meeting with Diehl-Armstrong and Rothstein.

After the interview on January 31, 2006, Stockton hired a lawyer, Charbel Latouf, of Erie, who got Stockton to be quiet. Clark pressed Latouf about what Stockton knew. Clark hinted that the FBI and the U.S. Attorney's Office had enough to indict Stockton, so Latouf should think about cutting a deal.

Latouf had followed the Wells case in the *Erie Times-News*, but he had learned very little from his client. Stockton wasn't revealing much, putting Latouf and his fellow lawyer, Mo Abdrabboh, from Detroit, in the perilous position of trying to protect a client who was pulling the silent treatment on his own attorney. Abdrabboh represented Stockton's girlfriend, K.W. How could Latouf negotiate for Stockton if he could not evaluate what Stockton could offer the U.S. Attorney's Office in return? Latouf dreaded surprises from a client, especially one in such a high-profile case.

Latouf and Abdrabboh flew to Seattle and sat down with Stockton in the hotel room in late 2006. Stockton gave vague answers and refused to come clean about all he knew. Latouf, thirty-three years old, and staring down the FBI and the U.S. Attorney's Office in the biggest case of his career, was ready to give up. He and Abdrabboh had traveled all the way to Washington for this wishy-washiness?

"If you're going to lie to me, I'm just going to let you get the needle and I'm out of here," Latouf said to Stockton. "I don't care."

Stockton collapsed onto the hotel room floor. He went into cardiac arrest. He lost control of his bladder. Latouf saw that Stockton was barely breathing. Abdrabboh left the room.

"He's dead, and you're leaving him here with me?" Latouf yelled.

Latouf slapped Stockton in the face. He shook him. No response.

Latouf telephoned the front desk, which called 911. Paramedics revived Stockton as Latouf and Abdrabboh, who had returned, looked on. He had suffered a miniature heart attack. Stockton recovered at a local hospital. His secrets survived, even if he was still keeping them buried in his memory.

———

Latouf worked out in the same downtown Erie gym as Clark.* He trusted the FBI agent like Latouf trusted no one else in law enforcement. Clark's easygoing manner made

———

*Latouf practiced with one of Clark's friends, Dave Ridge, who graduated with Clark from Cathedral Prep in 1978. Ridge is the younger brother of another of Clark's friends, Erie native Tom Ridge, a former Pennsylvania governor and the first secretary of the Department of Homeland Security under President George W. Bush.

Latouf comfortable. Latouf knew Clark was in pursuit of Stockton, but Latouf appreciated Clark's frankness and what Latouf considered Clark's sense of fairness. Clark, Latouf thought, would make sure Stockton, if he was indicted at all, would get a chance to review what he was up against before deciding whether to go to trial or negotiate a plea deal.

Within days after Stockton fell to the hotel room floor, Latouf called Clark and recounted Stockton's near-death experience. Clark was glad Stockton had not joined Wells, Pinetti and Rothstein as a dead person of interest.

Latouf was frustrated. He wanted to figure out how much Stockton knew about the Wells case, but could not; Stockton was wary. Latouf asked Clark to tell him something he could put before Stockton, a nugget to force Stockton to understand that the FBI was serious.

Clark wavered. He sympathized with Latouf, and he wanted Stockton to talk, but he did not want Latouf to use the FBI's information to lead Stockton, which would allow Stockton to play with the investigators and tell them what they already knew. Clark also worried Stockton would get the information but refuse to talk and then use what Clark had told him to help build a defense.

At the same time, Clark figured Stockton had to know something significant, based on information that included his taped prison calls with his girlfriend. Stockton was mentioned prominently in Makela's notes; he was Floyd, "the bushy hair" guy. Barnes had talked about Stockton. In addition, the FBI had tracked down Stockton's former wife in Minnesota. She said when she and Stockton lived in Erie in the 1970s, Stockton and Rothstein would hang out at the TV tower and that the two liked to talk about planning the perfect crime. The ex-wife, J.P., said Stockton liked to doodle. She said the McDonald's sign on the notes in the Wells plot resembled Stockton's handiwork. She believed the J-shaped handle of the cane gun signified the letter *J*, as in Jay Stockton.

Clark gathered more information on Stockton in January 2007. It came in after *America's Most Wanted* aired its fifth episode about the pizza bomber case, on January 6, 2007.* Two people called the FBI with information on the man they had known as Jay.

One caller, G.R., said he had been incarcerated with Stockton at the Airway Heights Correctional Facility, in Spokane, after Stockton was extradited from Erie on the rape charges in the fall of 2003. The caller said Stockton told him Wells was to receive $5,000 for wearing the bomb and that Stockton said he helped make the device. Another caller, T.P., said he had known Stockton as an inmate in 1999 and 2000; he said Stockton told him he had a plan to rob a bank by using a pizza deliveryman and duct-taping a bomb to his chest.

Clark considered all that evidence as he weighed whether to give Latouf something to bring back to Stockton. Clark decided the benefits of providing a nugget outstripped the risks. Clark was willing to give one detail to Stockton in the hope of getting twenty in return.

America's Most Wanted would air a total of seven episodes—a high number—on the Wells case, which the show called "The Erie Collar Bomber."

Clark told Latouf the evidence showed Stockton was at the TV tower site on August 28, 2003, not just on August 27, as Stockton had admitted.

The disclosure registered with Stockton, who had to have realized Clark and Wick were not bluffing: they had him. Who was ratting out Stockton? Diehl-Armstrong? Barnes? Had Rothstein said something before he died?

Latouf confronted Stockton with the information. He told Stockton the feds had solid evidence and that he needed to make a deal or risk an indictment, especially if Diehl-Armstrong or Barnes implicated him. If Stockton wanted a deal, Latouf wanted him to be the first person knocking on the door of the U.S. Attorney's Office.

Stockton revealed to Latouf—and Latouf relayed to Clark—that Rothstein had assigned him a role on August 28, 2003: Stockton said he was to go to the Kwik Fill gas station at 7760 Peach Street, next to the interchange of Peach Street and Interstate 90, just south of the Summit Towne Centre. Stockton was to wait there until Rothstein dropped a bag of cash in the gas station's Dumpster. Stockton then was to take that money—which Rothstein would have gotten from Wells—and put it inside a broken-down white van in Rothstein's driveway.

Stockton had put himself in the plot, to some degree. More than ever, Clark was glad Stockton had left that hotel room alive.

———

By mid-2007, what would become one of the most debated issues in the Wells case had fully developed: whether the

U.S. Attorney's Office should grant Stockton immunity, and, if so, to what degree.

The discussions started shortly after the interview at the office of Stockton's probation officer on January 31, 2006. Stockton's intransigence led Clark and Latouf to discuss immunity as a way to get Stockton to continue talking. Clark was careful not to make any guarantees on immunity; he knew any final decision had to come from the prosecutor, Marshall Piccinini.

Stockton initially told Clark he was interested in immunity. Clark took that as a sign Stockton was concealing details and was worried about getting indicted. Then Stockton said he wasn't interested. Then he got a lawyer.

The U.S. Attorney's Office sent Stockton a target letter, which explained he was the focus of a criminal investigation. Stockton would not cooperate. Clark countered by telling Latouf the grand jury was certain to indict Stockton. He recommended Latouf have Stockton come talk about the Wells case and use the discussions to broker a deal with the U.S. Attorney's Office.

To discuss the situation with Stockton, Latouf and Abdrabboh flew to Seattle, where they witnessed Stockton's collapse in the hotel room.

———

The information from Diehl-Armstrong, Barnes, T.P. and G.R.: Clark was sure the U.S. Attorney's Office could use all of it to get a grand jury to indict Stockton as an accomplice in the Wells case. The way the evidence had come together in mid-2007, the grand jury, in Clark's view, had more than enough to indict Barnes and Diehl-Armstrong as well; by meeting with Clark and Wick, Diehl-Armstrong and Barnes had all but talked themselves into getting indicted.

The U.S. Attorney's Office was more cautious. Piccinini considered giving Stockton some kind of immunity, to use him as a witness against Diehl-Armstrong and Barnes. The way Piccinini explained the situation to Clark, Piccinini was concerned the U.S. Attorney's Office lacked enough evidence against Stockton to convict him, so Piccinini might as well use him as an immunized witness.

Clark conceded that Piccinini had some good points on the quality of the evidence against Stockton. Considering even the taped phone calls from prison, and what Stockton had told Latouf about the Kwik Fill, Stockton *himself* had said nothing at that point that indisputably incriminated him. Barnes had every opportunity to say Stockton was deeply involved in the Wells case; he had insisted that Rothstein ordered Stockton into Rothstein's house on August 27, 2003, which raised questions about the extent of Stockton's participation in the planning of the scheme. Diehl-Armstrong herself had not implicated Stockton, though his name was in Makela's notes. Stockton and his girlfriend had been out west on vacation from August 16 through August 23, 2003—the FBI verified that.* The morning of August

---

*Stockton's girlfriend, K.W., told the Erie police they visited the Ingalls Homestead in South Dakota, a childhood home of Laura Ingalls Wilder, the author of *Little House on the Prairie*, and Yellowstone National Park.

28, Stockton had been painting at a house in northern Erie County—the FBI confirmed that, too.

All of that evidence, as Piccinini explained to Clark, suggested Stockton's involvement in the Wells case, if he was involved, was less than that of Barnes and Diehl-Armstrong. Piccinini needed more evidence to secure an indictment against Stockton.

Ultimately, only Piccinini and his bosses could decide on whether to immunize Stockton. An assistant U.S. attorney alone could not determine immunity; Piccinini would have to consult the Justice Department, in Washington, D.C. Clark, as an FBI agent, would never have control over such a determination—nor, Clark knew, should he. In the division of labor in the Justice Department, Clark was an investigator, responsible for getting evidence to support a case. The assistant U.S. attorney or the U.S. attorney was the prosecutor, responsible for bringing the case to trial. The decision on immunity rested with the prosecutors.

As if to emphasize that he understood his place in the pecking order, Clark during the investigation told Piccinini the two of them had to come together to make the case work: "You are it," Clark told Piccinini. "We are going to be connected to this case for the rest of our lives."

Clark throughout the case worked well with Piccinini, though the relationship between Wick and Piccinini was becoming so stressed that the two were barely speaking in 2007; Wick wanted an indictment, and Piccinini wanted to wait. Wick was already upset at missed opportunities, such as the belated discovery of Makela's notes.

Wick was concerned the U.S. Attorney's Office would never let him and Clark finish the case.

Clark kept his frustrations more muted. Though he would disagree with Piccinini, he kept their relationship cordial, even lighthearted. Whenever the Wells case would reach a critical milestone—when, for example, Barnes unveiled his knowledge of the plot after the meeting in the conference room at Piccinini's office—Clark, in his excitement, would drop to the floor of Piccinini's office and do ten, twenty, thirty pushups. Piccinini would laugh at the spectacle.

"You," he would tell Clark, "are out of your mind."

———

The U.S. Attorney's Office can bestow two forms of immunity on a witness. Transactional immunity, also known as full or blanket immunity, provides a witness complete protection from getting indicted, as long as that person provides truthful testimony. Use immunity, also known as letter immunity or informal immunity, provides much more limited protection to a witness and does not preclude prosecution.

Use immunity only prohibits the U.S. Attorney's Office from directly using the witness' statements, made in the form of a proffer, against him or her. Investigators can use as evidence any information they derive from the statements. If a witness with use immunity tells the FBI he hid a gun with a friend, the FBI can talk to that friend, get the gun and use the gun as evidence against the witness.

Use immunity typically involves statements a witness gives to investigators over the course of a single meeting on one day. The U.S. Attorney's Office outlines the application of the use immunity in a letter to the witness. In exchange for talking, the witness is made—in a term common among lawyers—"a queen for a day."

By mid-2007, Piccinini had decided to crown Stockton a queen for a day. Piccinini would offer no guarantee of full immunity; that evaluation would come later, after Stockton, with Latouf present, gave his proffer under the use-immunity guidelines. Stockton and Latouf accepted the queen-for-a-day offer, though not without trepidation. Latouf still was convinced that Stockton was keeping information from him. How far should Stockton go in the proffer? How much did he know? What should he hold back to get a better deal?

Piccinini and Clark traveled to Washington State to get the proffer from Stockton. Over Clark's objections, they left Wick behind. Latouf knew of some tension between his client and the intense Wick; before Stockton hired Latouf, Wick had confronted Stockton during the first interview at the Airway Heights Correctional Facility in July 2005. Latouf asked Piccinini that Wick not come to Washington for the queen-for-a-day proffer. Piccinini agreed, leaving Clark to break the decision to his crest-fallen partner. Wick wondered how was it that a defense lawyer was dictating the terms of an interview. Clark said he and Wick had good chemistry, and both knew how to handle Stockton. Piccinini did not relent.

At 9:00 A.M. on March 27, 2007, Piccinini and Clark arrived at room 1122 of the Grand Hyatt Hotel, at the corner of Seventh and Pine streets, in Seattle. Inside room 1122 were Latouf; Abdrabboh, K.W.'s lawyer; and

Stockton. Piccinini opened the conversation by giving a ten-minute explanation of queen-for-a-day immunity. He told Stockton he could not tell him, at this point, what the final deal would be, but that the only way Stockton could hurt himself is if he failed to tell the truth. If Stockton was truthful, the government could not directly use the proffered information against him.

Clark interviewed Stockton, who rambled for fifteen minutes. He said he could not remember things well because he was getting old and had smoked a lot of dope over the years.

"Oh boy, that's not good," Clark thought.

Stockton, whom Piccinini had just warned not to lie, was being elusive. Clark tried to nudge Stockton into coming clean.

"Listen," Clark said, "we have a lot to cover."

Piccinini interrupted. He was usually reserved, but not at this moment. He told Stockton he had not flown three thousand miles to listen to this bullshit. He said he and Clark were leaving, that Stockton had blown his one chance.

Latouf and Abdrabboh looked shocked.

Stockton said nothing.

Piccinini reiterated the evidence against Stockton. He said he and Clark had information that Stockton had talked about duct-taping a bomb to a guy's chest.

Stockton grinned, as if Piccinini's comments amused him. Clark interpreted it as a good sign, as if Stockton was saying to himself, "Holy shit, they do know."

Latouf pulled Stockton aside.

"You just got to tell the truth," he said. "This is going to be your only shot."

The interview restarted.

"All right," Stockton said, "let me tell you."

He gave his explanation of what happened.

About three to six months before August 28, 2003, Stockton said, he had watched a TV show that reminded him of another show he had seen years earlier—a show about a bank robbery in which a woman was forced to wear a bomb, and the heist succeeded. Stockton told Rothstein about the original show, and Rothstein told Diehl-Armstrong and those two liked the idea of robbing a bank. Rothstein and Diehl-Armstrong needed money.

Stockton suggested using a pizza deliveryman in the robbery because Rothstein enjoyed pizza so much. Rothstein said he knew just the person—Brian Wells. Diehl-Armstrong knew Wells through Ken Barnes.

A short time later, and about a month before August 30, 2003, Rothstein asked Stockton if he would cut two pieces of metal. He showed Stockton a schematic of a collar Rothstein wanted made. Stockton went to the garage of D.M., Rothstein's close friend, and used a welding arc to cut the two pieces of metal. Stockton fashioned them into a handcuff-shaped collar. He gave the device to Rothstein, who said he would take things from there.

Latouf and Abdrabboh stopped the interview. Stockton had just admitted to making part of the collar bomb, but this was the first time the lawyers had heard about it.

Latouf and Abdrabboh went out into the hall. They told Clark and Piccinini the interview could not go any further because they had no idea what Stockton was going to say. Everyone took a break.

Piccinini and Clark called their bosses. Clark was no longer both supervising and investigating the Wells case. Since August 2005, the head of the FBI office in Erie had been a special agent who had come from Washington D.C., Andrew Wilson. He had a law degree and had also served with the FBI in Chicago. Immediately upon his arrival in Erie, he reviewed the Wells file and agreed with the approach of Clark and Wick. Wilson told Clark that he would always support him until the end of the case— and Wilson would.

Clark spoke briefly to Wilson on the phone about Stockton. Latouf and Abdrabboh got reassurance that Stockton's information would help him get a deal, and that he was still, as of that moment, a queen for a day.

Stockton resumed talking. On August 27, 2003, the day before Wells was killed, Stockton said, he walked outside Rothstein's house and saw Rothstein talking with Diehl-Armstrong and Wells. Rothstein saw Stockton.

"Get back in the house," Rothstein said.

After the meeting broke up, Stockton said, Rothstein asked him to help load something into Rothstein's van—a device that weighed ten to fifteen pounds and was wrapped in a white T-shirt. Rothstein told Stockton it was "the fucking bomb."

Stockton said Rothstein explained the bank-robbery plot to him, including how a pizza order would be a part of it and how Stockton was to be at the Kwik Fill to wait for the money. Rothstein said he himself would be outside the bank, Diehl-Armstrong would set up the sites for the notes on the highway; Barnes would follow her. Rothstein said to be here, at his house, between noon and 1:00 P.M. the next day, August 28, 2003.

"I don't want to do this," Stockton said, according to his version.

Stockton said Rothstein told him he didn't have a fucking choice. Rothstein, he said, told him Diehl-Armstrong would kill him, that she didn't even like the way he looked.

The next day, August 28, Stockton returned to Rothstein's house at the designated time, after his housepainting job. Stockton walked to the site of the TV tower. He saw Wells, Diehl-Armstrong, Barnes and Rothstein, who stood near the open doors of his van. Rothstein carried a handgun.

Rothstein ordered Stockton to go to Rothstein's van and get the bomb. Stockton did, and walked toward Wells, who was crying. Stockton told Wells the bomb was not real.

Rothstein fired a single shot from the handgun. Wells, frightened, dropped to his knees.

Stockton thought Rothstein, his friend, would shoot him next, in the back.

Wells stood up. Stockton, frightened of Rothstein, put the collar around Wells' neck. Stockton tightened it.

Click.

Stockton told Wells the bomb wasn't real.

"It's fucking real," Rothstein said.

Stockton protested. Rothstein told him to go back to

the house. Stockton walked slowly. He looked back to make sure Rothstein would not shoot him. He walked in zigs and zags so he would be harder to hit with a bullet.

Rothstein walked into the house and told Stockton to go to the Kwik Fill. Stockton said he did, out of fear, but eventually left the gas station and went back to Rothstein's house. Stockton said he watched the footage of Wells on TV. A police cruiser idled on the dirt road next to Rothstein's garage.

———

Stockton said he knew nothing of the bank-robbery notes and nothing of the cane gun. He said he had no idea Roden had been in the freezer until Stockton was arrested on the fugitive-from-justice charges. At the time Wells was killed, Stockton said, he needed money to hire a lawyer to defend him against the rape charges in Bellingham. Robert Pinetti was involved in the plot, Stockton said. He said his job was to persuade Wells to cooperate. Barnes was paying Pinetti with drugs, Stockton said. He said Pinetti panicked after Wells was killed and that Barnes gave Pinetti the drugs—the methadone mixed with the alprazolam in the Xanax—that killed Pinetti. The deadly mixture had a name, Stockton said. It was called a "hotshot." He said Rothstein called it "super dope."

———

The interview with Stockton ended at 10:00 P.M. on March 27, 2007—or 1:00 A.M. eastern time. Clark went to bed that night confident: they had Stockton locked in.

With Stockton on the stand, Barnes and Diehl-Armstrong would be dead.

Clark left Seattle also wanting Stockton indicted; he wanted him as a witness and a defendant. The contents of Stockton's queen-for-a-day proffer, of course, would be off-limits as evidence, but the statements from Barnes, as well as evidence from the two people who had called *America's Most Wanted* about Stockton, would be enough to rope Stockton into the conspiracy and get an indictment. Stockton could plead guilty, Clark thought, testify against Diehl-Armstrong and Barnes, and get a deserved break at sentencing. Clark just wanted him charged with something.

Latouf was still pushing for full immunity, a possibility that Piccinini had yet to rule out. Latouf figured he had Piccinini's attention. Federal prosecutors, in Latouf's experience, were always open to flipping a codefendant into a witness to make their case a slam dunk.

As a prosecutor, Piccinini had to step through a thicket of legal complexities. One of them, as far as Clark could tell, was the concern that Stockton, without full immunity, would end up recanting his entire proffered statements, which would make him useless as a witness. Without Stockton's testimony, the case against Diehl-Armstrong and Barnes could weaken. Piccinini would risk having nothing.

Like any prosecutor dealing with potential codefendants, Piccinini had to weigh how to handle Stockton's testimony if Stockton were indicted. Piccinini had to consider the Bruton rule, named after a 1968 U.S. Supreme Court decision,

Bruton v. the United States. It deals with the Sixth Amendment right of a defendant to cross-examine witnesses and the Fifth Amendment right against self-incrimination.

The Bruton case prohibits prosecutors from using a defendant's statements to police against another defendant—unless the codefendant who made the statements agrees to testify and be subject to cross-examination. Without immunity or a plea deal, that is a precarious proposition for a codefendant. Immunizing Stockton to some degree would remove any Bruton problems; it would get him on the stand against Barnes and Diehl-Armstrong with no possibility for self-incrimination, unless Stockton lied.*

Clark understood the Bruton issues, though, unlike Piccinini, he was not bound by them. Clark knew what Stockton had said, and he knew Stockton was involved. Stockton's claim that Rothstein forced him to lock the bomb to Wells was not without problems for Stockton. If Stockton was so scared of Rothstein, why did Stockton go to the Kwik Fill? Why didn't he run away? Clark wanted Stockton indicted, but with a plea deal in place that would help Stockton but still put him in prison. Clark also realized that whatever Stockton said in the queen-for-a-day proffer could not be used against him.

The internal debate over immunity for Stockton illustrated, more than anything else in the Wells investigation,

---

*Another, more cumbersome solution to offset Bruton concerns is to try codefendants separately. In the Wells case, following such a strategy would have necessitated three trials: one each for Diehl-Armstrong, Barnes and Stockton.

how the approach of Clark, as an investigator, differed from that of Piccinini, as a prosecutor. Clark aimed as an investigator to uncover as much as he could, including a motive, in the Wells case. More information produced more leads, which produced more indictments. Clark evaluated each piece of evidence to find out whether he had the full story. Piccinini, in Clark's view, parsed evidence and testimony based on what he could present in court.

When Piccinini considered whether Stockton should get immunity, Piccinini, as was his job, placed the debate in the context of the adjusted reality of the courtroom. Piccinini, after all, was responsible for winning a conviction. When Clark considered whether Stockton should get immunity, he placed the debate more in the context of his overall understanding of what occurred on August 28, 2003.

Clark realized Piccinini had valid concerns, but he thought his concerns were legitimate as well. Between the two of them, Clark thought, a compromise could be in order: indict Stockton; require him to take the stand as part of the plea deal, thus negating the Bruton issues; and work to have Stockton receive a sentence that accounted for his cooperation.

———

Whether Stockton would get immunity, and what kind, remained unsettled on May 14, 2007, when a guest by the name of Floyd Smith left the Hampton Inn in Erie, Pennsylvania, for a law office downtown. "Floyd Smith" was really Floyd Stockton, who had traveled to Erie for more queen-for-a-day conferences with Latouf, Clark, Wick and Piccinini.

Latouf had told Stockton his continued cooperation would be worthwhile.

"Look," Latouf said, "there's a chance you could walk."

Stockton said he still couldn't believe that would happen.

Stockton was initially standoffish during his visit to Latouf's downtown office. He said he was unsure whom he could trust; he said almost no one in law enforcement had ever treated him fairly.

Stockton looked at Clark.

"He's never lied to me," Stockton said.

Stockton then sat in Clark's government-leased Ford Explorer as a passenger. He took Clark, Wick and Latouf on a tour of his whereabouts on August 28, 2003. At the TV tower, Stockton did not hesitate: he said he locked the bomb to Wells' neck, but unwillingly. Stockton cried and shook as he spoke. He said he had been scared that Rothstein, Diehl-Armstrong or Barnes would shoot him in the back.

"I'm a convicted sex offender," Stockton said he thought at the time. "No one will give a shit if I'm shot dead back here."

————

Stockton repeated the tour the next day, with Piccinini present. Piccinini would take the information to his superiors at the Justice Department and decide on what to do.

The tour group drove to the tower site. Stockton, still

a queen for a day, played himself. He directed everyone to certain spots, to show what happened on August 28, 2003. Wick played Wells. Clark played Diehl-Armstrong. Piccinini played Barnes. Latouf played Rothstein; in a bit of humor, Piccinini made that casting decision, based on Latouf's belly.

The miniature drama ended.

"Floyd," Clark said, "I don't know what's going to happen from here, but you stood up for yourself. You made K.W. proud, your father proud. You did the right thing."

Stockton turned to Piccinini.

"Marshall, I don't care what happens to me," he said. "I'm just doing this because it is the right thing. I don't care what you do. If I'm going to meet my maker or be incarcerated for the rest of my life, I've accepted it. I did it because it was the right thing."

———

Clark by now had come to agree with whatever might happen to Stockton: indictment with no immunity; full immunity, which would prohibit an indictment; or a plea deal in which Stockton would testify and get a sentencing break.

Clark trusted Piccinini's judgment. Most of all, Clark wanted the Wells case to go to trial. If immunizing Stockton would help accomplish that, great. If indicting Stockton or reaching a plea deal would help accomplish that, great. Clark would be ready either way.

Stockton testified before the grand jury in the Wells case on June 26, 2007. He got full immunity.

22

Fractured and Evil

During the queen-for-a-day proffers, Clark came to believe Stockton reveled in the give-and-take. Stockton seemed to both fear and enjoy the strain, the fact that his future wavered with every detail he disclosed. Stockton's lawyers scoffed at Clark's contention. Stockton had told them an indictment would not scare him. He just did not want to go to prison, they said. He wanted his story told.

Stockton, his lawyers said, hoped for a book or movie deal.

"Get in line," Clark responded. "Everyone who's touched this wants that. But they only have pieces, not the whole story."

By the summer of 2007, Clark had sorted through all the stories for four years. He and Wick had taken to calling all the persons of interest in the Wells case—Diehl-Armstrong, Barnes, Stockton and the dead Rothstein—the "fractured intellectuals," in a nod to Rothstein's cadre that went by the same name. They all possessed high intelligence, but twisted their brainpower to concoct a wicked plot. They all came up with different tales of what happened on August 28, 2003. Rothstein, Diehl-Armstrong, Barnes, Stockton: each was a kind of sinister Scheherazade, trying to stay free by spinning 1,001 stories.

Rothstein had denied knowing anything. Stockton, Barnes and Diehl-Armstrong said they did not participate or, if they did, the involvement was unknowing, unwilling or minor. Each fractured intellectual cast him- or herself in a different shade of evil.

Clark constructed his own narrative, what he believed was the most accurate account.

———

On August 27, 2003, Diehl-Armstrong, Rothstein, Barnes, Stockton and Wells gathered near Rothstein's house and then at the clearing at the end of the dirt road. Missing was Roden, whom Diehl-Armstrong silenced with a shotgun seventeen days earlier. Clark thought Roden was supposed to have done something in the scheme, though driving a getaway car seemed improbable, unless earlier incarnations called for Roden to drive Wells or even Rothstein to the bank. With Roden out of the way, Diehl-Armstrong, Barnes, Rothstein, Stockton and Wells were certain no one would discover their plan.

Roden's body in the freezer reminded them what Diehl-Armstrong would do to a snitch.

Diehl-Armstrong, as far as Clark could determine, came up with the bank-robbery plot, though she was not the mastermind behind all the details. Rothstein filled that role. In the late spring or early summer of 2003, Diehl-Armstrong first proposed her idea to Rothstein and the others. She was constantly complaining about her father, how he was giving away her fucking inheritance to those fucking vultures who were his neighbors and friends; she was going to put a stop to it and secure her inheritance. She solicited Barnes to kill her father; Barnes wanted $100,000 up front. Diehl-Armstrong proposed to Rothstein that they should rob a PNC Bank, the bank that had mistreated her, and use the money to pay Barnes. Pinetti, Wells' druggie friend, was recruited to persuade Wells to go along. Of all the participants, Pinetti was the most unreliable: he was wasted so much of the time.

Stockton said he got the idea for a collar bomb from a TV show, which Clark and Wick could never find. Perhaps the fractured intellectuals agreed to the plan to get Diehl-Armstrong to shut up about her father's money. More likely, Rothstein and the others participated because they needed money, too.

Rothstein insisted on a sale price of $250,000 for the homestead at 8645 Peach Street. That was the same amount of money Diehl-Armstrong said the bank robbery would yield. Maybe Rothstein figured he would need at least that much to placate his sister, who wanted the junk pile of a house sold and the estate settled. Maybe Rothstein hoped to use the money to try to stay in the house until he died of the cancer he knew was eating away at him.

Ken Barnes needed money to buy more crack. Wells, if what Barnes said was accurate, needed money to cover the drug debts he incurred, not because he used crack, but because he bought drugs for Jessica Hoopsick and his other prostitutes in exchange for sex in that sordid upstairs bedroom in Barnes' disgusting house. Robert Pinetti needed money for drugs and because he was closing in on bankruptcy. Floyd Stockton needed money to hire a lawyer to represent him on the rape charges. Diehl-Armstrong needed money because she could never get enough of it. She wanted her father dead so she could get more.

They were all obsessed with money, each of the fractured intellectuals. Their levels of violence and culpability differed among them, but their deceit and matchless desire for money pulled them together like magnets. For Diehl-Armstrong and Rothstein, their avarice fit with their obsessions to hang on to the past, to the prosperity their families once enjoyed. For Diehl-Armstrong, her father's money would keep her comfortable and secure; she was smart enough, after all, to deserve a fortune. She was Marjorie Diehl-Armstrong, the gifted granddaughter of wealthy grandparents who told her all that cash in their safe would one day belong to her, their rightful heir. Rothstein was desperate to hang on to a place to live. The Rola Cola plant was gone. So was the income it had provided; Rothstein had nowhere to go except the house of his late mother. Rothstein believed he deserved better, too—he, Bill Rothstein, the robotics genius, smart enough that he should be in Mensa, was only a substitute teacher?—but the house at 8645 Peach Street was really all he had left.

In their quests to cling to what once was, Diehl-Armstrong and Rothstein exhibited traits not unlike the worst characteristics of the city of Erie, where they had lived all their lives. Instead of focusing their energy and intellect on changing a course for the future, Rothstein and Diehl-Armstrong chained themselves to an era that had slipped away long ago. She was no longer the slim beauty with the multiple college degrees and a young life full of promise. He was no longer the heir to a family business that had made his father, Mad Man Matty, a local star. Diehl-Armstrong and Rothstein had made nothing of themselves, though they believed it was everyone else who had failed them.

Rothstein and Diehl-Armstrong, engaged to be married once, in better times, turned to each other. Rothstein turned also to one of his oldest friends, Stockton, who told the FBI he was never sexually involved with Rothstein but who was extremely close to him nonetheless.*

With help from their strange but smart friends, Barnes included, Diehl-Armstrong and Rothstein would use the bank-robbery plot to prove their brilliance, to show that

---

*Stockton told the Erie police of Rothstein, "As far as I know, he's not gay" and "I know he's had sex with girls; he's commented about it."

everyone else was fucking wrong. The bank-robbery plot gave the fractured intellectuals, who in their weirdness were rotten peas in a rotten pod, something to do. Once they started going with the plan, they would see it through to the end. The plot gave their maliciousness a purpose.

———

When Clark explained his theory to other agents, when he detailed to them the motivations of Diehl-Armstrong and Rothstein, they would often reply, as Clark's superiors did, early on, that none of it made sense: the whole bank-robbery plan was so bizarre that anyone with half a brain would realize it was too complicated to work. Why would Diehl-Armstrong solicit Barnes to kill her father instead of killing him herself? It's not like she had never killed a man. Why the complicated notes? For people who were supposed to be brilliant, Diehl-Armstrong and Rothstein did a lot of stupid things. It was all so irrational.

That was the point, Clark would explain, reaching back to his forensic-psychology training. The entire plot was irrational because the people who crafted it were irrational. The worst mistake investigators could make in the Wells case, Clark said, would be to gauge the evidence in the context of how normal criminals would behave. These are intelligent but abnormal people, Clark would explain, especially Diehl-Armstrong, whose mental problems and narcissism blinded her to reality.

As for Rothstein, Clark believed he simply did not care. He did not care whether the plot worked, whether

Diehl-Armstrong got her money, whether Wells lived or died. Sure, Rothstein would have liked to get money for himself, to keep his mother's house, to satiate his deranged needs. But those outcomes were all secondary. What mattered most to Rothstein was the game.

Rothstein knew he was dying of cancer when he helped undertake the scheme. Rothstein listened to Diehl-Armstrong's plan and ran with it; he saw it as his chance to create, before the cancer took him, the ultimate criminal masterpiece—a design in which he, Bill Rothstein, the grand manipulator, would decide whether someone lived or died.

Rothstein gave the plot's ultimate command: "Act now, think later or you will die." If Wells lived, according to Rothstein's design, the ploy would have worked: Wells would have handed the money to Rothstein before Wells was caught, and Wells would have exonerated himself by telling the police he was a hostage forced to wear the bomb. If the bomb were to go off and Wells were killed? The plan would have succeeded, according to Rothstein's design. Wells would have handed the money to Rothstein before he died, and his death would have eliminated Wells as a witness.

And, finally, if Wells were killed and no one got the money? Another success, for Rothstein. He would have killed a man and gotten away with it; if police were to catch him, Rothstein would be dead of cancer soon anyway. If Diehl-Armstrong turned on Rothstein, while he was still alive, and said he was behind the Wells plot, no one would believe her, because she was crazy. Rothstein, if he lived, would cut a deal, like he had done in the Louis Allessie case. Maybe he would kill himself. Either way, the Wells plot would be his perfect crime, his chance to show the world his genius. It would be William D. Schmuck's revenge.

———

As far as Clark could determine, the events of August 28, 2003, unfolded at the site of the TV tower in the way Barnes and Stockton described. Wells drove up, Diehl-Armstrong and the others were present; Rothstein took out the bomb and fired a shot in the air; Stockton and Pinetti tackled a petrified Wells, whom Barnes punched; and Stockton, for whatever reason, locked the bomb to his neck.

Clark pitied Pinetti. He didn't seem like a bad guy. He lacked the deviousness that made Diehl-Armstrong, Rothstein and Barnes so merciless. For whatever reason— drugs, money or both—Pinetti agreed to take part; his job was to persuade Wells to go along. Pinetti learned too late he had made a pact with a group of devils; then he was dead. Whether Barnes or anyone else gave him the drugs—the "hotshot," the "super dope"—he used to overdose, Clark could never be sure.

Clark pitied Wells, to a degree. Wells' presence at the meeting on August 27, as well as his attendance on the porch at the party at Barnes' crack house in June 2003, proved he agreed to rob the bank with the collar device locked to his neck. The fractured intellectuals did not choose Wells at random; Wells floated in their off-kilter orbit. Wells, according to his IQ and despite his demeanor, was not dumb, and he possessed street smarts; he knew his way around the underworld of Erie's lower east side. Wells' shaved pubic area, his penchant for prostitutes, his business with drug dealers, and, what Clark learned about later, Wells' psychopathic and paranoid tendencies as a teenager: these attributes indicated Wells had enough of a deviant and devious side to have willingly signed on to hold up the PNC Bank in the Summit Towne Centre, thinking the bomb would be fake.* Wells' death was a tragedy, but he was by no means an angel.

Wells' deceitfulness was no match for the unmitigated guile of Diehl-Armstrong, Rothstein and Barnes. Wells was in over his head: Wells in that regard both conspired in the pizza bomber plot and was victimized by it. Wells had to have been in a state of disbelief when the bomb was locked to his neck; he had thought the bomb would be phony, that his journey would be like the newspaper's Great Key Hunt. Had he known beforehand the bomb was real, Wells would have never driven down the dirt road. He had neither the wherewithal nor the demeanor to let someone put a live bomb on him.

Yet Wells, perhaps frightened of the notes' commands to act or die, still walked nonchalantly into the bank. Wells' slow pace undermined the plot. His slow pace gave the police enough time to arrive, which forced Rothstein to abandon his post outside the bank, where Wells was to give him $250,000, a ridiculously high amount for a bank robbery. Rothstein left the bank empty-handed.

---

*The psychological report on the sixteen-year-old Wells came to light in late 2011.

What was Wells thinking? Clark reminded himself not to attempt to understand this case through the prisms of rational thought and logic. Who would ever know why Wells acted as he did? His behavior would remain a mystery.

Many other elements of the case would remain unexplained or unsolved. Clark and Wick never found Rothstein's gold Mercury Marquis. They never found the dark blue car that Michael Douglas, the draftsman on his way to the movies, saw following Wells' Geo Metro. They never determined who wrote the notes, which Clark believed were typed and then traced.

Clark and Wick could never pinpoint why Diehl-Armstrong, Rothstein and the others picked August 28 to execute their plan. Clark and Wick thought astrology or numerology probably or maybe even American history influenced the choice. Stockton told Clark and Wick that August 28 supposedly marked an important event in the Vietnam War, though no particular battle or overseas event stood out on the date.*

Clark and Wick never figured out for certain how much each of the fractured intellectuals knew about the plot. Diehl-Armstrong, Barnes and Stockton, if they were to be believed on the subject, said they knew only parts of the

---

*On August 28, 1968, Abbie Hoffman helped lead the protests at the Democratic National Convention in Chicago. Hoffman interested Rothstein, a self-styled anarchist; Clark did not discount that the fractured intellectuals might have chosen August 28 as a paean to Hoffman, a countercultural hero.

plan. The complete file had to have rested in the mind of Rothstein.

Clark was certain, however, that, as often with the case with thieves, no one trusted the other in the pizza bomber plot. Diehl-Armstrong led the paranoia. She and Rothstein eyed each other, waiting to see who would break first and reveal Roden's dead body to the police. After the plot fell apart, with Wells' death, Diehl-Armstrong feared Rothstein had conned her.

She must have been apoplectic, Clark thought, when Rothstein told her he had no money, that their expertly planned bank robbery had gone bad. Was Rothstein telling the truth? Was he hiding the money? Diehl-Armstrong had no way of knowing at that point, so, Clark believed, she went to find out for herself.

Though Clark could never prove his theory, he believed Diehl-Armstrong stopped along I-79 that afternoon and climbed over the guardrail to grab the instructions that had been placed near the McKean Township sign. She wanted to get the note before the police found it. Clark also believed Diehl-Armstrong tore up that site looking for a stash of money she thought Rothstein might have been trying to keep from her. Diehl-Armstrong would have wanted what was hers.

———

The indictments were on their way in midsummer 2007. The waiting could not continue; the law was forcing the issue. The U.S. Attorney's Office had convened the grand jury in the Wells case eighteen months earlier, then had its term extended another six months. That extension was due to expire in early July 2007. Marshall Piccinini would have to ask the grand jury to indict before then, or he would have to convene a new grand jury and present all the evidence anew. That would be a time-consuming option.

Clark and Wick understood Piccinini's cautiousness, his desire to use as much time as he could to build a case. They understood why he wanted to wait until the last moment to ask the grand jury to indict.

Piccinini was always asking them to bring back more evidence. His hunches were usually correct. Piccinini especially emphasized the importance of Clark and Wick independently verifying, or debunking, the contents of Kelly Makela's notes.

Clark and Wick agreed on the soundness of that strategy. They followed through on Piccinini's requests that they interview people connected to events mentioned in Makela's notes. But Clark and Wick agreed between themselves that Piccinini by early 2007 had enough to indict Diehl-Armstrong, Barnes and Stockton. They were tired of waiting.

The frustration of Clark and Wick had peaked on February 16, 2007, at a meeting in Pittsburgh. It had been called by Piccinini's boss, Mary Beth Buchanan, the U.S. attorney for the Western District of Pennsylvania, based in Pittsburgh. Buchanan, who had done none of the groundwork on the case, summoned Piccinini, Clark, Wick and other prosecutors and investigators to her office to discuss the status of the Wells investigation.

Clark and Wick fumed as they sat through the meeting,

which some twelve people attended, with multiple representatives from the FBI, ATF and U.S. Attorney's Office. Clark was dismayed. He thought the briefings from the top officials in the room had left out important details. Clark did not want to breach protocol and second-guess those above him, but he wanted all the facts on the table. Like a schoolboy, he raised his hand. Buchanan called on him to speak.

Clark mainly reviewed what Barnes had told him and Wick, how Barnes' statements tightened the investigation. The others in the room weren't convinced. Indicting Diehl-Armstrong was a possibility, they said, but not Barnes or Stockton—at least not yet. Buchanan wanted more evidence.

———

The request left Clark demoralized—again. Even before the summit at Buchanan's office, he had survived calls from within the FBI that another veteran agent "scrub" his case file to see if he had missed anything. Clark was grateful the agent selected to perform the scrubbing declined, citing Clark's reputation for diligence. Just knowing that others in the bureau had asked for the review infuriated Clark.

Wick, who had been living out of a hotel in Erie for nearly four years, saw his marriage collapse during the investigation, a casualty, he believed, of his spending too little time at home. Clark's health suffered; his blood pressure rose so much he had to go on medication. The stresses increased every day, particularly with the public comments about why the hell this case was taking so long.

Diehl-Armstrong added to the anxiety. She apparently wanted Clark and Wick dead. They had learned of her threats two years earlier, in November 2005, from Jennifer Brininger, one of the inmates who had befriended Diehl-Armstrong. Brininger knew someone "on the outside" who was a member of the Latin Kings gang from New York City; Brininger said Diehl-Armstrong asked her to get in touch with her Latin Kings contact to see if that person could kill Clark, Wick and Kelly Makela.

"She wanted to know if Kelly Makela could be shot through the gate from 500 yards away," Brininger said.

Clark and Wick could never be certain about whether Diehl-Armstrong was serious in seeking to have Makela and them killed. Diehl-Armstrong said a lot of things when she ran her mouth, but she had also shot two men to death. For as long as the Wells investigation lasted, Clark and Wick worried whether Diehl-Armstrong had put them on a hit list.

———

The time eventually came for indictments. Clark and Wick had done all they could, to the satisfaction of the U.S. Attorney's Office. The grand jury's term was about to expire. On July 9, 2007, after nearly four years of investigation, Piccinini got indictments against Diehl-Armstrong and Barnes.

In a fit of celebration, Clark hit the floor for pushups.

PART III

RESOLUTION

23

"A Limited Role"

The United States District Courthouse in Erie fills a block on Perry Square, a park at the center of downtown that is as old as the city. The courthouse occupies the site of what once was one of Erie's grandest dwellings—a Greek Revival mansion built around 1829 for Rufus Reed, a merchant who financed the construction of Commodore Oliver Hazard Perry's fleet. Reed's father was Colonel Seth Reed, who built the Presque Isle Hotel, outside of which the surveyors placed the Erie Stone in 1795.

Erie got its first federal courthouse in 1895. The federal government in 1937 razed it and erected, on the same spot, a modern courthouse funded by $365,000 in New Deal money. A $34 million expansion and renovation in 2004 added a new main entrance and a glass atrium that fronts the southeastern edge of Perry Square; in the distance stands a statue of the park's namesake, triumphant in victory.

On the morning of Wednesday, July 11, 2007, three years, ten months and eighteen days after the bombing death of Brian Wells, television news trucks lined Perry Square near the federal courthouse. Reporters and FBI agents and ATF agents and state police troopers and courthouse staff streamed into the courthouse's glass atrium and down the hall. They gathered in a large jury assembly room converted to the staging area for the biggest news conference yet in the pizza bomber case. It was scheduled for 1:30 P.M.

The grand jury had returned indictments two days earlier, on July 9. The government would unseal them today.

———

The announcement of the indictments would come from Mary Beth Buchanan. Piccinini, Clark and Wick gathered in the room with everyone else.

Clark that morning woke considering the day his best in law enforcement. He and Wick had closed FBI Major Case 203 with what they were certain was unassailable evidence.

As he waited in the jury assembly room, surrounded by reporters and crowds of congratulatory agents and police officers, Clark, though jubilant, was beset by a feeling of dread. Wells' family had become unpredictable. They were angry.

Long gone were the days when Wells' sister would send a letter to the editor of the *Erie Times-News* that praised the FBI and pleaded with Wells' assailants, whoever they were, that "law enforcement can and will help you." As the Wells investigation lengthened, and more evidence surfaced in the newspapers and on TV about what Wells may have or may not have done, the Wells family soured on the FBI and the U.S. Attorney's Office and finally turned on them. No way, the brothers and sisters said, could their gentle brother Brian have been anything other than a victim. Under no circumstances, they said, would Brian have become knowingly involved with such a wretched group of misfits as Diehl-Armstrong, Rothstein, Barnes and Stockton.

The morning of July 11, 2007, Clark, Piccinini, Buchanan and others briefed Wells' mother and siblings about the content of the indictments. Clark thought the relatives might seem calm, but you never knew with the Wells family, especially Brian's brother John. He had flown in from Arizona and was the family's de facto spokesman. He had gone on TV before to disparage the FBI. After the meeting with Wells' family, Clark urged Buchanan not to let the Wellses attend the ensuing news conference. He knew the family was upset at the evidence that Wells had willingly participated, to a degree, in the plot. He worried that the family, if present at the news conference, would deny Wells was in on the scheme.

The U.S. Attorney's Office, with Buchanan in charge, responded that no one could bar the Wellses from a public building. Clark agreed, with reservations. The Wellses were entitled to have a news conference of their own, even somewhere else in the federal courthouse, Clark said, but he did not like the idea of the family being in the same room when Buchanan delivered what, for the Wellses, could only be taken as bad news. He said the news conference could turn into a circus.

Clark lost the argument to the U.S. Attorney's Office. One of the best professional days of his life quickly disintegrated into one of the worst.

———

Buchanan announced that the grand jury charged Diehl-Armstrong and Barnes with the same three felonies: conspiracy to commit armed robbery, aiding and abetting an armed bank robbery involving a death and aiding and abetting the use of a destructive device—the bomb—in a crime of violence. A conviction on the count of armed bank robbery would carry a life sentence because Wells died in the robbery. A conviction on the conspiracy charge would carry five years in prison, and a conviction on the destructive-device charge would carry a maximum sentence of thirty years to life.

The indictments alleged the conspiracy included Diehl-Armstrong's killing of Jim Roden, identified in the indictment as J.R. The indictments listed two unindicted co-conspirators, both of them dead: W.R., or William Rothstein, and B.W., or Brian Wells. Wells, the U.S. Attorney's Office said, had been involved, though to what extent remained uncertain.

"Earlier today we met with the family of Brian Wells,"

Buchanan said from the podium. "As prosecutors and investigators, we have not been able to discuss with them the details of this investigation. For some time they have wanted us to publicly disclose the role of their family member.

"We can only make decisions in a case based on what the facts actually are, not what we want them to be. Unfortunately, our investigation has led to the belief that Brian became involved in a limited role with a group of individuals who planned to rob the PNC Bank.

"We do not know the extent to which the others planned on him dying that day, but we do know unfortunately that Brian participated in a limited role in the planning and the carrying out of this robbery. Sadly, the plans of the other individuals were much more sinister than Brian's—much more sinister—and he died as a result. It may be that his role transitioned from that of the planning stages to being an unwilling part in the scheme."

Other officials spoke, but Buchanan had to return to the question of the day: what did Brian Wells know? The reporters kept asking for an explanation.

"We're not exactly sure how much the robber knew," she said. "We know that he was involved in a limited extent with the planning of this. We don't know what he knew about the construction or how this bomb would be activated or when it would be activated. In fact, we're not even sure that he was absolutely positive that this bomb was going to be detonated.

"We can't talk about why he became involved. We can't comment on what his motives might have been. We know from the information we've collected he was involved in the planning stages. We have reason to believe that certainly at the point where the bomb was strapped to his neck that he did express a strong desire to terminate. However, for whatever reason, unfortunately he did go forward and make the bank robbery."

Buchanan said Wells was coerced into the plot just before the bomb was locked to his neck, but that Wells nonetheless did not abandon the conspiracy. She described him as both a participant and a victim.

"There were opportunities when he could have let people know what was happening, and that is why," Buchanan said, "he was both."

The catcalls sounded throughout the room. Clark groaned. Wells' relatives were the source of the discontent.

"Liar!" Wells' sister Barbara Wells shouted at Buchanan. "Liar!"

Buchanan discussed the bomb locked to Wells' neck. Barbara Wells got louder. She suggested Buchanan strap a bomb around her own neck.

"Let's have it reenacted and see what you do, Mary Beth!" Barbara Wells yelled.

Buchanan made no direct response. A reporter asked her about the family's fury.

"We knew this was going to be very difficult for them to accept," she said.

Several minutes later, Buchanan said she would take no more questions. She and the officials and investigators left the room, though they already had lost control of it.

Wells' family had hijacked the news conference, proclaiming a tale of betrayal and rage that, for the TV cameras, overshadowed even the indictments.

John Wells stepped to the podium. This was his news conference now.

"I would like to let everyone know that Brian was a complete innocent murder victim in this case," he said. "There's no evidence to suggest otherwise, or you would have heard that evidence today.

"My brother is a brutal-murder victim. He does not know any of these people. The fact that he delivered Rothstein a pizza does not make him a co-conspirator. When he delivered pizzas to the DA, that did not make him a prosecutor. When he delivered pizza to Hamot Medical Center, that did not make him a doctor. When he delivers pizzas to a murderer, that does not make him a co-conspirator. I have not seen any evidence to suggest he knew these people in any way other than he might have delivered them a pizza."

John Wells said he wanted Diehl-Armstrong and Barnes prosecuted "to the fullest extent of the law, but I don't want my brother used to prosecute them."

His voice rose.

"When you have a bomb locked to your neck and the federal authorities chop your head off to get the bomb off, there was no way Brian put that on himself," John Wells said. "Nineteen hours after that bomb went off, the federal authorities chopped his head off to get that collar off. Brian did not put that collar on himself.

"He did not know any of these people. That is why they had to lure him to the tower to clamp the bomb on him. They grabbed him at gunpoint. If you're a co-conspirator, you don't put a bomb on yourself after you have been shot at."

John Wells derided the police for not calling the bomb squad sooner.* He tore into Buchanan, the FBI and everyone else who investigated the case.

"I can't imagine that they're trying to get the public to believe this," he said. "There is no satisfaction in this because these two people [Diehl-Armstrong and Barnes] aren't the only people involved.

"This whole case has been unbelievable from the beginning. Where's the evidence? There is no evidence. You can't link a man without evidence."

A reporter asked John Wells why the U.S. Attorney's Office would say his brother was involved if he really was not.

"It's easier for them because they didn't do their job," he said. "The truth will come out. It's sad that these people just came here on national TV and are going to be made to look stupid.

"I'd like to see their evidence."

---

*John Wells was the executor of his brother's estate, which he opened in 2004. The Wells family at the time filed court records indicating the estate was planning to file a suit against unspecified parties, but the estate never took such action.

———

Clark felt sick. Nearly four years of grinding detective work, and this is what the public was going to remember: not the indictments, the solving of the case, but the image of John Wells raging on national television, yelling about his brother's head getting chopped off, questioning the integrity and intelligence of Clark and all the other investigators.

Clark headed back to his office. His mind went over all the information he and Wick had compiled. Clark pledged to answer, in public, at trial, John Wells' question, "Where's the evidence?"

24

Mental Illness

I t would be far too presumptuous to conclude that the bank-robbery scheme was purposely designed so Diehl-Armstrong and Barnes would avoid the death penalty if caught and convicted. But that is what happened. Wells' participation in the plot, however uncertain or limited, removed the possibility that the U.S. Attorney's Office would seek capital punishment.

The United States Code, Title 18, Section 2113 (e) allows for the death penalty for "whoever kills someone during a bank robbery." Mary Beth Buchanan told reporters that Wells' role precluded the government from charging Barnes and Diehl-Armstrong with actually killing him and committing a homicide during a bank robbery. If Wells had been a party to his death, how could the government charge someone with murdering him? Wells died as part of a bank robbery, but he was not like a bank employee or bank customer whom the robber shoots and kills. At Piccinini's request, the grand jury indicted Barnes and Diehl-Armstrong of participating in an armed robbery involving not a murder, but a death, an offense that carries a maximum sentence of life.

The precision of the indictments impressed Clark. He had long ago come to appreciate the crushing power inherent in an expert application of Title 18, the volume of the United States Code that concerns crimes and criminal offenses. Piccinini had mined Title 18 to find the offenses that best fit the activities of Diehl-Armstrong and Barnes. He had obtained an indictment that charged each of them as aiders or abettors. To prove his case in court, Piccinini would not have to show that Barnes or Diehl-Armstrong directly robbed the PNC Bank. He would only have to demonstrate that Diehl-Armstrong and Barnes had done something, no matter how big or how small, to further the heist: in for a penny, in for a pound.

The inclusion of Jim Roden's death in the indictment was another example of Piccinini's acumen. The indictment alleged Roden's death was an "overt act" that showed the involvement of Diehl-Armstrong in the bank-robbery plot; the grand jury in the indictment accused her of killing Roden to keep him "from disclosing the bank robbery plan that was being formulated by the co-conspirators." At trial, Piccinini would be able to strengthen the case against Diehl-Armstrong by presenting the jury evidence, in sickening detail after sickening detail, that she had already pleaded guilty but mentally ill to gunning down her boyfriend, whose body was found stuffed in Rothstein's freezer.

The grand jury alleged a total of twenty overt acts contributed to Barnes and Diehl-Armstrong's complicity in the fatal bank-robbery plot. Others included her solicitation of Barnes to kill her father; Diehl-Armstrong and Barnes gathering at the tower site on August 27 and August 28, 2003; Barnes and Diehl-Armstrong driving on I-79; Barnes and Diehl-Armstrong using binoculars to peer at Wells just before the bomb exploded.

Diehl-Armstrong's slaying of Roden was the overt act that resonated with Clark the most, the element of the indictment that best exemplified the sweep of the investigation. Roden's death and Wells' death, two events that some investigators for years had treated as unrelated, were finally tied together.

———

Arraignments are typically among the most uneventful of court proceedings. The newly indicted defendant and a lawyer appear before a judge, who reads the charges, listens to the defendant plead not guilty and sets bond. The defendant and the prosecutor leave, to meet again during the more challenging events in the case, such as pretrial hearings and the trial. As if signaling how unorthodox Diehl-Armstrong's case could become, her arraignment proved to be unusual—before it even occurred.

On July 12, 2007, a day after Buchanan announced the indictment, the government was arranging to drive Diehl-Armstrong from the State Correctional Institution at Muncy to the federal courthouse in Erie for her arraignment. Clark and Wick planned to drive to Muncy to get her. The investigators' involvement—federal marshals typically handle such transports—led Diehl-Armstrong's lawyer, Tom Patton, to ask for a hearing before the federal magistrate judge in Erie, Susan Paradise Baxter. Patton, the assistant federal public defender in Erie, wanted Baxter to prohibit Clark and Wick from picking up Diehl-Armstrong at Muncy and driving her back to Erie. Patton feared that Diehl-Armstrong, who never stopped talking, would say something incriminating to Clark and Wick, who knew her better than any other investigators.

"She is mentally ill, has been diagnosed with a bipolar disorder for the past thirty years," Patton said in court. "I have met with her in Muncy several times. She is almost constantly in a manic state. She is on no psychotropic medications. She cannot control herself in the manic state without speaking."

Baxter denied Patton's request, but the government's victory was moot. Patton decided the best way to keep Diehl-Armstrong from unleashing statements would be to keep her out of court as much as possible. He later had Diehl-Armstrong waive her right to be present at her arraignment. He pleaded not guilty on her behalf on July 17, 2007. Patton, in this instance, had been able to keep his new client under control.

On November 7, 2007, Ed Palattella picked up his desk phone at the *Erie Times-News* and was startled to hear the voice on the other end of the line. "Hello, Ed," she said. "This is Marge Diehl-Armstrong."

Palattella had for months written Diehl-Armstrong to call him. She finally decided to do so, against instructions from Patton. By now, Diehl-Armstrong had become what most defense attorneys loathe: a runaway client. The call to Palattella lasted eleven minutes and forty seconds. He barely said anything. She talked from the moment Palattella accepted the collect call, from SCI Muncy, until she hung up.

"I am 100 percent innocent," she said. "I am trying to get extricated from this maze. I am trying to see daylight."

Palattella asked her to explain what she did, and where she was, on August 28, 2003. She refused. She said Rothstein set her up. She didn't want to say anything more specific. She knew the feds would listen to the tapes from the phone calls.

"My time is running out here," she said. "I am going to get framed for life."

She hung up and called back several minutes later. Palattella got her on the subject of the men she had killed in her life.

"I am not a man hater at all," she shouted. "I am in a prison full of dykes. I am the only person here who is not gay."

Diehl-Armstrong called Palattella again the next day, and the day after that and the day after that. Starting on November 7, 2007, Diehl-Armstrong, with few exceptions, such as when she was in transit between prisons, called Palattella collect at least once a day, every weekday, for three years straight. She sometimes called three or four times a day, often phoning seconds after she had hung up, apparently having bullied every other inmate away from the prison pay phone. She talked nonstop each time.

Palattella sometimes was tempted not to answer—the caller ID on his desk phone displayed the number for the prison when she was on the line—but he never knew what she was going to say. He never wanted to blow a chance of her admitting to something, though that never occurred. Palattella got used to hearing Diehl-Armstrong's voice, grew accustomed both to hearing her demand that he do something—call her personal lawyer, Larry D'Ambrosio; look up something for her on the Internet; send her something in the mail—and complain when Palattella did not meet those requests. She said the feds were railroading her.

"I am a very forgiving person, if you knew me," she said. "I am always between dumb and dumber and a rock and a hard place."

During another call, she quoted Plato: "He who commits injustice is ever made more wretched than he who suffers it."

Getting phone calls from Diehl-Armstrong was a better way to communicate with her than seeing her in person. Palattella had done that once, at the Erie County Prison. It had been a disaster. She seemed surprised that Palattella, forty-one years old in 2007 and five feet eight inches tall, didn't have more height. Looking at Palattella in person seemed to distract her from whatever focus she had. She appeared to be disappointed in him.

In a phone call to Palattella several days after that visit, Diehl-Armstrong spewed some of the vilest language he had ever heard from her, as she called him a "fucking fag" (knowing that Palattella was married) and mocked his ability to cover her case. She was upset at something he had written, about how the district attorney's office was not going to charge anyone in the burglary and robbery at her house on May 30, 2003. Diehl-Armstrong wanted Palattella to accept that she had nothing to do with the Wells case; when he refused to give her that assurance, she ripped into him. She said she would never call him again. It was one of those phone calls where he was glad that, after thirty minutes, her time on the prison phone automatically ran out.

Diehl-Armstrong apologized the next day. She kept calling. She said she needed someone to talk to, someone to understand her. Palattella thought the only difference between him and the other people she tried to telephone was that he would accept her calls. In an odd way, he came to look forward to her hypercharged chats and hyperbole and irreverence and black humor.

"I'm the pickle in the middle with hell on all sides," she said.

Her case, she said, is "the worst thing that happened in American history."

"You know that saying that a grand jury would indict a ham sandwich if the prosecutor asked them to?" she said. "Well, I am the ham sandwich, that's what I am. I am the scapegoat."

Still another time, Diehl-Armstrong told Palattella her epitaph: "Death by legal system."

And once, when Palattella misheard her pronounce the letter *H*, she swiftly shot back a diabolical response: "An *H*!" she shouted over the phone. "An *H*, as in *hell*."

Diehl-Armstrong could get you laughing so much over the phone that you could forget her past—for a moment. Palattella would remind himself of this each time she hung up: the woman on the other end of the line, no matter what she said, had already killed two men and was accused of being part of a plot in which another was blown up. No matter what she said, Palattella would remind himself, she was a killer.

Diehl-Armstrong's antisocial and violent personality traits were, for whatever reason, fully ingrained in her psyche, inseparable from her brilliance. Medication might modulate her impulses, according to Palattella's reading of her psychiatric history, but medication would never eliminate her ill-willed desires, obsessions and compulsions. Diehl-Armstrong was a sociopath. She used her intellect to menace and murder. Like other manipulative master killers, such as Ted Bundy, who she said was unlike her, Diehl-Armstrong employed her tolerable and even attractive traits—her quick wit; her sweeping knowledge of pop culture and history; her looks, at one time—to lure and ensnare her victims, all of them men.

———

In his nearly twenty years of covering the courts in Erie County, Palattella had watched many good defense attorneys and just as many bad defense attorneys. He considered Diehl-Armstrong's court-appointed lawyer, Tom Patton, one of the best. Patton, who was thirty-nine years old in 2007, was originally from Illinois and had made his career as an assistant federal public defender. He knew the intricacies of federal law and was committed to his clients with an intensity that Palattella admired.

Patton was a realist: he knew when the mighty federal government indicts your client, your client is all but done. Ninety-five percent of the time, in the federal system, an indictment ends in a guilty plea. Patton still made the U.S. Attorney's Office fight for everything in court. He was the loyal opposition, whose job was to keep the other guys honest and let them know when they had gone too far.

"This is trying to use a sledgehammer to push in a tack," he once complained to a judge about a prosecutor's application of federal law.

Diehl-Armstrong wanted Patton fired.

Her request was nothing new. She had berated the attorneys in her previous cases, including Leonard Ambrose, considered the best defense lawyer in northwestern Pennsylvania, whom her parents had hired to represent her in the Bob Thomas homicide case. Diehl-Armstrong, in general, detested public defenders—"public pretenders," she called them—though she also believed, in her arrogance, that no lawyer, no matter how he or she was paid, could know more about the law and her case than she did.

Diehl-Armstrong on January 6, 2008, petitioned the judge in the Wells case, U.S. District Judge Sean J. McLaughlin, seated in Erie, to let her fire Patton, whom she called "despicable." McLaughlin declined her request but did not rule out hearing it again later.

———

Patton went ahead defending Diehl-Armstrong. He proceeded on a course that would determine when and even if her case would go to trial. Patton asked McLaughlin to schedule a hearing to determine whether Diehl-Armstrong was mentally competent.

Patton was not seeking to establish an insanity defense, and, because the federal system has no plea of guilty but mentally ill, he was not trying to set the stage for that outcome, either. Patton believed Diehl-Armstrong suffered a bipolar disorder so severe that she was mentally unfit to assist in her defense. It did not matter that an Erie County judge, Shad Connelly, had found her mentally fit for trial in September 2004, in the Roden case, in which she eventually pleaded guilty but mentally ill to third-degree murder. McLaughlin would have to review Diehl-Armstrong's mental health anew.

The competency hearing occurred in McLaughlin's second-floor courtroom on May 22 and 23, 2008. Patton's main evidence was Diehl-Armstrong's past: ten mental-health professionals had diagnosed her with a bipolar disorder over the previous thirty years, including in the cases of Thomas and Roden. Patton's main witness was Robert Sadoff, M.D., a psychiatrist from Philadelphia who had diagnosed Diehl-Armstrong with a bipolar disorder starting in 1985, in the Thomas case. Sadoff's finding had led to seven consecutive court rulings that Diehl was mentally unfit to stand trial, until she was found competent, in 1988, and was acquitted.

Sadoff, under questioning from Patton, cited the other psychiatrists and psychologists who had also diagnosed Diehl-Armstrong as bipolar. If ten people "from different places observe that, and I observe similar things, then to me it is a no-brainer," Sadoff testified. "She is bipolar. She is extremely bright. But that doesn't take away the fact that she is bipolar."

Patton asked Sadoff about the condition of Diehl-Armstrong's houses over the years, including her hoarding of junk and the government-surplus butter, cheese and hundreds of pounds of other perishables. He said her behavior was psychotic.

"It is the breakdown of the personality that leads to the chaos we see," Sadoff said.

Patton entered into evidence a report of a psychologist who examined her on April 29, 1985. The psychologist, Gerald Cooke, came as close as anyone in attempting to trace the origins of Diehl-Armstrong's mental illness, including her anorexia at age twelve. He wrote:

> She describes her mother as "schizy" and as either being too overprotective or too underprotective at different times. She also described her at times as being

domineering and cold, and at other times as being overly warm and affectionate and possibly superficial. She says her mother made up her mind that Marjorie was going to be an M.D. when she grew up.

She blames her mood swings on "genetics and inconsistent treatment by my parents. . . ." [H]er moods swings are egosyntonic. That is, to some degree she regards these as part of her identity and more of a positive than a negative factor. . . . [S]he may perceive them this way because they then become an excuse for her behavior. In a sense it is the manic illness and her mood swings that she then blames for her behavior rather than blaming herself. . . .

She describes both her father and mother as having manic and depressive periods. . . . She also feels that her parents would have preferred a boy and tried to raise her as a boy to some extent. . . .

She indicates that she sees a relationship between the anorexia and the beginnings of sexual development, and she said she had many incorrect notions such as the fact that she could get pregnant if she kissed a boy. She says she stopped eating because she was afraid of sexual attention. . . .

It is my opinion that Ms. Diehl has shown the seeds of severe mental illness since her early childhood.

Patton submitted a report that a psychiatrist, David Paul, wrote on August 1, 1985. The report said Diehl-Armstrong—then Marjorie Diehl—told him she stopped menstruating when she was anorexic.

She tied her anorexia in with rebellion against her parents. . . . She stated she felt pressured by upwardly mobile parents to "perform," and the anorexia was also seen as defense against the sexual advances of males, as she had an early maturation.

Marshall Piccinini presented a bold argument to Judge McLaughlin in May 2008. He contended the entire psychiatric record in Diehl-Armstrong's case—the record of all her medications, her psychiatric counseling, her psychological testing—showed she had been misdiagnosed throughout her life as suffering from a bipolar disorder. Piccinini said Diehl-Armstrong really suffered from a personality disorder, not otherwise specified, with borderline, paranoid and narcissistic traits.*

Piccinini said psychiatrists and psychologists first mistakenly diagnosed Diehl-Armstrong with a bipolar disorder more than thirty years earlier, in the early 1980s, because she exaggerated her symptoms to get Social Security benefits; she started receiving them in January 1984 after a psychiatrist diagnosed her as manic depressive in 1983. Other psychiatrists had deferred too much to that original diagnosis of a bipolar disorder, Piccinini said. He

---

*The *Diagnostic and Statistical Manual of Mental Disorders, Fourth Edition, Text Revision*, classifies a bipolar disorder as an Axis I disorder, in which the symptoms are most acute and typically psychotic. The *DSM-IV* classifies a personality disorder as an Axis II disorder, in which the symptoms are typically neurotic and less severe than those of an Axis I diagnosis.

argued they never adequately or independently documented the signs that would justify such a diagnosis.

Piccinini's main witness was William J. Ryan, a forensic psychologist with the Federal Bureau of Prisons. He had interviewed Diehl-Armstrong at the Metropolitan Correctional Center, a federal prison in lower Manhattan, where she had been sent for the mental-health review in preparation for the competency hearing before Mc-Laughlin. Ryan said his thirty-day examination of Diehl-Armstrong revealed she suffered not from a bipolar disorder that rose to the level of a severe mental illness, but from a personality disorder that was separate from a mental disease, and whose main characteristics were narcissism and paranoia.

Ryan said Diehl-Armstrong, unmedicated for three years, was fit for trial. He called her a "conversational bully" who nonetheless behaved calmly for him in prison, after he told her he was going to find her mentally fit for trial—an outcome Diehl-Armstrong said she desired.

"She seemed to me a different person," Ryan testified about Diehl-Armstrong's personality change when he told her his intentions. "She was perfect."

Ryan amazed Jerry Clark, who, with his background in psychology and forensic therapy, was well versed in the language of mental illness. For Clark, Ryan represented the first psychologist or psychiatrist who had encountered Diehl-Armstrong and who was willing to think differently, to challenge the previous diagnoses of a bipolar disorder. Clark agreed with Ryan that Diehl-Armstrong was neurotic but that her neuroses were more in line with a personality disorder rather than a serious mental illness such as a bipolar disorder. For Clark, she was mentally ill but also crazy like a fox.

In his eight interviews with Diehl-Armstrong, Clark had seen her manic side, her pressured speech, her unrestrained fugues, her flights of ideas, her unquenched rage as she disgorged an endless stream of profanities. But Clark never witnessed what he thought would have been solid proof of a bipolar disorder: deep depression. True manic-depressives cycled from mania to depression. As far as Clark could tell, Diehl-Armstrong was stuck in the manic mode. She was never really down, and certainly never so down, so severely depressed, that she was incapacitated and, for instance, would not get out of bed.

Clark had experience with the severely mentally ill. While in college, during his internship in the psychiatric ward at Erie's Saint Vincent Health Center, he saw patients so manic the staff had to hold them down to force them to take Thorazine. He remembered one patient who would visit the grocery store and rearrange all the cans on the shelves. That, to Clark, was true mania.

Diehl-Armstrong, through her squalid houses and other weird habits, exhibits signs of her neuroses, Clark thought. But, like Ryan, Clark ultimately considered Diehl-Armstrong a deranged person who was a master manipulator, not a severely mentally ill manic-depressive who had no understanding of daily life. Clark had experience with manipulative mentally ill as well.

Before he started at the DEA, in 1990, Clark had worked as a forensic therapist at another Erie hospital,

Hamot Medical Center. His year in the job drove him to go back into law enforcement. Clark saw too many mentally ill people he thought were capable of at least trying to help themselves, but did nothing. They enjoyed manipulating the system. Clark worried he would lose his mind if he stayed around them much longer.

Clark looked back at that time; he looked at Diehl-Armstrong and concluded she suffered from a straight antisocial personality disorder, nothing more. Clark realized the distinction was a fine one. He believed Diehl-Armstrong was mentally ill but not to the degree that the defense was contending and certainly not to the degree that, under the strictures of federal law, would ever make Diehl-Armstrong incompetent to stand trial.

"Ms. Armstrong was calculating and unscrupulous on more than one occasion, also typical of personality disorders," William Ryan wrote in his evaluation. "She was also manipulative, demanding and intrusively advocated for her own needs and desires. She was typically unwilling to convenience anyone else, but repeatedly sought conveniences for herself."

Clark, sitting in the courtroom, agreed with every word.

———

Tom Patton countered with another witness who, like Sadoff, was from Diehl-Armstrong's past: attorney Leonard Ambrose, who successfully represented her in the Thomas case. Ambrose said he was unable to work with Diehl-Armstrong effectively until she was medicated.

Ambrose said Diehl-Armstrong talked constantly, but less so while she was on lithium carbonate, which regulated her moods.

"It was literally, in my mind, the case from hell," Ambrose testified. "With medication, it would kind of cut off these talks, so you could kind of have some window so you could communicate with her. It would take off the high, what I would call the nonstop verbiage."

Patton questioned Ryan's report. He said it concluded Diehl-Armstrong was a difficult person because she simply had an unpleasant personality.

"My client is not difficult because she is just a nasty person," Patton said. "She is difficult because she is mentally ill."

Piccinini referred to Diehl-Armstrong's behavior in court during the two-day competency hearing, where she had sat quietly most of the time. Piccinini said she exhibited no signs of hypomania and that she has been stable while not on medication.

Diehl-Armstrong had displayed what was, for her, fairly placid behavior in court. She had, for the most part, calmly studied papers. Her outbursts had been few. She had yelled at Ambrose when he spoke of his difficulties with her in the Thomas case. She had shouted "Liar! Liar!" during testimony that she had given statements connecting her to the Wells case; she had called Piccinini and Clark "corrupt"; she had said, apparently to herself, that "I am innocent. Period"; and, during testimony about the deaths of Thomas and Roden, she had shouted "Self-defense!" During breaks in court, when McLaughlin was not on the bench, she had talked, but not incessantly so.

During one break, after criticizing the U.S. Attorney's Office, she caught the eye of Clark, who was seated at the prosecution table, across from her.

"Jerry Clark," Diehl-Armstrong said to him, "you're a dumb ass, too."

Clark smiled.

———

At the end of each of the hearing's two days, Diehl-Armstrong telephoned Palattella as soon as she got back to the Erie County Prison.

"I don't think either of them really explained me," she said of Ryan and Sadoff.

She told Palattella that an unnamed psychic had recently communicated to her that she is innocent in the Wells case. She said the psychic implicated other people, including her codefendant, Ken Barnes.

"She is right on the money," Diehl-Armstrong said.

———

During one long break in the hearing, Clark and Jason Wick drove Diehl-Armstrong to the FBI office in Erie to get her fingerprinted and photographed. The FBI usually books someone following an arraignment, but, because Diehl-Armstrong had waived her appearance at her arraignment, in July 2007, Clark and Wick had to process her on this day.

Diehl-Armstrong, handcuffed and wearing a tan prison

uniform, left the FBI office and declared her innocence and criticized the investigation to the TV reporters who were waiting outside. She got into the backseat of Clark's Ford Explorer. Patton sat next to her. Clark drove and Wick sat in the front passenger seat. Clark was to take Diehl-Armstrong back to the Erie County Prison.

"I'm hungry," Diehl-Armstrong said. "I missed lunch. Can you stop?"

She accepted Clark's offer to stop at the drive-through at a Wendy's. She discussed the TV reporters.

"Sorry I had to talk to them like that," Diehl-Armstrong said. "They ask stupid questions. If you don't respond, it makes you look guilty. You have to give them an answer."

Diehl-Armstrong spoke to Clark.

"I wish this was under better circumstances," she said.

Clark pulled into the Wendy's. He asked Diehl-Armstrong what she wanted to eat.

"A Triple," she said.

"A Triple?" Clark said. "You can't eat a Triple, Marge."

"Yes I can."

She asked him to supersize her order: large fries, large Coke.

Clark got the order. He parked in the Wendy's parking lot so Diehl-Armstrong could eat. Wick unlocked Diehl-Armstrong's handcuffs from her leather belt, though the cuffs remained locked to her wrists. She ate by grabbing the Triple and fries with her shackled hands. Grease dripped onto her lap.

"Jerry," Diehl-Armstrong said, "are you mad at me?"

"Why would I be mad at you, Marge?"

"Because I called you a name in court."

"I didn't take it personally," Clark said. "I had a disagreement with your attorney and I didn't take that personally, either."

"Jerry," she said, "why did you turn on me? We were all getting along. You guys were nice to me. I thought I was helping you."

"Marjorie," Patton said, "don't say any more."

"I would love to answer you, Marjorie, but I can't," Clark said.

"I want to take a polygraph or a truth serum," she said. "Why don't you give me a polygraph?"

"I thought Marshall Piccinini was taller," she said, starting to ramble. "Girls in the pod [in prison] said he was tall with dark hair. He was short with white hair."

Diehl-Armstrong turned to Patton. She said he was doing a better job at the competency hearing than she thought he would. She thanked him.

"You need to see me more often," she told Patton. "Spend more time with me."

In between sentences, Diehl-Armstrong continued to eat the Triple and fries. Her handcuffed hands were like claws as she broke the burger and the bun and the fries into small pieces. She let the pieces fall into her lap, where they made a pile. She took each piece from the pile and stuffed it into her mouth. Clark thought she ate like she feared this meal would be her last.

25
Guilty Plea

Judge McLaughlin's fifty-nine-page ruling on Diehl-Armstrong's competency, released on July 29, 2008, captured the depth of her journey into mental instability. In clinically precise language, McLaughlin cataloged both Diehl-Armstrong's mental problems and the efforts of so many professionals to try to help her. McLaughlin found Diehl-Armstrong's past too powerful to ignore. He rejected the findings of Piccinini's main witness, William Ryan, who said Diehl-Armstrong did not suffer from a mental defect in the form of a bipolar disorder.

"In short," McLaughlin wrote, "Dr. Ryan's diagnosis can only be accepted as accurate by concluding that every other clinician who has diagnosed the Defendant with bipolar disorder did so in error. I do not find that the record supports that conclusion."

McLaughlin ruled Diehl-Armstrong mentally incompetent to stand trial, but only because of how the bipolar disorder affected her ability to assist her attorney, Tom Patton. McLaughlin narrowed a review of Diehl-Armstrong's competency to her relationship with Patton. McLaughlin found Diehl-Armstrong understood the legal system and the charges against her but could not adequately help Patton prepare for trial. McLaughlin wrote:

> When he tries to sit down and communicate with the defendant about her case, she becomes belligerent and abusive, irrational in her demands and incapable of understanding either the illogic of her own positions or the importance of heeding her counsel's advice. Rather than meaningfully interact with her attorney to confront the evidence against her, she will simply demand that Mr. Patton obtain a dismissal of all her charges or grant her prosecutorial immunity with no apparent understanding as to why this is not rationally possible under the circumstances.

McLaughlin ordered Diehl-Armstrong to undergo four months of psychiatric treatment while in the custody of the Federal Bureau of Prisons. He said he would review her competency again after he received another mandatory psychiatric report, which had to be done in 120 days.

———

As far as anyone knew, Ken Barnes had never suffered from a verifiable serious mental illness. Clark never believed Barnes had such problems. Clark had always thought Barnes' brain had short-circuited years ago, not due to a mental illness, but because he overloaded it with crack. "Every last penny he spent was on cocaine," one of Barnes' lawyers said at the sentencing in Barnes' drug case in Erie County Common Pleas Court in August 2006.

In that case, a probation officer wrote in a presentencing report that Barnes had admitted to using "marijuana, crack, cocaine, opiates, stimulants, depressants and hallucinogens." Barnes said he started using drugs and drinking alcohol at age seventeen; described his current state of health as "just fair"; and he listed his ailments: poor eyesight, poor lung capacity (from the drug use and constant smoking) and "appendectomy, tonsil removal, heart catherization [sic] 3 times, electrocuted, diabetes, high blood pressure, etc." Barnes said he had received treatment from a psychiatrist but did not know when, where or why. After he was jailed at the Erie County Prison in the drug case in March 2006, Barnes complained of depression and was prescribed Prozac. That was the extent, in the official record, of his mental-health issues.

Barnes' lawyers in the Wells case nonetheless decided to pursue an initial defense that he was mentally incompetent to stand trial. They filed a motion before McLaughlin on March 31, 2008, asking him to hold a competency hearing. One of Barnes' lawyers, Alison Scarpitti, said Barnes had a history of mental illness. After meeting with Barnes in prison, Scarpitti said, she believed Barnes needed a psychiatric exam.

The U.S. Attorney's Office quickly undermined the

defense's contentions. Piccinini's evidence rested with Ricky Barnes, Ken's half brother, and Ricky's conversations with Ken at the Erie County Prison in 2006 and 2007. According to Ricky, Ken told him he had no credible mental problems and would feign mental illness to avoid a conviction in the Wells case. Ken told Ricky he would cause a mistrial by getting up and screaming in the courtroom. Ken said he realized the promise in raising a "psych defense" because of the relatively light seven- to twenty-year sentence Diehl-Armstrong got for pleading guilty but mentally ill to third-degree murder in the slaying of Jim Roden. Nobody believes Diehl-Armstrong because she is crazy, Ken Barnes told his half brother; "Who's to say I'm not crazy, too?"

McLaughlin never had to rule on whether Barnes was mentally fit to stand trial. His defense lawyers dropped that strategy. On September 3, 2008, while Diehl-Armstrong's mental health remained under review, Kenneth Eugene Barnes, age fifty-four, walked into McLaughlin's courtroom and pleaded guilty in Criminal Case No. 07-26 Erie: *The United States of America v. Marjorie Diehl-Armstrong and Kenneth Barnes*. He pleaded guilty to two of the three charges against him— conspiracy to commit armed bank robbery and aiding and abetting the use of a destructive device in a crime of violence. Piccinini, in exchange, dropped the charge of aiding and abetting an armed bank robbery, which carried a life sentence because Wells was killed.

Even with the plea, Barnes faced a sentence of thirty-five years to life. He agreed to cooperate against

Diehl-Armstrong, leaving open the possibility that he could get his initial sentence reduced later, based on his testimony if she ever went to trial.* But no matter how much time McLaughlin might lop off the sentence, Barnes was on his way to spending what would likely be the rest of his life in a prison in the federal system, which has no parole. His time as a free man, fixing TVs, taking apart computers, skirting the law while running a crack house for whores and telling Diehl-Armstrong he would need $100,000 up front to kill her father, was finished.

Barnes spoke softly as he answered "yes" and "no" to McLaughlin's questions at the plea hearing. Barnes' chance to address the judge at length would come months later, at his sentencing. Today, at this hearing, Barnes disputed none of the information in the indictment about his involvement in the Wells case. Justice was Barnes' motive to plead guilty, said Scarpitti, one of his lawyers. Barnes, she said, "doesn't want to see people who should be punished get away with it."

Ricky Barnes attended the hearing, but not to support his half brother. He said he was glad Ken Barnes pleaded

---

*A U.S. Attorney's Office can vouch for a defendant's cooperation in two ways. If the cooperation occurs before sentencing, a prosecutor may submit to the sentencing judge a 5K motion, so named after Section 5K1.1 of the Federal Sentencing Guidelines. The judge may use that information to justify a lesser sentence. If the cooperation occurs after sentencing, the prosecutor may submit to the sentencing judge a Rule 35 motion, after Rule 35 of the Federal Rules of Criminal Procedure. In that case, the judge may use information in the motion to reduce the original sentence.

guilty. He said he was proud of his contributions to the government's case.

"He's never been any type of family to me," Ricky Barnes said after the hearing. "The types of things he has done in his past, I wouldn't want to be related to him."

Ken Barnes, wearing handcuffs and a green prison uniform, shuffled his feet as he walked. In 2006, while watching a basketball game at the Erie County Prison, he suffered a severely broken leg when someone ran into him. Doctors placed a metal rod in the leg. Barnes had lost weight. He was pale. His lawyers said his diabetes was getting worse.

Barnes would have been dead by now without the health care at the Erie County Prison. He looked worn out. Barnes, who had told Ed Palattella in a letter on May 7, 2007, that he was innocent in the Wells case, that "they have no one to put this on," and that "this case may never be solved," had given up.

———

Clark felt vindicated. He had known for weeks that this guilty plea was going to happen. He was a friend of Barnes' other lawyer, Jamie Mead, a former assistant U.S. attorney. Clark and Mead would discuss the case during their occasional lunch-hour runs through downtown Erie. Piccinini knew of these discussions, in which Clark would recount what Barnes said during those fifteen interviews. Clark had read Barnes his rights. He knew McLaughlin would never suppress those statements—the only real hope Barnes had to beat the indictment. Mead and Scarpitti agreed. Barnes' plea was set.

Clark, despondent after the press conference announcing the indictments in July 2009, was energized at Barnes' plea hearing. He wanted to speak up when Barnes confirmed all the details of his role in the pizza bomber plot. Referring to Wick and himself, Clark wanted to say, "And we were exactly right."

Diehl-Armstrong did not think her case was in trouble. She called Barnes a liar hours after the plea hearing, in her daily phone call to Palattella.

"I am not cut from the same cloth as Ken Barnes," she said. "I am higher on the food chain. I am going to be telling the whole truth and nothing but the truth."

———

Barnes' sentencing hearing, on December 3, 2008, lasted an hour. One of Wells' sisters, Jean Heid, who had written the letter to the editor to the *Erie Times-News* in 2004, addressed McLaughlin for nearly half that time. Heid held a framed photograph of her brother as she invoked the Bible and said he had been crucified by the bombing and was at peace in heaven.

Wells, Heid said, was "an innocent man caught in the snares of evildoers through no fault of his own."

Heid turned toward Barnes.

"Brian was made to be an unwilling pawn in your senseless killing," she said.

Barnes wore an orange jumpsuit, the trademark color for problematic inmates at the Erie County Prison. He apologized briefly to McLaughlin and Heid. He referred to Wells.

"What happened to him," Barnes said, "was something that was not supposed to happen."

Barnes faced a mandatory minimum sentence of thirty years for the count of aiding and abetting the use of a destructive device in a crime of violence. He faced a maximum sentence of five years on the count of conspiracy to commit bank robbery.

Barnes' lawyers asked McLaughlin for no more than the mandatory minimum sentence. They claimed Barnes had a minor role. Piccinini asked for more than the mandatory minimum sentence. He said Wells' death was "so much more depraved" than what occurs in typical crimes and that Barnes deserved more time. Piccinini called the case "one of the most bizarre criminal acts we have ever seen," and he said the bank-robbery plot sometimes "seems completely unthinkable."

"They did more than just think about it," Piccinini said of Barnes and his cohorts. "They put it into play. An act such as this in this country cannot be tolerated."

McLaughlin sentenced Barnes, fifty-five years old, to forty-five years in prison—a penalty that would keep him incarcerated until he turned one hundred. McLaughlin said Barnes "was intimately involved in the planning of the robbery and gave advice on what components could be used to make the bomb." He said Barnes knew Wells was "likely a dead man" after the bomb was locked to his neck. He called Barnes coldhearted.

"The callousness and complete lack of regard for human life exhibited by this defendant is, in a word, chilling,"

McLaughlin said. "This case represents the unfortunate combination of the incredibly bizarre and the sadly tragic."

Barnes left the courtroom. He knew he eventually would return, to testify as a star prosecution witness when Diehl-Armstrong went to trial. Forty-five years was a lot of time. Barnes hoped he could parlay his testimony into something less.

"It all depends on what happens with Marjorie," his lawyer Alison Scarpitti said. "So we are just waiting."

Diehl-Armstrong had no problem with forty-five years for Barnes.

"He got what he deserved," she snarled over the phone to Palattella.

———

Diehl-Armstrong could not listen to the testimony any longer. It was April 27, 2009. McLaughlin was holding another hearing on her competency. On the stand was Piccinini's main witness this time around, Leslie Powers, a forensic psychologist for the Federal Bureau of Prisons. She had examined Diehl-Armstrong during her four-month stay at the Federal Medical Center (FMC) at Carswell, a specialized women's prison in Fort Worth, Texas. Powers found Diehl-Armstrong competent to stand trial. That conclusion did not anger Diehl-Armstrong. She was upset at Powers' description of her behavior at FMC Carswell.

"I noted her to do three things," Powers testified. "She watched television a lot, she slept and she went down to the cafeteria to eat."

Diehl-Armstrong shouted from the defense table.

"How could I when I was on unit restriction all that time!" she said. "I couldn't go down to the cafeteria to eat. That's a lie right there!"

"Ms. Armstrong," McLaughlin said, "hang on a second."

"I couldn't go down, Your Honor," Diehl-Armstrong said, undeterred. "She says I go down to the cafeteria to eat. I was forbidden. . . . I was on restriction; how could I go down when I ate on a tray every day! I didn't go down at all. You got me mixed up with somebody else."

"Ms. Armstrong, I would like you to remain in the courtroom . . . ," McLaughlin said.

Diehl-Armstrong interrupted.

"They threw the six misconducts out, the lieutenants did, they expunged them from the computer," she said, bombarding the courtroom with words. "I had one in six years."

"Ms. Armstrong. . . . ," McLaughlin said.

"I'm done with her," Diehl-Armstrong said, cutting off the judge and referring to Powers. "I don't care what she says."

"Hang on a second," McLaughlin said. "I'm not done with you."

"I don't care," she said. "I don't care anymore. You know they framed me for something I didn't do. . . . I don't care anymore. You can say what you want."

"Ms. Armstrong, I want you to remain in the courtroom if you can," McLaughlin said. "I'm going to give you one warning."

"I won't say another word," Diehl-Armstrong said.

"Hang on a second," McLaughlin said. "If you be quiet, you can stay here. One more outburst, take her out in the holding cell. Let's go."

Diehl-Armstrong was quiet after that.

For McLaughlin, the conversation represented a pivotal moment in the competency hearing. In a later ruling, he wrote the exchange showed three things: that Diehl-Armstrong can be redirected to stop her rude behavior, in this case, erupting in court; that she often uses "a maladaptive communication technique"—pressured speech—to get her point across; and that she can engage in rational thought.

Diehl-Armstrong had been correct about not eating in the cafeteria; Powers later acknowledged that she herself was wrong, that the staff at FMC Carswell had indeed restricted Diehl-Armstrong so she could not eat there. Diehl-Armstrong, just as she had been when she confronted the PNC bank manager about access to her mother's safe-deposit box, was, in this instance, correct. Her reaction in court might have been over the top, but she was justified in disputing Powers' testimony.

The courtroom exchange, McLaughlin wrote in a sixty-four-page opinion filed on September 8, 2009, shows "that the Defendant—though often impulsive and lacking good judgment—is not irrational."

McLaughlin found Diehl-Armstrong competent to work with an attorney and stand trial. McLaughlin said he agreed with Powers over William Ryan, the Federal Bureau of Prisons psychologist who had examined Diehl-Armstrong for the previous competency hearing, in May 2008. Ryan, who had also said Diehl-Armstrong was competent, examined her for a shorter period of time than Powers did, McLaughlin said. He said he found more persuasive Powers' argument that Diehl-Armstrong suffers from both a bipolar disorder—a diagnosis Ryan rejected—and a personality disorder. McLaughlin said he agreed with Powers' analysis that the "bipolar disorder was in a state of relative quiescence during her incarceration at FMC Carswell and that the symptoms during that time did not suggest the presence of any mania."

McLaughlin said he recognized Diehl-Armstrong's bipolar disorder to be a mental defect or disease, but he said the disorder, at this point, was not making Diehl-Armstrong mentally unfit for trial. McLaughlin wrote:

> I am not persuaded at this juncture that the Defendant's proscribed behavior is necessarily indicative of mental incompetence or detachment from reality. . . .
> The Defendant's refusal to heed the advice of her lawyer may be unwise in the extreme, but it does not necessarily demonstrate an inability to consult with her lawyer with a reasonable degree of rational understanding.

The ruling satisfied Clark. It was hard for Clark to be unhappy with a decision by McLaughlin, whom he greatly respected. The ruling was thorough and fair and thoughtful, traits that lawyers had seen McLaughlin display since President Bill Clinton appointed him to the federal bench in October 1994, when he was thirty-nine years old.

If any judge possessed the qualities necessary to preside over the pretrial hearings and trial of Marjorie Diehl-Armstrong, it was Sean J. McLaughlin, who was fifty-four years old in 2009. He was known among prosecutors and defense attorneys to be evenhanded almost to a fault, often allowing counsel or a plaintiff or a defendant to make a point long after another judge would have ended the conversation. McLaughlin rarely raised his voice in court; he was patient. He was a judge who, despite listening daily to the details of crimes or seeing civil suit after civil suit filed on his docket, still enjoyed his job.

———

Diehl-Armstrong retained her allies as her trial drew closer. At the competency hearing on April 27, 2009, her most vocal supporters, other than Tom Patton, whose job was to back her, were Wells' sisters Jean Heid and Barbara Wells.

"I didn't have anything to do with it!" Diehl-Armstrong hollered to the sisters during a break.

"I tried to solve the crime," she said. "They are trying to frame me."

Heid, standing in the gallery, said she agreed with Diehl-Armstrong. Heid said Brian Wells was innocent.

"And the truth will prevail," she said.

Diehl-Armstrong shouted in agreement.

"You got it, girlfriend," Barbara Wells shouted back.

"She deserves her day in court, and the truth needs to come out," Heid yelled about Diehl-Armstrong.

"I'd like to know who killed my brother," Heid said during another break.

"Jay Stockton built the fucking bomb, I heard," Diehl-Armstrong shouted.

"The only thing absent from this courtroom is the truth," Heid said.

———

Marjorie Diehl-Armstrong got to talk to a federal judge one-on-one. The conversation occurred in Judge McLaughlin's chambers on September 17, 2009. Diehl-Armstrong still wanted to fire Tom Patton. Now that he had ruled Diehl-Armstrong competent for trial, on September 8, McLaughlin had to decide whether to grant her request.

McLaughlin met privately and separately with Diehl-Armstrong and Patton in his chambers. Each conversation lasted about thirteen minutes.

McLaughlin took the bench. He told Diehl-Armstrong he was allowing her to fire Patton, "one of the preeminent defense attorneys in the area." McLaughlin said Diehl-Armstrong had "a deep-seated distrust and antipathy" toward Patton and that he had become "a distinct psychological stressor for her."

McLaughlin told Diehl-Armstrong that, as an indigent defendant, she was entitled to a lawyer, but not a lawyer of her choice. He warned her she would get "one bite at the apple" to fire Patton, but if she continued her uncooperative behavior with her next lawyer, she could "potentially waive your right to counsel."

"Could you please try to find someone who is aggressive, who will put his heart and soul into this case?" she shouted.

McLaughlin cut her off.

"Ms. Diehl-Armstrong," he said, "this is my courtroom, not yours."

He said he would assign her qualified counsel from a list of area defense attorneys approved to represent poor clients in federal court.

Diehl-Armstrong sat at the defense table. She had gotten her way. Tom Patton, who had achieved no small victory by initially defeating the U.S. Attorney's Office on the issue of her competency, would no longer sit next to her in court.

Patton got up to leave.

"Good luck, Marge," he said.

26
Cancer

Diehl-Armstrong got a new lawyer on September 25, 2009. McLaughlin appointed Doug Sughrue, a thirty-six-year-old in private practice in Pittsburgh. Diehl-Armstrong at first praised the appointment, saying it was the big break her horoscope had predicted would happen. Sughrue got to work. He met with Diehl-Armstrong to prepare for trial, scheduled to start in late August 2010. Sughrue brought women's clothing catalogs—Talbot's, Coldwater Creek—to the Erie County Prison so Diehl-Armstrong could pick a dress to wear.

Sughrue, who had a calm manner, a gently sardonic outlook and an expansive sense of humor, soon listened to Diehl-Armstrong berate him as no more effective than Patton. Diehl-Armstrong asked McLaughlin to let her fire Sughrue. McLaughlin refused.

"That pattern which emerges," he said at a hearing, "is one where the defendant is never satisfied with counsel, whoever it might be, because she tends to view herself as smarter and more informed than anyone else."

"I don't want to hear this!" Diehl-Armstrong shouted.

———

By the spring of 2010, Sughrue was spending less time on legal strategy and more time tracking Diehl-Armstrong's health. She had cancer.

Though her life had been replete with serious mental problems, Diehl-Armstrong's physical health had generally been good. She suffered from hypothyroidism and glaucoma, and was on medication for both, but that was it—until the lymph nodes in her neck swelled in January 2010. In March, doctors at Millcreek Community Hospital, just south of Mama Mia's Pizza-Ria on Peach Street, removed a cancerous lump from her neck. By April she was waiting on the results of a PET scan so doctors could figure out what kind of cancer she had—and how long she had to live.

"I have fucking cancer somewhere," she told Palattella over the phone on April 7, 2010. "We are all terminal in this world. It's not like it makes me a bad person. We are all going to die sometime; death is part of life. But I'm not ashamed. A lot of people get cancer. I just happen to be one. It's out of my control."

Her focus had shifted.

"I'm fighting for my life here," she said. "That is the most important thing right now. I don't even care about the Wells case. The case has taken a back burner, which is crazy, because before I thought about it all the time."

Her cancer would not change her defense. She said she would never admit to being part of the Wells plot.

"I'm telling you that if I died today, I would never confess that. I am not going to say I did something that I didn't do. This case is killing me."

"I hope they all rot in hell," she said of Clark and Wick. "If they ever came near me on my deathbed, I'd spit in their fucking faces. I solved this case for them."

———————

Clark wondered how many people were going to die in the pizza bomber case, which by now seemed cursed. At this rate, cancer would claim Diehl-Armstrong. The only people still alive would be Barnes, who was in prison and in poor health, and Stockton, who was in poor health from his heart problems and had immunity. Clark knew Diehl-Armstrong's case, with its competency issues, would take a long time to bring to trial. He just never thought the lengthy passage of time might encompass her death.

Piccinini told Clark Diehl-Armstrong's cancer prognosis would determine whether a prosecution would occur. If she only has several months left, Piccinini said, the U.S. Attorney's Office was not going to seek a conviction, only to see her die soon after a guilty verdict.

Clark also wanted no part of taking a dying person to trial. However, if that was to be the case with Diehl-Armstrong, he said he would want her to admit her guilt or somehow take some responsibility for the Wells case before she died.

Otherwise, Clark said, "there's no resolution."

———

Ken Barnes once said Diehl-Armstrong, when soliciting him to kill her father, told him her father was worth $12 million and that she was due to inherit all of it. In actuality, Harold Diehl, upon the death of his wife, Agnes Diehl, in 2000, was worth about $1.8 million, primarily in municipal bonds. And in actuality, Harold Diehl willed only $2,000 of that to his daughter.

Diehl-Armstrong learned of this in the spring and summer of 2010, while she was in prison and undergoing cancer treatment. She had her personal lawyer, Larry D'Ambrosio, who had her power of attorney, petition an Erie County probate judge to appoint a financial guardian for her father, now ninety-one years old and suffering from Alzheimer's disease at the Pennsylvania Soldiers' and Sailors' Home, in Erie.

D'Ambrosio, citing financial records, calculated Harold Diehl's worth at $1.8 million, a figure that went undisputed. D'Ambrosio claimed a guardian was necessary because of Diehl's dementia and because he had been dissipating his assets by giving away money to his friends and neighbors. Diehl-Armstrong, suffering from cancer and facing charges that could put her away for life, wanted to make sure money would be left for her when her father died.

There would be—but only $2,000.

Harold Diehl's assets in May 2010 amounted to $185,601,

according to court documents. Diehl had left Diehl-Armstrong $100,000 in a will in 2000, but he had executed a new will in 2005 in which he bequeathed her only $2,000. In the meantime, Harold Diehl had indeed given away the bulk of the $1.8 million to his other relatives and friends and neighbors—the people he felt truly cared for him.

Diehl's lawyer said Diehl disinherited his daughter in the 2005 will because of how she had treated him in the dispute over her mother's safe-deposit box in 2000. Diehl-Armstrong in that case had called her father an abusive alcoholic, a characterization Harold Diehl's lawyer said was false.

More than anything, Harold Diehl's lawyer said, Diehl-Armstrong's "vitriolic attacks" on her father led him to change the will and leave her $2,000.

"It is an unusual circumstance where neighbors are favored over a child," the lawyer said, "but this is an unusual fact pattern."

The disinheritance outraged Diehl-Armstrong. She likened the situation to *Bleak House*, the Dickens masterpiece in which a large inheritance dwindles to nothing as expensive legal fees consume the estate in an endless fight over who should get what.

"I know I am in the right here," she told Palattella. "God put me in this family. I have the birthright. I have the bloodline."

———

The initial prognosis for Diehl-Armstrong's cancer classified it as incurable and terminal. The cancer had originated in a breast and spread to her glands. It was adenocarcinoma. How long she had to live was still unknown in midsummer of 2010. The Regional Cancer Center, in Erie, had ruled the cancer terminal in the first prognosis, but Diehl-Armstrong was to get a second opinion. The outcome of that review would determine her legal fate. Piccinini was skeptical she would live much longer.

"I've just never heard of someone having metastasized breast cancer with lymph node activity that exists having such a rosy prognosis," he told McLaughlin at a hearing on July 1, 2010. "I'm a little bit concerned in hearing more about that."

Piccinini said how long she had to live was important, as was her quality of life under treatment.

"If we are left in the end, because these things are not all that predictable, that she could live for years without side effects, then we would go forward," Piccinini said. "If I'm dealing with someone who is suffering from the side effects of the cancer or from treatment, I'm less inclined, as the representative of the U.S., to go forward at this time and criminally prosecute her."

McLaughlin agreed to wait for the second opinion. He postponed Diehl-Armstrong's trial, which he had scheduled for August 30, to October 12, 2010.

"I'm doing this somewhat reluctantly," McLaughlin said. "For all we know, this woman could, and hopefully she will, live for many years.

"It has been very, very difficult to get this case to trial."

———

The prosecution would go on. Magee-Womens Hospital of the University of Pittsburgh Medical Center reported in August 2010 that Diehl-Armstrong would live for at least three to seven years.

McLaughlin accepted the report. He set jury selection in Diehl-Armstrong's trial for October 12.

Doctors prescribed Diehl-Armstrong Arimidex, an estrogen-blocking drug, to treat her cancer. She said it had not spread. She said her doctors called it "occult cancer," from the Latin *occultus*, meaning "hidden." Though her doctors believed the cancer originated in a breast, she said, they found no cancer there, but only in her lymph nodes.

"My cancer is hidden," she told Palattella. "My cancer is microscopic."

She had turned her attention to her trial.

"I have to testify," she said. "I am the only one who can save myself. It is the only way I can bail myself out from my worthless lawyer. I have nothing to lose, and everything to gain, from testifying."

———

If she took the stand, Diehl-Armstrong would have plenty to try to rebut. In the days before October 12, McLaughlin ruled against Diehl-Armstrong and Sughrue in every defense request. McLaughlin declined to change the venue or venire for the trial, saying the potential jury pool—residents of the seven counties of northwestern Pennsylvania—would be large enough to yield an impartial panel. He refused to suppress any of the statements Diehl-Armstrong gave to Clark and Wick. He ruled Clark and Wick coerced none of the statements; that they read Diehl-Armstrong her Miranda rights; that she understood what was going on (for example, McLaughlin ruled, Diehl-Armstrong repeatedly declined to discuss certain topics with Clark and Wick); and that her personal attorney, D'Ambrosio, was present during most of the interviews.

The jury would hear everything Diehl-Armstrong had told the investigators.

————

She had a chance to avoid a trial. Piccinini in 2009 and into 2010 offered her a deal: plead guilty in the Wells case, and the U.S. Attorney's Office would ask for a sentence of no more than twenty-five years. Diehl-Armstrong would serve that sentence concurrently, or at the same time that she served her sentence of seven to twenty years for Roden's murder. Once Diehl-Armstrong finished the twenty years, she would have to serve only five years in the Wells case. Five years for a bank robbery in which the robber died when a bomb locked to his neck exploded? It was a good deal.

"This is like signing up for five years for another murder," Clark thought.

Piccinini had several reasons for making the offer. He told Clark a guilty plea would eliminate the possibility of appeals—appeals that would center on the complicated issue of mental competency. Piccinini knew the evidence was solid, but trials could be uncertain. And Diehl-Armstrong had cancer. Even with the plea, she would be in prison for another eighteen years, including five for the Wells case. She would be seventy-nine years old when she finally got out—if she did not die first.

Diehl-Armstrong and Sughrue considered the offer. Clark thought the phone would ring and Piccinini would be on the other end of the line, telling him she was pleading guilty.

The call never came. Diehl-Armstrong rejected the plea deal. She said she was innocent. She was concerned she would never get paroled in the Roden case if she pleaded guilty in the Wells case.

By October 2010, Diehl-Armstrong had already served seven years of the seven-year minimum sentence in the Roden case.* She said she was positive the Parole Board soon would free her; she was correct when she said the guards at SCI Muncy had described her as a hard worker in prison, a model inmate. Prisoners like that impressed the Parole Board, she said. Why, she said, should she risk parole by pleading guilty in the Wells case and having the Parole Board hold that plea against her? She was going to be acquitted anyway, she said.

---

*When she was sentenced to seven to twenty years in the Roden case on January 7, 2005, Diehl-Armstrong got 475 days of credit, or about a year and three months, for the time she had been in prison since her arrest. Including the 475 days, Diehl-Armstrong in October 2010 had been incarcerated about seven years, making her eligible for parole.

Diehl-Armstrong told Palattella she would never accept the plea offer from the U.S. Attorney's Office.

"I'll tell them not only to wipe their ass with it," she said, "but to shove it up their ass."

Clark knew that, even if she were acquitted in the Wells case, Diehl-Armstrong would not win parole, not with her history of fatally shooting two men. Diehl-Armstrong wanted to hear none of that reasoning from Piccinini or Sughrue. Clark thought that prison time had become irrelevant to her. She was dying.

27
Trial

The five faces stared back at the jurors: Bill Rothstein, smiling, in his bib overalls and thick beard; Ken Barnes, with his pasty complexion and jowls and hollow look; Marjorie Diehl-Armstrong, in the middle, with her long, raven-black hair and piercing blue eyes; Brian Wells, with his big eyeglasses and wide-eyed expression; and, off to the right of the jury box, to the side of the other four faces, Jim Roden, with his sharp cheekbones and shattered gaze.

Marshall Piccinini referred to each of the five faces as he delivered his opening statement at Marjorie Diehl-Armstrong's trial in the courtroom of U.S. District Judge Sean J. McLaughlin shortly after 1:00 P.M. on October 15, 2010. The U.S. Attorney's Office had blown up photographs of the five faces to movie-poster size and placed the portraits on easels. At the base of the easels for Diehl-Armstrong, Rothstein and Barnes rested blown-up photos of their respective junk-ridden houses. The faces haunted the courtroom, especially because three of the people were dead, with one blown up by a bomb and the body of another found in a freezer. Diehl-Armstrong's portrait was uncanny: here she was in the photo; there she was, just several feet away, seated at the defense table, in the flesh.

——————

For three days Piccinini and Doug Sughrue had worked to pick the sixteen people who now sat in the jury box and peered at the photos. They had chosen twelve jurors and four alternates from a pool of forty-one potential jurors. Jury selection had gone unexpectedly quickly, knowing the pizza bomber case had been a national news story for seven years and two months. Seven women and five men comprised the core twelve. They and the alternates answered fifty-one questions on paper, about their jobs, their ability to keep an open mind, their views on mental illness. They then answered questions in person, as Piccinini and Sughrue probed their biases.

Diehl-Armstrong, wearing dark-colored dresses, did not sit stoically during jury selection. She criticized the process, she barked at Piccinini, she mused about her legal predicament. She targeted her wrath mostly at Sughrue, who, after a verbal lashing, would lean back in his chair and crack a wry smile.

"Leave me the fuck alone!" she shouted at him on October 12, the first day of jury selection.

She questioned Sughrue's strategy by referring to a signature event of the Second World War.

"I'm tanking like the Bismarck," she said.

She did not let up.

"I'm really sick of you," she told Sughrue on October 13.

That same day, as she reviewed a written jury questionnaire, she became enraged. Someone had misspelled a word.

"How fucking stupid are these people?" she said.

Her chattering drew a rebuke from McLaughlin, who was sitting in on the questioning of the prospective jurors and had tired of Diehl-Armstrong's interjections.

"Ms. Armstrong," he told her as he asked her to calm down, "I'm trying to work here."

Diehl-Armstrong showed more restraint, but only for a time. This was her stage, this trial, perhaps the biggest criminal trial in the history of Erie County, a trial the national news networks were covering. She was the star of this performance, the center of attention. As she trundled into the courtroom from the holding cell, you first noticed her size; she had gained weight since her most recent competency hearing, making her the largest person in the room. She walked with a confident gait but with an air of resignation, almost as if she thought the trial was a bother but had decided she would commit to it because she was going to be here anyway.

As the marshals unlocked her handcuffs, and before

she sat down, she would turn around and scan the gallery. She would start talking to a reporter or someone else she knew, or she would sit, sigh, jabber and even hiss at Sughrue. She would say what she wanted. She would do whatever she wanted. She would not stay quiet. She would not go unnoticed.

———

Jerry Clark, as the lead investigator, sat at the prosecution table with Piccinini. Jason Wick sat behind them. Piccinini got up to address the jury. Spectators, including Wells' relatives, packed the gallery.

"In the summer of 2003," Piccinini said at the start of his sixty-five-minute opening statement, "a group of twisted, intellectually bright, dysfunctional individuals hatched a violent plot to rob a bank on Peach Street, in Erie, Pennsylvania. In this violent crime, the defendant, Marjorie Diehl-Armstrong, depicted here in the middle; her lifelong friend, William Rothstein, next to her; and another friend by the name of Kenneth Barnes, engaged in a twisted scheme to convince this man on my right, Brian Wells, to assist them in plotting a bank robbery, and convinced him to wear what initially was likely a nonactive destructive device around his neck attached by a collar, and rob the bank."

Piccinini did not place a blown-up photograph of Floyd Stockton in the courtroom. He did not mention Stockton in his opening statement.

Piccinini explained how Roden's death fit into the case. He described the subplot to have Barnes kill Harold Diehl for his money. He said Diehl-Armstrong, accused as an aider and abettor, "was liable for the acts of the others." He said Diehl-Armstrong, Rothstein and Barnes ended up outwitting themselves and turning on each other when their plan went awry. The plot, Piccinini said, was too complicated to succeed. He said Wells could have never survived and that the bank-robbery notes were a ruse to confuse and distract investigators.

"This group of dysfunctional, highly intelligent individuals completely outsmarted themselves," Piccinini said. "They outsmarted themselves, they overthought, they overplanned, and that overplanning, that overthinking, that overpreparation, ended up resulting in their demise.

"And their plan, ladies and gentleman, failed miserably. It tanked like the *Bismarck*."

Diehl-Armstrong looked up from the defense table. She smiled but was quiet, for that moment.

She did not stay silent for long.

She began to mutter to herself and Sughrue, often making comments loud enough for the jury to hear.

"Lie," she said at one point during Piccinini's remarks.

"Oh my God!" she shouted at another.

Sughrue spoke for twenty-five minutes. He talked of the burden of proof, a concept he said most of the jurors had heard about on television, on *Law and Order* or the *CSI* shows. He asked each juror to keep an open mind. He said Diehl-Armstrong had information on the bank-robbery plot, but never participated in it. Diehl-Armstrong, he said, met with Clark and Wick to help them solve the case. She knew some things.

"Why?" Sughrue said. "Because she was around these people. For goodness' sakes, Jim Roden's body was in William Rothstein's freezer, right along that tower road. No one is going to change that. She was around and observed things."

Sughrue said he would not dispute much of the evidence.

"Where we disagree with the government," he said, "is whether the evidence will show Marjorie did things for the same reason that the government is claiming she did them."

―――――――

Toward the end of the day on October 15, the first for testimony, Piccinini played Government Exhibit 2—a videotape of the news footage of Wells in the Eyeglass World parking lot, with the bomb locked to his neck. The tape showed him before and after the explosion; it did not show the explosion itself.

Upon seeing the aftermath of the blast, one juror turned and looked away.

―――――――

The testimony took nine days. The government presented seventy-one exhibits, with many of them including multiple pieces of evidence. The defense presented thirteen. The government exhibits included the notes for and carried by Wells, surveillance photos of Wells in the bank, the revolver and walkie-talkies found in Rothstein's van, videotapes of Rothstein's tours of his and Diehl-Armstrong's houses, a videotape of Barnes' interview with Erie police over the burglary and robbery at Diehl-Armstrong's house, audiotapes of Rothstein's 911 calls about Roden's body, and the notes Kelly Makela took in prison. Other exhibits were photographs of the cane gun, which the FBI had taken apart to search for fingerprints and other pieces of evidence; a model of the collar and bomb; and photos of the actual collar. Piccinini did not enter the collar itself into evidence: the videotape of Wells getting blown up adequately conveyed the device's lethal purpose.

The trial, including jury selection and jury deliberations, lasted three weeks. Thirty-nine witnesses testified—thirty for the government and nine for the defense.

Piccinini's witnesses took the stand from October 15 to October 22, with one rebuttal witness on October 27. The government witnesses included Kelly Makela, now Kelly Makela Roberts, and five other inmates who spoke to Diehl-Armstrong in prison; Tony Ditomo; the motorists, including Tom Sedwick, who said they saw Diehl-Armstrong on the highway; Michael Douglas, the UPS driver, and Michael Vogt, the draftsman who slammed his car's brakes near Rothstein's house on August 27, 2003; the chief bank teller, Barbara Lipinski, now Barbara Lipinski Eisert; Kirk Yeager, the FBI bomb expert; the state police troopers who were on the scene at the Eyeglass World parking lot; Jessica Hoopsick; Ken Barnes; Jason Wick; and Jerry Clark.

Sughrue's witnesses testified from October 25 to October 27. He presented two main witnesses: Larry D'Ambrosio, Marjorie Diehl-Armstrong's personal lawyer, and Diehl-Armstrong.

───────────

Ken Barnes barely lifted his feet as he walked out of the holding cell and through a side door of the courtroom on October 21. He had lost weight since McLaughlin had sentenced him to forty-five years in prison in December 2008. Diehl-Armstrong, who had been sighing dismissively throughout the trial, glared at the witness stand and at Barnes, her erstwhile fishing buddy, with whom she and Jim Roden had shared all those good times on the South Pier.

Barnes testified about his plea and sentence. He repeated to the jury everything he had told Clark and Wick about Wells, Hoopsick, Rothstein, Stockton, Robert Pinetti and Diehl-Armstrong, including how he had been in the car with her when she drove the wrong way on the interstate. He said he never intended to kill Diehl-Armstrong's father, though he said she offered him $250,000 to do so.

"I wasn't going to kill her dad," Barnes testified. "All I was going to do was take half the money and I was going to go to Buffalo and buy a lot of crack and come back and be a millionaire. That didn't work because I smoked my own product too much."

Barnes told the jury what happened at the TV tower site the day before the bank robbery. The jurors fixated on him. He described how Rothstein had ordered Stockton back into Rothstein's house, leaving Barnes at the scene with Rothstein and Diehl-Armstrong and Wells.

"And Marjorie was measuring his neck to see how the collar was going to fit," Barnes said.

"Liar!" Diehl-Armstrong screamed from the defense table.

"I didn't lie," Barnes shot back. "And after that—"

McLaughlin interrupted.

"Mr. Barnes, excuse me one second," he said. "Members of the jury, would you be so kind as to go back into the jury room for just one second, please."

McLaughlin raised his voice slightly as he spoke to Diehl-Armstrong. He told her he would remove her from the courtroom if her disruptions continued. She would watch her trial on closed-circuit TV, in the holding cell.

"You are now on notice," McLaughlin said.

Her disruptions subsided.

Barnes testified for two hours and forty minutes. He had a lot to confess to the jury, a lot to say he was sorry about. He lamented punching Wells in the face and forcing him to wear the collar bomb on August 28, 2003.

"I regret doing that, because back then I was just thinking of my own greed about getting the money," Barnes said. "I really wasn't concerned for his health and safety at that point."

"What were you concerned about?" Piccinini asked.

"I was concerned about getting the money so I could take off and bring some crack."

"You went over and hit him while he was being jumped by this group of people?"

"Yeah, and I'm not proud of that," Barnes said.

Barnes admitted he had misled the investigators initially to avoid trouble so he could keep dealing drugs. He said a spiritual change of heart led him to tell the truth, plead guilty and get nearly half a century in prison for Wells' death.

"I've had nothing but nightmares about what I saw on TV when he got killed," Barnes said.

"I'm real sick with diabetes, shoot insulin twice a day and I don't know how long I'm going to live. My thing is I want to be clear with God, be on the right side of God before I die. So I just decided to come in here and tell the whole thing and get clean."

———

Diehl-Armstrong seethed during Barnes' testimony. If McLaughlin had not cautioned her about her outbursts, she probably would have shouted at him, especially during cross-examination. Sughrue questioned Barnes' motives. He brought up the burglary and robbery at Diehl-Armstrong's house on May 30, 2003. Sughrue was trying to show that Diehl-Armstrong would have had no desire to be around Barnes, let alone plan the Wells case with him, if she suspected he had broken into her house with the crackhead biker.

Barnes said he did not break into the house. He said he told two of his friends that Diehl-Armstrong had plenty of cash and would be a good target; he said he cased her house with the friends. But he said those friends burglarized her house themselves, without telling him about the heist beforehand. For Diehl-Armstrong, who had derided the police and the district attorney for not filing charges over the burglary and robbery, Barnes' testimony vindicated her in this one instance: she had indeed been burglarized and robbed, her privacy violated, just as she had told the police. She had not been lying. She was not crazy.

If Diehl-Armstrong got any consolation from that sliver of Barnes' testimony, it quickly faded. Barnes continued to bury her. On cross-examination, he remained consistent in what happened on August 28, 2003. He said he had no problem with his forty-five-year sentence and the likelihood of dying in prison. Responding to an incredulous Sughrue, Barnes said no one had guaranteed him a lesser sentence in exchange for his testimony.

"If they do it, it's their choice," Barnes said. "Nobody said they were going to. Nobody said they promised me or anything. They may. If they don't want to, what am I supposed to do? I don't care.

"I'm doing forty-five years. I got my life set up in the prison," Barnes said. "You know, it's a little city within itself with walls all the way around, nothing but concrete. But yet, I've got my own little room, my own little piece of heaven. I can live and be my own man.

"Now, if I was out here on the street, I would have to

pay rent, gas, electric, medication, all that stuff, on my $630 a month SSI. I couldn't do it. There is no way possible. In there I get all my stuff for free. I get three meals a day, a hot and a cot. I get my medication and everything I need."

"Maybe life is harder for you running a crack house?" Sughrue asked, almost with a shout.

"If I was out there running that crack house," Barnes said, "chances are nine times out of ten, the way the conditions, things are today, with the economy, the crimes and the drug scene—yeah, they probably would have taken it down and I probably would have spent anywhere from twenty to life in jail, depending on the amount they might have confiscated or whatever."

Barnes spoke about his new life, his life in prison,

"I got a life that I can just live out and not have to worry about anything," he said. "The only thing I want to do is tell the truth and get this straightened out once and for all so that I can have God forgive me for the parts I've done and the parts I didn't."

Floyd Stockton did not testify. He had been on the government's witness list, but he never showed up at trial. He did not testify because he nearly died.

Stockton had recently suffered two strokes, one of which weakened the left side of his face. Stockton—who had collapsed in cardiac arrest in that hotel room in Seattle in 2006—underwent emergency open-heart surgery, with a triple bypass, on October 8, 2010, at Skagit Valley

Hospital, south of Bellingham, Washington. By his side had been K.W., his longtime girlfriend who was now his wife. The hospital discharged Stockton on October 12, the same day jury selection started in Diehl-Armstrong's trial. His doctors said he was in no condition to travel.

When Piccinini told Clark about Stockton's near-fatal scare, Clark thought Jay Stockton was pulling off a farce, that he was again trying to slink away from trouble. Piccinini decided against asking McLaughlin to postpone the trial. So much had happened in the case already, including Diehl-Armstrong getting diagnosed with cancer, that risking a long delay and more uncertainty seemed imprudent.

Clark had been looking forward to Stockton's testimony. Like Barnes', Stockton's words on the witness stand would confirm that Clark and Wick had followed the correct path all along by locking their investigation onto Rothstein and his cohorts. Clark and Wick had finally broke down Stockton, who admitted his role. Stockton's surgery would deny Clark and Wick the opportunity to witness his testimony, the final prize of their interrogations.

Through the work of Charbel Latouf, his lawyer, Stockton had received the deal of a lifetime: he got full immunity. Because of his bypass surgery, the deal got even better: Stockton did not even have to testify at Diehl-Armstrong's trial; he avoided what would have likely been an intense cross-examination by Sughrue.

With no Stockton, Diehl-Armstrong's jury and the public would never know the full story of the pizza bomber case—and they would not know why Stockton got immunity. The arrangement would remain cloudy, its existence widely known but its terms unexplained to the public.

Piccinini, Clark and Wick could do nothing about the absent witness. Stockton, his immunity deal the subject of so much tension during the investigation, was recovering at home on the other side of the country. For the doctors who had performed the triple bypass, Floyd Arthur Stockton Jr. was just another patient with a worried wife and an unhealthy past.

"This is a pleasant 63-year-old, half a pack a day smoker with a family history of coronary artery disease in his father who died in the early 1970s," according to Stockton's hospital discharge summary. "The patient is accompanied today by his spouse."

———

Jerry Clark resembled a medical examiner during some of his four hours of testimony. He explained how a drug overdose killed Pinetti, how cancer killed Rothstein, how Roden's shot-filled body ended up in the freezer in Rothstein's garage.

Clark's time on the stand was cathartic: finally, he could tell the public all he knew. As Clark left the prosecution table and walked to the witness box, his nerves flared. He felt more anxious than he had been as a witness in his twenty-six years in law enforcement. He thought of his father, the cop he most admired. He calmed down once Piccinini asked him one or two questions.

Clark recounted the eight interviews he and Wick and

David Gluth conducted with Diehl-Armstrong, as well as his discussion with Rothstein after he called 911 about Roden's body, and how Rothstein gave him the alibi about being in North East with Diehl-Armstrong on August 28, 2003. Clark encapsulated Diehl-Armstrong's position: that she was only at certain places on August 28, 2003, because Rothstein directed her to be there, and that Rothstein framed her in the Wells case because she refused to marry him.

As for Barnes' insistence that he was in the wrong-way car with Diehl-Armstrong, Clark testified that Diehl-Armstrong "denied being with Ken Barnes that day, but said her vision is not good, that someone possibly could have been with her in her vehicle without her knowing it." She insisted her eyes were too myopic for her to have been a lookout, either.

For Ed Palattella, who was covering the trial for the *Erie Times-News*, Diehl-Armstrong's emphasis on her deficient eyesight was enough evidence to finish her. Diehl-Armstrong, the manipulative, domineering, supersmart paranoid, had insisted she had no idea someone might have been in a car with her because her eyesight was so poor. Her explanation was absurd.

———

The pace of the investigation became a subject of inquiry. Clark answered a question the jurors probably raised as soon as they learned the basic facts of the case: if Wells was killed in August 2003, why wasn't anyone indicted until 2007?

"The evidence that has been developed and testified to here in this courtroom, did it take months and days and years to develop?" Piccinini asked Clark.

"It took a long time," Clark said.

Piccinini asked Clark about Roden's death and the Wells case.

"In the initial stages and over the first couple years of the investigation, was there a significant link that was made during the course of the investigation?"

"Early?" Clark said.

"Yes," Piccinini said.

"No, there was not."

Piccinini spoke of the overlap of law-enforcement agencies, how the state police and Erie police investigated Roden's murder at the same time the federal agents conducted the collar bomb investigation.

Piccinini: "With regard to the evidence they developed, witness statements, the letters and notes that were written by Kelly Makela, the evidence seized at the houses that were searched, did all those items remain in the possession of local law enforcement authorities?"

"Yes, it did," Clark said.

Piccinini: "In the content of Kelly Makela's letters, where she indicates the collar bomb case was connected to Roden's death, was that information turned over to federal investigators as part of the collar bomb investigation?"

"Eventually," Clark said, "but not initially."

Piccinini: "After Marjorie Diehl-Armstrong is convicted and sent to prison for the murder of James Roden, was it at that point in time that the information gathered by local authorities in their local investigation was turned over at your request to the feds?"

"That's correct," Clark said.

———————

Diehl-Armstrong's trial took on the tone of a normal court proceeding during most of the government's case. Diehl-Armstrong heeded McLaughlin's caution and rarely made a scene when the jury was present. She gave a thumbs-down during the testimony of one former inmate. Her yammering at Sughrue grew louder during the testimony of another former inmate, who said Diehl-Armstrong told her she acted as a lookout.

"Ms. Armstrong, you have to be quiet," McLaughlin said in a raised voice.

"Can I ask you a question, Your Honor?" Diehl-Armstrong said.

"No, you cannot."

———————

Just as Stockton's surgery gave Piccinini one fewer witness, an unexpected circumstance eliminated a defense witness. Sughrue had wanted to call to the stand Robert Sadoff, the psychiatrist who first examined Diehl-Armstrong in 1985. Sadoff never appeared. He was on his way to Nepal. Diehl-Armstrong's trial had moved more quickly than expected, creating the conflict with Sadoff's schedule. McLaughlin ruled Sadoff unavailable. He ruled Sadoff's testimony about Diehl-Armstrong's mental state would have been inadmissible in any case, because Diehl-Armstrong was not pleading insanity.

Sughrue had wanted Sadoff to testify that Diehl-Armstrong's mental illness made her less inclined to cooperate with Rothstein and the others to carry out the bank robbery. In a report on Diehl-Armstrong he submitted on October 11, 2010, the day before jury selection, Sadoff wrote:

> Because she is paranoid, she has great difficulty cooperating and working with others. She also has great difficulty in exercising control of her impulses with respect to her behavior. When she is manic, she is likely to act impulsively in order to achieve her personal goals, which may not be shared by others. With her borderline personality traits, she sees events either in black or white and with very little shades of gray. She tends to focus on the extremes rather than the middle ground. She is also destructive.

Sughrue might have had a better time arguing the admissibility of Sadoff's planned testimony if Sadoff had been available. On October 25, the first day of the defense's case, he was following through with his plans to fly to the Himalayas.

Floyd Stockton's absence from the trial did not preclude Sughrue from raising questions about why the government had not charged Stockton. A pursuit of that kind of defense, however, would have required Diehl-Armstrong to acknowledge that she was intimately involved in the Wells plot, and that she saw Stockton do certain things that should have led to charges. She maintained she had nothing to do with the scheme; Stockton never became a focus of her case.

Sughrue built Diehl-Armstrong's defense around his two main witnesses, both of whom testified in a manner that often left those in the courtroom gallery shaking their heads or even laughing.

Larry D'Ambrosio, now seventy-eight years old and wearing a hearing aid, testified just before Diehl-Armstrong, his friend and client of some forty years. D'Ambrosio grimaced as he took the stand. His face soured as he turned toward McLaughlin.

"I want to apologize to the court and everyone," D'Ambrosio said. "I drank some tainted fruit juice last night. I threw up all night, had diarrhea and only slept a couple of hours. I don't feel so well, but I will try to do my best here today."

Though called to the stand by Sughrue, D'Ambrosio's testimony benefited both the defense and the government. He told Sughrue he never heard Diehl-Armstrong admit anything to Clark and Wick, including her having information about egg timers. D'Ambrosio said he believed Diehl-Armstrong had information that might help the investigators, but he said she never implicated herself, not even when she went on the driving tour and he sat next to her in the backseat.

"Jerry was asking more of hypothetical questions," D'Ambrosio said of the interviews.

He described Diehl-Armstrong as "a poor little girl" and said he had visual evidence that Clark and Wick knew the grand jury had wrongly indicted her. He said he saw the proof at the news conference U.S. Attorney Mary Beth Buchanan held to announce the indictments on July 11, 2007. D'Ambrosio recalled Buchanan talking about the allegation that Diehl-Armstrong killed Roden to silence him. D'Ambrosio said he was standing next to Jason Wick.

"I looked at Jason; he looked at me," D'Ambrosio testified. "All of the sudden he was perspiring like it was raining."

"What were your thoughts whenever you heard the facts that were alleged in the indictment?" Sughrue asked.

"I thought that's outrageous," D'Ambrosio said. "Jason knows that; that's why he's perspiring so heavily like that. He wouldn't look at me."

D'Ambrosio was testifying he knew the thoughts of another person based on sweat. Piccinini objected, McLaughlin sustained the objection and Sughrue ceased that line of questioning.

On cross-examination, D'Ambrosio tried to be conciliatory toward Piccinini, though he had just called into question the credibility of the government's investigators.

"Marshall . . ." D'Ambrosio said, trying to plead with Piccinini.

"Don't call me Marshall," he shot back.

Piccinini presented evidence that D'Ambrosio, prior to the issuance of the indictments, visited Ken Barnes at the Erie County Prison while Barnes was awaiting prosecution in the drug case. Based on Barnes' account of that meeting, Piccinini said, D'Ambrosio wanted to get Barnes out on bond so he could flee and never testify against Diehl-Armstrong. D'Ambrosio denied that scenario, but said he had discussed with Barnes "whether [Barnes] was actually in the car with Margie" driving the wrong way on I-79.

"I went to find out on my own," D'Ambrosio said.

"Isn't it true," Piccinini said, "you discovered from Ken Barnes that she in fact was in the car that day?"

"Yes," D'Ambrosio said. "I believed him then."

Diehl-Armstrong's personal lawyer, her confidant for decades, had just corroborated the testimony of the main witness against her. Barnes, D'Ambrosio said in so many words, had told the truth about the wrong-way car ride.

———

D'Ambrosio testified he always was looking out for Diehl-Armstrong. Clark figured D'Ambrosio probably was trying to help her, to some degree, when he advised her to speak to the FBI. D'Ambrosio had hoped to get her a deal. That plan collapsed, maybe because D'Ambrosio was in over his head or because she was more deeply involved in the Wells case than even D'Ambrosio knew.

Either way, D'Ambrosio had intertwined his affairs with those of his client. The situation opened him up to scrutiny from Piccinini and Sughrue.

D'Ambrosio testified that Diehl-Armstrong signed a movie deal with a California production firm, SilverCreek Entertainment, on July 17, 2007—eight days after the grand jury indicted Diehl-Armstrong and Barnes.

Sughrue argued the contract created a conflict of interest for D'Ambrosio, because Diehl-Armstrong, under the law, could not profit from the movie deal if she were convicted. That, Sughrue said, gave D'Ambrosio an incentive to have her talk to the federal agents all along and eventually get found guilty, so he could collect all the money. D'Ambrosio acknowledged the arrangement with SilverCreek Entertainment but would always maintain that if Diehl-Armstrong were convicted and the movie made, he would use the money for her appeals.

Piccinini had a different take. He agreed the contract gave D'Ambrosio an incentive—but to testify that Diehl-Armstrong never said those things to Clark and Wick, a contention designed to get her acquitted. With a verdict of not guilty, Piccinini said, Diehl-Armstrong and D'Ambrosio could both make money on a movie.

D'Ambrosio was under attack from both sides.

D'Ambrosio called Clark "a great guy," and he said Clark and Wick treated Diehl-Armstrong honorably. He also testified Diehl-Armstrong did not tell Clark and Wick what the investigators wrote in their interview reports. D'Ambrosio characterized the whole situation as a misunderstanding, a kind of honest mistake between two good-hearted federal agents and a well-meaning but mentally ill woman who yearned to help them solve a big case.

Piccinini: "You're basically testifying that if Special

Agent Clark wrote in his report and testified that your client provided Rothstein two kitchen egg timers, you're saying that never happened, isn't that true?"

"That's correct," D'Ambrosio said. "I believe that Jerry Clark really believes, truly believes that she told him all that. But he asked hypothetical questions and to me those answers were in the way he interpreted them."

Sughrue did not offer relief to D'Ambrosio, his own witness. He asked about Diehl-Armstrong's decision, based on D'Ambrosio's advice, to sit for the eight interviews.

"Did you have anything to gain or lose during those interviews?" Sughrue asked.

"No," D'Ambrosio said. "I was just looking out for Margie's interests, trying to get her to the point where she can help them, then they could help her and speak on her behalf at the parole hearing. That's the main gist of it."

"And how did that work out?" Sughrue said in a deadpan tone.

"Objection," Piccinini said.

"Sustained," McLaughlin said.

D'Ambrosio never responded to Sughrue's question. But the answer to the question of how things had worked out was not hard to find.

The answer was several feet away: Diehl-Armstrong was sitting at the defense table, ready to testify and explain herself in yet another case in which a man was dead.

28

In Her Own Words

Marjorie Diehl-Armstrong launched into a verbal reverie that lasted some five hours and twenty minutes over the one and one-half days she was on the witness stand. This is how her testimony started:

Doug Sughrue: "Make sure you sit in the chair so we can see you, okay? Are you comfortable?"

Diehl-Armstrong: "Comfortable as you can be in the witness chair, I guess."

She then spoke, nonstop, about all the houses she once owned, all the fur coats that once lined her closets, all the jewelry she had once collected, all the things she had once inherited. Sughrue interrupted Diehl-Armstrong's fevered chatter long enough to ask her the same question about all of the items.

"Were they the worst or the best?" Sughrue said.

"They were the best," she said.

"They were the top-of-the-line items," she said. "I had good stuff."

"Cheap or expensive?" Sughrue said.

"Expensive."

"So you were a woman of means then?"

"Definitely," Diehl-Armstrong said. "But I was not a money-hungry-type person that was a status seeker. I just happened to acquire a lot of valuable items. Although I have quite a Bohemian streak in me . . . I'm not into conspicuous consumption, but it just so happened, I was gifted with a lot of things that were very valuable."

Diehl-Armstrong talked so fast and without prompting that Marshall Piccinini objected because she was not responding to a question, just uttering all these things on her own.

The conversation was slowed by Sughrue.

"When you were raised, Marge, were you raised in poverty, or were you raised with money?"

"I was always raised with a lot of money."

"When you went to high school, were you in the bottom of your class or the top of your class?"

"Top."

"Were you ever at the bottom of anything?"

"No."

———

Sughrue waded through the onslaught of words. He tried to establish that Diehl-Armstrong, before she went to prison, owned so many precious objects, and had so much money, either in cash or tied up in easily liquidated assets such as real estate and jewelry, that she had no reason to want to rob a bank or have her father killed over her inheritance. She already had enough money.

Sughrue shifted the discussion to Diehl-Armstrong's childhood. He wanted her to explain the origins of the mental illness the jury had been hearing about for days. He asked her to reflect on her troubled girlhood, during which, she would also tell the jury, she struggled as an anorexic child prodigy.

"My father was an abusive alcoholic and my mother protected me from him," Diehl-Armstrong said.

"In what ways?"

"He was sexually molesting me as a child and as an adolescent. He even tried when I lived there until I was twenty-one. My mother always tried to be a buffer and protect me. She was a good woman."

"Was she always able to protect you?"

"No."

"How did that make you feel towards your dad?"

"I didn't like him very much."

Diehl-Armstrong's allegation of child abuse surprised Jerry Clark, who had no reason to believe the claim. In all his interviews with Diehl-Armstrong, she had never said she was molested as a child. None of the thirty years of psychiatric reports that Clark had reviewed quoted Diehl-Armstrong as saying her father sexually abused her.

Later in her testimony, she said, "The relationship between my father and me is good." She said that "he has a lot of evil in him; he has some good in him, too."

Years later, Ed Palattella would ask Diehl-Armstrong why she had never before, until her testimony, alleged her father had molested her.

"I don't like to broadcast that stuff," she said. "People don't understand."

———————

Diehl-Armstrong had testified for ninety minutes. She had not yet mentioned Brian Wells. Sughrue tried to guide her through her family history. Judge McLaughlin told her to answer Sughrue's questions.

"Mr. Sughrue is not tailoring these questions to get what I need to say to these jurors," Diehl-Armstrong said.

She told the jurors how she met many of the men in her life, including Rothstein and Roden and Larry D'Ambrosio and Richard Armstrong, her only husband. She described herself as old-fashioned, in that she always thought the guy should pick up the girl. She said the guys always had something to look at when they tried to pick her up. When she was in her twenties, she said, she attracted them with her smooth skin and her straight and shiny teeth.

"When I was young I was a model; I was good-looking," she said. "But of course I put on a whole lot of weight here in the prison in the last eight years . . . sitting around mostly over this case. Before I got diagnosed with cancer, you know it's supposed to be terminal now, on top of everything else.

"But when I was young, I was pretty doggone good looking and a model and all, if I do say so myself, not to be bragging about it. My one husband had a good saying, 'Beauty is only skin deep and a lot of them ought to be skinned.' So I don't put a lot of importance on judging a book by its cover or by what a person looks like. It's what's in the heart that counts with me."

———

Sughrue steered the testimony to the events of August 28, 2003: "Let's talk about how you met or if you knew Brian Wells."

"I never met Brian Wells and I never knew Brian Wells," Diehl-Armstrong said.

"Until . . ."

She interrupted Sughrue.

"*Never*; not until," she said.

"You became aware of him?" Sughrue asked.

"I became aware of him that day that he died," she said. "Because on the day that he died, that night, I went to my home on Carter's Beach [east of Erie] and turned on the television. And his death was being televised. And I didn't pay a lot of attention to it, which I probably should have in retrospect."

———

Diehl-Armstrong explained how she was diagnosed as bipolar, how her mental disease is "all in a continuum, the depression and the mania. My mania is hypomania." She said hypomania gave her the will to persevere.

"I've been in prison eight years," she said. "Then they give me this indictment, which is not valid. But I have fought it. I've had the wherewithal, without psychiatric [help], because I'm hypomanic and I tell myself, 'You can survive this.' Even with terminal cancer, I tell myself, 'You can get paroled. . . . You can get yourself out of there, get a cure.' There's hope. Hypomania gives you hope."

Sughrue asked her if the hypomania had enabled her to focus on her federal case.

"Yeah, because I taught American history, I'm a loyal American," she said. "To think the United States government thinks that I'm trying to rob their banks and bomb them is really a devastating thing. It's like that guy with that anthrax, that committed suicide with Tylenol when he got indicted. It's a horrendous thing to get indicted by a grand jury."

She wasn't done discussing her mental illness.

"I have bipolar disorder," Diehl-Armstrong said. "I get depressed and manic at the same time. I'm a rapid cycler, which means it can change really one minute to the next. Now the only problem it gives me is sometimes perceiving situations and people; it makes me more vulnerable and easily victimized by people. It does not make me sociopathic, which I've never been diagnosed, or violent, which has never been or had any incidents at all."

Diehl-Armstrong started to go on about an inmate she knew who had killed her father by setting his house on fire. Sitting just below McLaughlin, near the witness stand, was the stenographer, Ron Bench. For nearly one hundred minutes, save some breaks, Bench had been typing as fast as he could to keep up with Diehl-Armstrong.

She got ready to elaborate another thought. McLaughlin spoke first.

"Ms. Armstrong," he said, "we want to get the whole story in, but we're going to be here a long time if you don't listen to and respond to the questions, okay?"

"Okay," she said.

McLaughlin looked down at Bench and his stenotype machine.

"Ron," he said, "are you doing all right?"

"Yes," Bench said.

"He's very good," Diehl-Armstrong said. "I used to do that job for a doctor. He's very good."

"Ms. Armstrong, you're right," McLaughlin said. "He's very good. He's doing a good job.

Go ahead, Mr. Sughrue."

"I'm sorry for giving you such a hard time," Diehl-Armstrong said as she looked down at Bench.

Sughrue could not resist.

"Were you the best at it or the worst at it?" he asked Diehl-Armstrong.

"At what? My job?" she said. "I typed over 100 words a minute. Being a little manic helps for that."

The sound of laughter rippled through the gallery.

————

Diehl-Armstrong's free-form answers to even the simplest of questions lengthened her testimony. So did a more practical consideration: she had to explain what she knew about both Wells and Roden.

Diehl-Armstrong did not deny she killed Roden. She said she fired the shotgun not because he was going to tell the police about the bank-robbery plot. She said she was frustrated that he was not doing enough to help her find the men who burglarized her house on May 30, 2003.

"I had an anger in me after I couldn't do anything when I was victimized like that," she testified. "It was worse than being gangbanged in your own home. I cannot explain it. I had never been victimized like that before. It just set me off.

"I was just fed up to the brim," she said. "I couldn't take it anymore."

She said she knew Roden had not robbed her, but she was still angry with him. Her comments recalled Rothstein's testimony at her preliminary hearing in the Roden case in January 2004.

"I did blame him for introducing me to Ken Barnes and bringing him into my house," Diehl-Armstrong testified of Roden. "Ken Barnes to me was the devil himself. If he had never entered my doorstep, this shit wouldn't have happened to me. I had a good life before I met Ken Barnes."

Diehl-Armstrong said she was furious that Rothstein stuck Roden's body in the freezer. She said she never touched Roden's body and had nothing to do with the freezer.

"It's an absolute lie that I said, 'You should have bought an upright, you cheap son of a bitch, because it's easier to cut up the body.' It's a filthy rotten lie. I was absolutely livid that he bought a freezer and put him in it. I said, 'Who do you think you are, Jeffrey Dahmer? What are you, an idiot? What the fuck is going through your mind, idiot?' I was arguing with Bill, threatening to go to the police; that is why he ended up going to the police on me. That is the only reason."

———

Diehl-Armstrong called Rothstein evil and devious. Yet she told the jury Rothstein was the only man she trusted enough to help her dispose of Roden's body.

"He loved me," she said, "but he was mad at me because I didn't want to marry him. He was even talking about marriage when he saw Roden's dead body, and going into his house and having sex, cleaning up and showering, then sleeping in the bed with him.

"I said, 'You got to be nuts.' I said, 'I just got out of one mess here; I'm not getting into another one with you. I remember what you were like when we were engaged. I didn't particularly like your personality then.' I says, 'What am I going to do? Jump from the frying pan into the fire? I already got enough problems. I can't handle what's on my plate with Roden here.'

"And he says, 'Don't worry about him; he'll keep.' That's exactly the phrase he used, 'He'll keep.'"

Diehl-Armstrong acknowledged she was around Rothstein daily in August and September 2003. Not because of the bank-robbery plot, she said, but because Rothstein had Roden's body in his freezer and had $78,000 of her money. She said she wanted Rothstein to clean her blood-stained upstairs apartment on East Seventh Street more quickly, but he did not. She said he told her he was involved in an unspecified "business project."

By August 27 and 28, 2003, she said, "There wasn't anything I could do but wait for William Rothstein. William Rothstein was in control of my actions. What I wanted done, the only thing I was really worried about was getting Jim Roden's body out of the freezer and buried properly."

Sughrue got in a question about whether she planned the bank-robbery plot.

"If Ken Barnes says to this jury that you were at Bill Rothstein's house on the twenty-seventh, is that right or wrong?"

"I wasn't at Bill Rothstein's house planning any freaking bank robbery," Diehl-Armstrong said. "That's a fucking lie. Kenny Barnes was doing that, I wasn't."

Rothstein incensed her, she said, when he told her he had something more important to attend to than disposing of Roden's body.

"What's more important than a dead body in the freezer in the garage, for Christ's sake?" Diehl-Armstrong testified. "Is there anything more important than that?"

———

On August 28, 2003, she said, she drove her red Jeep Cherokee to meet Rothstein at the Shell station at Peach Street and Robison Road. She said Rothstein had asked her, for some unknown reason, to be there specifically at 1:30 P.M. She said she saw Barnes at the Shell station. She said Rothstein told her to put up with Barnes for a few minutes, despite her anger at him over the house burglary and robbery, "because he's part of a plan I'm doing with him on this business project."

Barnes pumped $10 of gas into her Jeep, she said. She said Rothstein made a call on the pay telephone. After the call, she said, she told Rothstein she was hungry for lunch.

"He says, 'I just called in a couple of pizzas. A guy that I know, that's a friend of mine, is bringing them up from a place on Peach Street,'" Diehl-Armstrong testified. "I said, 'Oh, really?' I says, 'Maybe I'll come around and get a piece.' He says, 'No, it's for the guys.' He says, 'You're going to have to go somewhere else to get your lunch today.'"

Diehl-Armstrong said she drove to KFC by herself, ate two chicken dinners on special, went to Barnes & Noble and read in her Jeep until she decided to leave. She said traffic was backed up on Peach Street for some reason, and that she had a hard time seeing because "my vision is poor." She said she stopped at Rothstein's house, saw his van, but did not go in his house. She said she drove to her Carter Beach Road house, where she said she turned on the TV and "for the first time laid eyes on the man that is known as Brian Wells."

———

Diehl-Armstrong called the inmates who had testified against her liars. She said she didn't drive on I-79 on August 28, 2003. She said she never solicited Barnes to kill her father. She said Clark and Wick "ruined her life," and she said she never incriminated herself in the statements she made to them. She said she cracked the case for the feds by telling them Rothstein was involved.

"They would have never solved this case if I hadn't fed them all the facts to Jerry Clark," she said. "I am the original one who pointed them in the right direction. They [the feds] thought it was this black guy. . . .

"They thought it was other people," she said, "these skinny white guys, they have sketches of them all over . . . I thought that, too, I did. That's why I didn't come forward. And then it dawned on me, 'Hey, wait a minute, this sounds like something Bill Rothstein would do.' And he knows about bombs.

"More and more information started to hook up in my head where I could remember about what he said to me. I put two and two together, I said, 'Bingo; I'm just going to point in his direction and see if it's lucky, if it's right.' And I didn't even know for sure. But I really sensed it was the right thing to do."

———

Under questioning from Sughrue, she called herself "the whistleblower" in the Wells case. She said Rothstein and

Floyd Stockton were the true culprits. Her words flowed in a torrent.

"He and Floyd Stockton, that's the guy who did twelve years for rape, that he was harboring as a fugitive in his home, the one who got immunity: They made a deal with the devil and put it on me. But the one that said he put the bomb on him to the grand jury and made the bomb. Floyd Stockton, the one that had the bypass because God does not like ugly. I'll tell you what, Floyd Stockton was living with Bill Rothstein. . . ."

"Objection, Your Honor," Piccinini said.

McLaughlin: "Ms. Armstrong, if you hang on a second. If you recall our conversation, this is question and answer . . ."

Diehl-Armstrong referred to Sughrue in her response.

"Yeah, I hope this all wraps up pretty soon because I'm about ready to leave," she said. "He's not asking me the right questions. I don't think I can get my story across anyway. I just don't feel like I can even tell anything to these people . . ."

McLaughlin cleared the jurors from the courtroom.

"Can I leave?" she said loudly as they filed out.

"No, you can't," McLaughlin said.

"I don't even want to deal with it," she said.

With the jury gone, Diehl-Armstrong told McLaughlin she did not care anymore, that she wanted to testify without Sughrue, if she continued to testify at all.

"Can I just leave?" she said. "I'm allowed to leave if I want to; it's my trial."

She turned to Sughrue.

"I can't take you any more, I really can't," she said. "You're driving me crazy here. I can't take it; you're asking me stupid questions. You're confusing me. You sound more like a prosecutor than you are a defense attorney. I don't even think the jury is even understanding anything I'm trying to say."

McLaughlin asked her to take a break and reconsider. She decided to stick with Sughrue.

Sughrue neared the end of his direct examination. He zeroed in on Larry D'Ambrosio. He reviewed with Diehl-Armstrong how, with her in prison, D'Ambrosio, with her power of attorney, had taken over all her assets, including her real estate, and had gotten rental income from them. D'Ambrosio would always maintain that he handled her properties appropriately and that he "never made a dime off them" and was holding the East Seventh Street house in trust for her. Sughrue went over the contract she and D'Ambrosio had signed with the movie producer; Sughrue said it could benefit D'Ambrosio over her if she were convicted. Sughrue had Diehl-Armstrong acknowledge that D'Ambrosio was giving her $100 a week in prison commissary money. It was the only money, she said, that she had left.

Diehl-Armstrong was reluctant to criticize D'Ambrosio.

"I had to be careful because Larry is the only lifeline I have," she said. "And the only friend or family I have in the world. And I do need my commissary money. But let's face it: I sure as hell don't agree with everything Larry

D'Ambrosio has done to me. But I'm not saying Larry D'Ambrosio is lying; he's not lying.

"He's telling the truth about how they twisted everything and they're trying to just politically end this case and use me for a scapegoat because I'm mentally ill and don't have money and I have no family. And I'm already in it, they want to bring up the murder charges, they use the Roden motive as the evidence, otherwise it wouldn't even be mentionable to the jury."

"Hang on a second," McLaughlin said. "Mr. Sughrue, do you have any more questions?"

"One more," Sughrue said. "But you were fearful of saying anything about Larry because then you lose that $100 a month?"

"I can't afford to lose it," she said.

———

Marshall Piccinini had juxtaposed the odd and the ordinary in his case to the jury. Diehl-Armstrong, Rothstein, Barnes: they were the odd ones, the dysfunctional criminals who fashioned the scheme that ended in Wells' death. The ordinary were people such as Tom Sedwick, Michael Douglas, Michael Vogt—people who were going about their daily business when they witnessed something that the FBI would later use to tie Diehl-Armstrong to the Wells case.

On cross-examination, Piccinini pounded at Diehl-Armstrong, she of the exceedingly strange behavior, with evidence from the ordinary. She did not deny the evidence that was inescapable, such as Douglas, the UPS driver, seeing her at the Shell station pay phone. She said she was there only at Rothstein's request and for reasons she never understood. Kelly Makela and the other inmates were liars, she said; Sedwick was confused. Diehl-Armstrong said she was simply misunderstood, by everyone, especially Clark and Wick.

Piccinini brought up Rothstein's alibi, that he told Clark he and Diehl-Armstrong were together in North East all day on August 28, 2003. Why would have Rothstein said that, Piccinini asked Diehl-Armstrong, if he had been trying to set her up in the Wells case?

"Because Bill Rothstein was making a fool of the police," she said.

———

She again mentioned how she would get paroled in the Roden case. Her comments echoed what she said after she was acquitted in the Bob Thomas case, in 1988, and what she said at her sentencing in the Roden case, in 2005.

Once she gets out of prison, Diehl-Armstrong said, "I'm not having any more relationships with anybody. I won't have to worry about getting in any trouble again."

———

Diehl-Armstrong said the government was using her, a mentally ill old woman dying of cancer, to end the Wells case to avoid embarrassment. She was nearly yelling at Piccinini.

"It's a political case is what this is . . . ," she said. "But they don't know what the hell they are doing; they've been screwing this case for years. If you had such a good idea, why did it take you all those years until you talked to me to even arrest me? I didn't even get indicted until 2007. This happened in 2003."

———

Piccinini referred again to all the witnesses against Diehl-Armstrong, all those ordinary people and innocent bystanders who had no conflicts of interests and no ulterior motives. He asked Diehl-Armstrong why they would all lie.

"Isn't it true," Piccinini said, "that all of these individuals, according to you, came together and conspired to frame you with regard to the collar bomb case, true or false?"

Diehl-Armstrong did not give a one-word answer.

Her voice rose as she droned on for several minutes. She called the inmates "crack whores and drug addicts." She described Barnes as a reprobate homosexual and "scumbag." She said Larry D'Ambrosio was more believable than Barnes and . . .

Piccinini broke in above the din.

"Your Honor," he said. "I have no more questions."

———

On redirect examination, Diehl-Armstrong told Sughrue of her testimony, "I'm under oath, so you know I'm not making it up."

Sughrue entered into evidence Defense Exhibit 1, a

document in which he and Piccinini stipulated that Diehl-Armstrong's eyesight was 20/200 in each eye. A measurement of 20/200 is considered nearly legally blind. Diehl-Armstrong persisted in her claim she might not have seen anyone in the car with her if she had been on I-79.

———————

Diehl-Armstrong did not get the last word. After Sughrue rested, Piccinini called one rebuttal witness, Jason Wick.

At the trial's start, Wick felt like he was going to explode with so much pressure. As the end of the trial approached, he was more relaxed. He, like Clark, had come to live with the Wells case, had come to accept that he and Clark had done their best. The anger had subsided.

Wick testified about the statements he and Clark took from Diehl-Armstrong. He said they misinterpreted nothing. Piccinini asked Wick about the news conference on July 11, 2007.

"Did you see Larry D'Ambrosio there next to you?" Piccinini asked.

"I did not," Wick said.

"Did you make any comments to Larry D'Ambrosio about the case?"

"No, sir."

"Were you sweating profusely, as he testified to?"

"I was not."

"That's all I have," Piccinini said.

29
Verdict

Piccinini countered the confusion with clarity. In his closing argument, he sought to slice through Diehl-Armstrong's jungle of verbiage, convoluted justifications and obscenity-laced declarations. Piccinini focused on two words:

Death and *greed*.

"Ladies and gentleman," Piccinini said at the start of his eighty-five-minute address, "this ludicrous, over-thought, overworked desperately failed plan to rob the bank was hatched on the heels of greed."

Diehl-Armstrong knew what was going on, he said. She knew that Brian Wells, wearing a maniacal device he learned too late was real, was on his way to die. Piccinini reviewed what the witnesses said happened at the tower site on August 28, 2003.

"There's only one reason to have to shoot a gun and force Brian Wells to wear this device, and everyone back there, including her, knew it," he said. "This thing was live. This thing was a ticking time bomb. Everyone knew it. No one stopped it."

Piccinini said Diehl-Armstrong's statements—the so many things she told so many people over so many years—did her in.

"She was involved in it up to her eyeballs," he said.

————

Sughrue attempted clarity as well. His words were also two: *sympathy* and *manipulation*.

In a ninety-five-minute closing argument, he asked the jurors to treat Diehl-Armstrong fairly but not to feel sorry for her. The request brought to mind her problems: her mental illness, her cancer, what Sughrue characterized as her vulnerability.

"I'm not asking you to like Marjorie Diehl-Armstrong as she sits there, making these remarks," Sughrue said. "Your job is not to like her, your job is not to invite her over for dinner or have a birthday party for her."

Sughrue blamed two of Diehl-Armstrong's friends, Rothstein and D'Ambrosio, who by now had become just as familiar to the jury as Diehl-Armstrong. D'Ambrosio, Sughrue said, had a conflict of interest in the way he handled Diehl-Armstrong's affairs. He called D'Ambrosio "the person that was supposed to protect her property, protect her assets, protect her money, protect her right to sell her own story, and now owns it all."

To prove Diehl-Armstrong's guilt, Sughrue argued, the U.S. Attorney's Office must do more than show "that she only kept bad company, that she associated with members of a conspiracy," referring to Rothstein, Barnes and the other participants in the bank-robbery plot. The government, Sughrue said, "has the duty to prove to you that she is guilty beyond a reasonable doubt of each and every element of each and every offense for which she is charged."

"I would submit to you that after considering all that evidence, you'll find my client not guilty of conspiracy, not guilty of the armed bank robbery, and not guilty of the use of an explosive device in furtherance of the bank robbery."

———

Piccinini spoke to the jury one last time, on rebuttal.

"This lady that you saw during the course of this trial, you saw her testify—she is not subject to manipulation," he said. "Things need to go Marge Diehl-Armstrong's way. When you cross-examine her and ask her a question, things need to go her way. When her own attorney asks her a question, things need to go her way. When you saw her sitting there, it's all about her. Nobody could ever manipulate her."

———

Jerry Clark liked Doug Sughrue. He found him straightforward and reasonable and resolute in his defense of Diehl-Armstrong. As the trial got longer, Clark thought Sughrue got stronger, culminating in a closing argument that was well done. Sughrue had taken a very difficult case with an impossibly difficult client and, by making D'Ambrosio another main character, had turned the evidence over in such a way to possibly create some doubt among the jurors.

At the end of the closing arguments, Clark worried, if only a bit. Piccinini had done an excellent job: the evidence had come together to obliterate Diehl-Armstrong's claim that Rothstein framed her. But you never knew with Marjorie Diehl-Armstrong. Most everyone thought the evidence against her in the Bob Thomas case was indomitable, too.

———

The jury got the case on the morning of October 29, a Friday, and deliberated eleven hours and thirty minutes over two days. The seven women and five men delivered their verdict on Monday, November 1, at 1:52 P.M. They reached the same decision on all three charges: conspiracy to commit armed robbery, aiding and abetting an armed bank robbery involving a death and aiding and abetting the use of a destructive device in a crime of violence.

Guilty.

Guilty.

Guilty.

Judge McLaughlin set sentencing for February 28, 2010. The mandatory sentencing provisions made the penalty certain: life plus thirty years.

Diehl-Armstrong sat quietly at the defense table. No shouting. No screaming. No cursing.

She leaned toward Sughrue. She spoke just above a whisper. She told him she wanted to appeal.

"You didn't do your job," she growled.

Marshals led her out in handcuffs. Sughrue shook hands with Piccinini and Clark and Wick. Sughrue walked outside the courthouse and commented on what evidence most hurt Diehl-Armstrong.

"Her own statements," he said.

Over the past year, Sughrue said, he had grown accustomed to Diehl-Armstrong's behavior.

"She's smart," he said, "but hard to please."

———

Across from the northwestern edge of Perry Square, a distance that is a short walk across the park from the federal courthouse, is the Erie Club. The majestic Greek Revival building went up in 1848 as the home of Charles Manning Reed. He built the mansion for his young bride. Charles Reed was the only son of Rufus Reed, whose grandfather helped settle Erie and who once lived in the mansion where the federal courthouse stands today.

The private Erie Club bought the Charles Reed mansion in 1905. The building is on the National Register of Historic Places, the result of the club's costly but successful effort to preserve the mansion's original beauty. Its most striking feature is its main entrance, framed by a white colonnade and graced by bronze sculptures of twin Greek nymphs bearing lamps above their lovely faces and flower-strewn hair.

On the evening of November 1, 2010, Jerry Clark met

his family at the Erie Club for dinner. His wife, his two children, his mother, his sister, his two brothers and their families: they had gathered to celebrate the end of Major Case 203. Clark had rarely seen his family over the past three weeks. He had been around Piccinini and Wick and even Diehl-Armstrong more than his wife and children.

Clark's family asked him to give a speech. Clark stood, reluctantly, but struggled for words. He was overwhelmed. The difficulties, the frustrations, the moments of elation from the pizza bomber case flooded over him. Jerry Clark, special agent of the FBI, the lead investigator in the strangest, most disturbing and most violent bank-robbery case any agent would ever know, could not speak. He broke down crying. As he gazed at his family surrounding him in the bright dining room, as he looked out the sweeping windows of the Erie Club and took in Perry Square and saw downtown Erie, his hometown, lit up in the darkness, Clark shed tears of relief.

30

"What Might Have Been"

A sentence that carries a penalty greater than life has no practical value, but its symbolic power is immense. It is as if the courts of the mortal realm are reaching into the next life to guarantee that the earthly conviction extends into damnation. Short of a death sentence, nothing is as final in the American justice system as a sentence longer than life.

Judge McLaughlin applied the Federal Sentencing Guidelines to Diehl-Armstrong's case. As he told the crowded courtroom at the start of her sentencing hearing, at 10:35 A.M. on February 28, 2011, the exercise was academic. Diehl-Armstrong faced a mandatory sentence of life plus thirty years. All that was left was for McLaughlin to impose it.

Brian Wells' sister was unsatisfied. Jean Heid read aloud a five-part statement. Heid's comments were atypical for a victim's family at a sentencing: instead of praising Clark and Piccinini and Wick and the others who had brought Diehl-Armstrong to justice, she condemned them. There was no justice, Heid said, not for the Wells family, not for her brother.

"We strongly believe that some who played a role in my brother Brian's murder are still free," Heid said. "This is a chilling reality. Simply put, we believe that this entire investigation lacks integrity, reeks of a massive cover-up and has used Brian as a scapegoat."

Heid said she believed Rothstein set up Diehl-Armstrong. She described her brother as a "forced victim" and criticized the state police for not removing the bomb from his neck in the Eyeglass World parking lot. She questioned Piccinini's handling of Stockton, wondering whether "a deal had been made with one of the persons responsible for this sick and twisted crime."

"Brian is dead," Heid said. "He cannot defend himself against the untrue charges of being a co-conspirator. He cannot tell us who put the collar bomb around his neck. The prosecutor has an immense responsibility to clearly distinguish between the criminals and the victim, Brian.

"The criminals cannot be allowed to continue to roam free to claim new victims. To those who know in their hearts the truth of Brian's innocence but remain silent: Please, I beg of you, to speak up now.

"We have unshakable faith and hope," Heid said, "that Brian will be released from the false accusations against him."

———————

At the start of the hearing, Diehl-Armstrong got noisy and McLaughlin threatened to remove her. She then quietly waited her turn to talk about Brian Wells and, of course, herself.

"My heart goes out to the family," she said. "My heart goes out to his sister. I haven't heard more wisdom than she just spoke. The true killers are still out there. Floyd Stockton is in Washington. I read the grand jury testimony myself, that he told the grand jury he alone put the bomb on Wells.

"I am not a person that wanted to see Brian Wells dead. I didn't even know Brian Wells. I'm not a crazed killer that goes around here wanting to kill and injure people. I am not that type of woman. I never have been."

She vowed to overturn her conviction so she could get paroled and rejoin society as a "good, decent person."

"I am not crazed," Diehl-Armstrong said. "I haven't been on psych meds in all the years now since I've been in prison. As long as I'm not being abused by some crazy guy, I don't need to be on them because I'm not a crazy person.

"I've had mental-illness problems," she said. "I haven't made the best choices. I've made my mistakes and I'm paying for them. But I'll be damned if I'm going to take the heat for . . . [the] men that killed this guy."

Diehl-Armstrong ripped into Doug Sughrue, who sat next to her at the defense table. "I don't think he can find his butt with both hands," she said.

"Ms. Armstrong," McLaughlin said, "you've got twenty seconds to wrap up."

Her words filled every last moment.

"You know there's an old Arkansas proverb," she said. " 'If it doesn't come out in the wash, it will come out in the rinse.' "

She was shouting.

"Someone get me a real lawyer; let the truth come out please! To my dying breath let the real truth come out!"

No blown-up photographs stood in the courtroom as Marshall Piccinini spoke this time. But the names and the unforgettable images hovered like ghosts and ghouls: Brian Wells, Robert Pinetti, Bill Rothstein, Ken Barnes, James Roden, Marjorie Diehl-Armstrong. Floyd Stockton, too, though Piccinini did not mention his name.*

Brian Wells, Piccinini said, "was caught in the snares of evildoers." The pizza bomber case showed the malicious can set their traps anywhere—including Erie, Pennsylvania.

---

*Neither Piccinini nor David J. Hickton, Mary Beth Buchanan's successor as U.S. attorney for the Western District of Pennsylvania, has publicly acknowledged Stockton got immunity. Piccinini has said that everyone who could have been prosecuted in the Wells case was; with Rothstein dead, the implication is that the U.S. Attorney's Office believes it could not have prosecuted Stockton.

"There are many themes to why people become involved in criminal activity," Piccinini told McLaughlin. "You see regularly crimes of opportunity, crimes of passion, crimes of greed, crimes related to drug abuse. But this particular case was motivated by greed and was completely characterized by evil. The jurors in this case saw the depths of human depravity."

Piccinini turned to Diehl-Armstrong.

"She is a manipulative, conniving and deceiving woman," he said. "Those are the things that make up this woman. Not some sympathy with regard to the government picking on this poor, unfortunate woman who suffers from mental illness.

"She does have mental illness. But when you combine this woman's serious mental illness with her personality disorder, her narcissism, her paranoia, her deception, her manipulativeness, you combine that in one person with evil and this is the type of crime that results. The combination of Marjorie Diehl and her propensity toward violence in this particular case proved deadly."

———

Jerry Clark and everyone else in the courtroom knew what was next. Clark was glad to hear it. He was pleased to witness the end.

"It is unnecessary at this point to rehash in any detail the specifics of this crime," Judge McLaughlin said. "They are well known. I do think, however, that its bizarre nature, coupled with the equally bizarre and sociopathic personalities that perpetuated it, have tended to obscure what this case is really about. And that is that this defendant and her conspirators sent a man to his certain death and, in so doing, risked injury or death to many other people.

"In addition, this defendant murdered James Roden by shooting him with a shotgun, so as to prevent him from divulging this plot.

"To be sure, this defendant does have a long history of mental illness. But there are other people with these conditions who do not solicit others to kill their father or shoot someone in cold blood to silence a perceived threat or seal a man's fate by strapping a ticking time bomb to his neck.

"Given this defendant's violent and erratic past, the sentencing goal of protection of the public confirms the appropriateness of a life term, as does the related sentencing consideration of deterring others from so cavalierly and callously taking human life.

"Finally, it is worth noting that the presentence report reflects that Ms. Diehl-Armstrong was an excellent student who graduated 12 out of 413 students in her high school class. She then went on to obtain a bachelor's degree in sociology as well as a master's degree in education.

"All of which begs the question," McLaughlin said, "as to what might have been."

The judge ordered Marjorie Diehl-Armstrong to rise.

He sent her away forever.

Epilogue

One afternoon in late April 2011, when spring had finally thawed northwestern Pennsylvania, Jerry Clark was driving on West Eighteenth Street, in Erie's Little Italy, when he saw her. There she was, Jessica Hoopsick, still walking the streets.

Clark shook his head as he drove toward her. He was saddened; at Diehl-Armstrong's trial, Hoopsick had said she was getting help to stay clean, but she clearly had failed. Clark thought her testimony had turned out to be a rare time of sanity in her disordered life.

Clark wondered how many people on West Eighteenth Street realized who Hoopsick was, other than her being a prostitute. She had been one of the pivotal figures in the nationally known pizza bomber case—not because of what she did, but because of who she was. She was Brian

Wells' connection to Ken Barnes, who was a friend of Marjorie Diehl-Armstrong, who was a friend of Bill Rothstein. The Wells case, in many ways, had hinged on information from this woman whom Clark was pulling up to at this moment.

Despite Hoopsick's cooperation, Clark still thought she had kept some things to herself. As the person who was perhaps closest to Wells, Hoopsick had to have known more of why he got caught up in the events that ended on August 28, 2003. Clark would always wonder what else she knew.

Clark called to Hoopsick.

"Jess," he said. "Jess, what are you doing?"

Hoopsick stopped.

"I've been at this years, Jerry," she said. "I can take care of myself."

Clark said he worried about her. He said they went back a long time.

"Jess," he said, "eight years we've been at this."

"Yep," she said.

Hoopsick kept walking.

Clark drove near her. He had one more point to make.

———

Clark had been out driving this April afternoon on business. He was still working for the FBI, though he was having difficulty adjusting to life after Diehl-Armstrong's conviction and sentence. The thrills had been many. Shortly after the guilty verdict, FBI Director Robert Mueller phoned Clark with congratulations. Other agents asked Clark about the case. People on the street asked him about the case. He got interview requests from national news outlets all the time.

Clark also felt lost. In the more than seven years he had worked on the Wells case, a lot had changed in the Erie FBI office, without him having the time to really notice: a new computer system, new agents. Clark felt as though the Erie office had grown up since August 28, 2003. He had been, because of all his work on the Wells case, and through no fault of anyone's, somewhat left behind.

His caseload posed other issues. He spent part of his time after Diehl-Armstrong's sentence giving some of the $100,000 in reward money to some of the former inmates and other witnesses who had provided critical information. Most of the amounts were around $1,000. After distributing that money, Clark wondered what was next. What other cases was he to work on now that the pizza bomber investigation was over? What case could be more complex or challenging? How could Clark ever top Major Case 203?

———

Clark would retire from the FBI on June 30, 2011, at age fifty, to join a consulting firm in Erie that specializes in security projects nationwide. He would also get a doctorate in criminology with a focus on public-service leadership. His thesis would concern restoration of competency for mentally ill defendants—a subject he came to understand well in his dealings with Diehl-Armstrong.

Clark would teach criminal justice at local colleges, and become an assistant professor at Gannon University.

After one class, a student would tell Clark how the student remembered only a few things about the Wells case. That was a long time ago, the student would tell Clark; he had only been a kid then. Clark would laugh.

Clark would come to enjoy this: whenever he would talk about the Wells case in class, his students would tell him it was one of the most intriguing stories they had ever heard. The investigation was lasting.

Jason Wick, five years younger than Clark, would stay with the ATF. He would remarry and regain a settled personal life. He and Clark would remain close friends, and often speak with each other daily.

Clark would also stay in touch with Marshall Piccinini, who would continue at the U.S. Attorney's Office in Erie. Clark would never forget those pushups he did in Piccinini's office, and the prosecutor's excitement the day Ken Barnes finally confessed all.

Barnes, who testified that he had come to like prison, would have his forty-five-year sentence halved in light of his cooperation and testimony in the Wells case. U.S. District Judge Sean J. McLaughlin would grant the reduction on June 6, 2011, leaving Barnes, then fifty-seven years old, to serve another twenty years in federal prison, rather than the approximately forty years he would have had left on the original sentence. Barnes would still seem destined to die behind bars.

Floyd A. Stockton Jr. would remain free. The last known residence for him and his wife, K.W., would be in Washington State. The couple would attempt to move to central North Carolina in the fall of 2011 but would return to Washington after the local paper published a story on Stockton's past, including the Wells case. Stockton's immunity deal would stay intact.

Larry D'Ambrosio, Marjorie Diehl-Armstrong's personal lawyer, would turn seventy-nine years old in 2011. He would continue to practice law and stay in touch with Diehl-Armstrong while she was in prison, and would send her money. He would still bristle at the claims from Diehl-Armstrong's trial that he had mishandled her affairs.

"That was just a ruse to make it look like I was feeding her to the wolves. That is ridiculous," D'Ambrosio would say.

"I'd do anything for Marge. She knows that. I'm probably the only friend she has in the world."

Marjorie Diehl-Armstrong would appeal her conviction and sentence. She would proclaim her innocence to anyone who would listen. Those people would include Ed Palattella, who would still regularly take her calls at the *Erie Times-News*.

Doug Sughrue, her long-suffering court-appointed lawyer, would file the first appeal, to the Third U.S. Circuit Court of Appeals, in Philadelphia, on November 4, 2011. Diehl-Armstrong, angry that she had been unable to fire Sughrue, would file her own appeal, on November 18, 2011. She would call her appeal brilliant. She would fulminate against the jury.

"I'm just trying to figure out what idiots thought I was guilty of this," she would tell Palattella.

She would be unrelenting in her dissection of the evidence, which she said did nothing to establish her guilt. She said she never confessed to anything and that she would have taken the five-year plea deal had she been guilty.

"It is all bullshit, piled on bullshit, piled on bullshit," she would say. She would add: "There is no way in freaking hell I had anything to do with this happy horseshit.

"I take responsibility for what I do, but I didn't do it," she would say. "And I will never, ever admit it, because I didn't do it."

Of Floyd Stockton, she would say, "He is free as a bird, because he got a real lawyer."

She would take no psychiatric drugs in prison; her only medicine would be for her glaucoma and cancer, which would appear to go into remission. The only health issue that would worsen for her in prison, she would say, would be her eyesight. She would say her vision had become even closer to legal blindness.

"I'm very myopic," she would say. "It's absolutely freaking ludicrous that anyone in their right mind would want me as a lookout."

Then she would laugh.

She would say she never felt better, despite the cancer. She would say she would outlive all the "pieces of shit" who investigated and prosecuted her.

"The Lord is blessing me," Diehl-Armstrong would say. "The cancer has stopped and gone away."

———

On that afternoon in late April 2011, Jerry Clark did have one last word with Jessica Hoopsick as she tried to walk away from him on West Eighteenth Street. From here, Clark thought, she would probably eventually find her way across town, to Parade Street on the lower east side.

Clark brought up Brian Wells.

"Jess," he said, "if you ever have more to tell me, I always want to hear it."

"I told you everything," Hoopsick said.

"I don't know whether you have," he said.

She walked away.

Jerry Clark drove on.

ACKNOWLEDGMENTS

The pizza bomber case touched on the lives and careers of a seemingly endless number of people. We are appreciative of so many of them for their assistance during the investigation and the subsequent writing of this book. Our literary agent, John Talbot, was enthusiastic about our idea from the start, as was our editor at The Berkley Publishing Group, Tom Colgan. We thank them both.

Jerry Clark: I consider myself extremely blessed to have been associated with so many fine individuals in my twenty-seven-year law-enforcement career. I am deeply grateful to the many law-enforcement officers I have met along the way who taught me the professional skills and personal values I relied on throughout this investigation. I especially would like to thank the case agent for the federal Bureau of Alcohol, Tobacco, Firearms and Explosives, Jason Wick, a great friend and confidant who was directly involved in the success of the investigation. Thank you to Erie attorney Phil Friedman for his advice in the pursuit of this book.

I am very fortunate to have an unbelievably close and loving family, including my mother, Sandy; my sister,

Mary Beth; and my brothers, Greg and Chris. To my father, Gerald Sr., who as a onetime law-enforcement officer would have been very proud, I miss you and think of you daily. To my wife, Danielle, and our children, Michael and Isabelle, I am so lucky to have you, and thank you for your patience, love and enduring support.

For every law-enforcement officer who participated in the pizza bomber investigation, I am extremely grateful. For all of the law-enforcement officers who dedicate their lives to the pursuit of safety and justice, you are my heroes.

Ed Palattella: Since 1990, I have been fortunate to work at the *Erie Times-News*, a midsize newspaper with large-scale talent. I am indebted to the Mead family, who owns the paper, and the publisher, Rosanne Cheeseman, and particularly my colleagues in the newsroom. Topping that long list are executive editor Rick Sayers; managing editor Pat Howard; the managing editor for news, Doug Oathout; and information-technology chief Rich Forsgren, who headed the photo department during much of the case. Many in the newsroom wrote pieces on the investigation or put up with me constantly chattering about it, most notably courts reporter Lisa Thompson, police reporter Tim Hahn and urban-affairs reporter Kevin Flowers. They, along with the other reporters and editors, are great journalists and good friends.

This project also never would have proceeded without the good humor and support of my family, including my mother, Patti; my brother, John; and my sister, Evelyn. My father, the late Edward Sr., was a fine attorney who valued strong writing; I hope Jerry and I acquitted ourselves well. I cherish my wonderful listeners: my wife, Chris, and our children, Henry and Nina. They never wearied of me, Jerry or our tales about Marjorie Diehl-Armstrong and the bank robber with the bomb locked to his neck. I can't thank them enough.

ABOUT THE AUTHORS

JERRY CLARK, Ph.D. retired as a special agent with the Federal Bureau of Investigation in 2011, after the conclusion of the pizza bomber case and after twenty-seven years in law enforcement, including careers as a special agent with the Drug Enforcement Administration and the Naval Criminal Investigative Service. He graduated from Edinboro University of Pennsylvania; the City University of New York John Jay College of Criminal Justice, where he received a master's degree in forensic psychology; and Capella University, from which he received a doctorate in public service leadership. He is an assistant professor of criminal justice at Gannon University in Erie, Pennsylvania, where he is also director of risk analysis and mitigation at McManis & Monsalve Associates. He lives with his wife and two children in Erie.

ED PALATTELLA joined the *Erie Times-News* in 1990. He has won a number of awards, including for his investigative work and coverage of the pizza bomber case. He arrived in Erie, Pennsylvania, after reporting for the

Point Reyes Light, in Marin County, California. He graduated from Washington University in St. Louis and Stanford University, where he received a master's degree in journalism. He lives with his wife and two children in Erie.